CROSS CURRENT

A Tale of Racial Conflicts Leading to the
World War II Internment of Japanese-
Americans

Kenn Sherwood Roe

Kenn Sherwood Roe

authorHOUSE®

AuthorHouse™
1663 Liberty Drive
Bloomington, IN 47403
www.authorhouse.com
Phone: 1 (800) 839-8640

Published by AuthorHouse   02/03/2016

ISBN: 978-1-4343-5942-1 (sc)
ISBN: 978-1-4343-5943-8 (hc)

Library of Congress Control Number: 2007910164

Print information available on the last page.

**Based upon a true story
and characters,
their names have been changed.**

Setting photos by the author.

To Grandchildren:
Kendall, Nathan, and Sam

Author's preface or post-script - an explanation and an apology

Few young readers - few adults for that matter - realize that while larger campaigns raged around the world in history's most destructive and significant war, a smaller struggle was occurring early on the Pacific Coast of the United States, as the Japanese Empire attempted to bring the conflict closer to the American people. Fear, rampant rumors, the encroaching Japanese submarines, and the devastating military setbacks in a struggle for survival, made humans ripe for emotional reactions.

This is that story. The facts are historical, and meticulously researched; the setting is still lovely, much in parklands and open space now. The villages and towns mentioned are thriving today, except the mileage between has been compressed in this work, for convenience sake, and for dramatic effect. Many of the characters did exist, their names changed.

The frightening incident, on December 10, of a mammoth Japanese submarine emerging from the sea to ignite an ineffective bombardment from new gun emplacements, did happen. The details are accurate, although the incident is little known or recorded.

Amongst the countless sources researched, I am especially indebted to an over-sized book: WORLD WAR TWO, A 50th ANNIVERSARY

HISTORY, by the writers and photographers of the Associated Press 1989, for invaluable information, particularly those facts on the relocating and incarceration of the Japanese-Americans.

My deepest thanks go to an old friend, Jan (Makimoto) Muto, who lived through the ordeal and whose family was imprisoned in Camp Amache, near Granada, Colorado. Her personal memoirs have been invaluable for their sensitivity, perceptive recollections, and historical perspective.

The racial strife in the schools is a composite of what occurred along the Pacific Coast before the incarceration of Japanese-Americans.

The battle practices described actually crisscrossed the Bodega Bay region some six months to a year later than the time frame of the story. They were incorporated to depict the serious intensity building along the Pacific Coast.

This writer apologizes to the locals and to the many visitors, and vacationers who love, or discover this remarkable region. First, the Sea Ranch did exist, but, was situated more inland, next to the brackish streams described. The Burton and Yamoto ranches are quartered, now, into sections of homes and fruit trees.

Second, this writer took, "poetic license" to remove a quaint, isolated colony called Dillon Beach, established in 1888, snuggled on the bluffs overlooking that magnificent sweep of ocean and beach, where so much action took place. The editorial decision is ironic, because the popular vacation escape, has been a second home for this writer's ancestors and family. Sorry friends, neighbors, relatives, and lovers of Dillon Beach.

The armed resistance of a Japanese rancher cannot be verified through old newspapers and historians, although discussed by now deceased neighbors and my relatives. If a rumor, it spread like "wildfire" in Sonoma and Marin Counties (setting of the story). Authorities have noted that defiances at that time apparently ended peacefully and were not publicized to keep locals from emotional reactions. Such tactics were common in that era to ensure positive morale for fear of foreign invasion. The incident, if it occurred, as believed, was used for dramatic effect in this work.

1

Panting heavily, Brick Burton pushed through the tangled brush paralleling the old ranch road, the beam of his flashlight splashing, penetrating the dark. Moonlight crinkled the far sea and cast eerie shadows across the land. From the foot of the hill, he had heard the sirens, and the screeching tires, and he had seen the bright lights silhouetting the ridge. He emerged now where the furrowed earth opened under rows of fruit trees; there he dropped to his knees and stared with horror. Ahead, sheriff's deputies and national guardsmen had surrounded the house; most were positioned behind trees or makeshift barricades. Several spotlights from cars raked the building, penetrating the recesses, flashing against the dark windows. A powerful light, stationed on a truck, held steadily on the front yard, probing the porch and the door, giving the setting a carnival brilliance. "Oh, Lord," Brick mouthed. It was like in his dreams - the devastating nightmare - but, without gunfire - yet.

A man on a bullhorn continued speaking, his words metallic and grating. "You are completely surrounded. Surrender now and nobody will get hurt," he said firmly. From inside the house, another man, not sounding like Mr. Yamoto, screamed back his defiance.

"We have tear gas," growled the man on the speaker. "If you don't come out peacefully, we will force you out. It's not just us sheriffs you're opposing, but, the whole USA. We got the FBI here, too. You want to hear from one of them?" A spotlight punctured the dark to seek out a cavernous window from where Yamoto's voice had seemed to come. But, he apparently vanished before the beam had found him, a ghostly shadow in the night.

Brick made little gasping sobs as his throat tightened. Where is Toby, he thought again, remembering the strange dream that still haunted him - the dream about his friend tattered, and cradled as if asleep in Mr. Yamoto's arms. Brick rose and hurried closer, his footsteps soundless in the soft-plowed dirt. His lungs and sides ached still from the exhausting rush up the hill. But, now he didn't notice. He moved up behind some soldiers crouched protectively in an outer ring of apple trees. Then, he saw his father appear briefly in the light-glow to be ordered away by a man in uniform. His father seemed to be looking around. Was he expecting Brick?

Neighbor Ezra Hamilton had phoned the Sea Ranch, that something was happening at the Yamoto's, as there were sirens and lights. And Brick's family would be listening intently to Uncle Burnie's radio with the special police band, most certainly his mother, hoping to hear something. Brick envisioned her crying, her face taut with fear and confusion. There, too, was Aunt Sathia puttering about, and Uncle Burnie comforting the women, probably pacing the floor, despite his bad heart. Brick expected them to be furious when eventually he faced them, especially since he had sneaked away despite their warnings. But, for his friend, Toby, there would be no other choice. "Toby's inside somewhere with his father, inside where there could be shooting." Brick worked the words, sour in his mouth. Burnie had picked up a brief contact on the radio between sheriff's units - something about an unconfirmed disturbance - a possible confrontation. The cold fact made his stomach flutter and go queasy. Toby could be hurt, even killed, Brick knew. Toby had shared earlier, the possibilities.

Then, they had heard distant sirens. Keenly aware of the tension building in the Yamoto family, Clarence, Brick's father, had accelerated his truck toward the Yamoto ranch, refusing to take his son. Brick had begged, implored to go. "It's Toby. It's Mr. Yamoto, our friends," he had wailed in frustration.

"I don't want you involved," Clarence had shouted back.

"Why are you going?"

"To Learn what's happening."

Brick had decided to take it on himself to reach Toby.

All Japanese had been ordered to report to assembly centers for shipment to detention camps, inland, this April 7, 1942; but, Mr. Yamoto was apparently resisting, for he would lose his precious ranch, all that was his life's work; it would be confiscated and sold by someone else at a good profit, with none of the proceeds coming to him. The War, only a few months along, was causing great fear for those living along the Pacific Coast, especially since American forces were suffering terrible defeats all over the Pacific, and since Japanese subs were known to be prowling a few miles offshore, sinking merchant ships, and even shelling coastal facilities. Many believed an invasion by the Japanese was inevitable. "I've got to do something," Brick said aloud. Hot and flushed from the climb, he found himself shivering suddenly.

"Burn the Jap out," someone bellowed.

"Damn it, Yamoto, this is it," the man on the horn announced, his voice gnarly. "I'll give you two minutes - and then we're gonna fill your house with tear gas." Two sheriff's deputies edged forward with fat-barreled guns.

Mr. Yamoto shouted something. From Brick's angle, the words were muffled. But apparently others understood, because a disquieting hush settled over the soldiers and over the lawmen. A few of the officials raised their heads.

"Hold fire," the man on the bullhorn ordered. "Let the boy come out. The Jap's going to let the kid out."

Mr. Yamoto called, "I beg you, let my boy go. Don't hurt him." His voice went high with emotion. "Don't harm my son. This is not his cause. You understand?" Brick heard the pleas distinctly this time.

"It's okay," said the lawman on the horn. "It's okay. We want your boy. We won't harm him. Now you be smart. You come, too, Yamoto. You come with him."

3

"No!" Yamoto's voice seemed to rip through his throat. "No, just my son."

Brick saw the officer with the horn look around at the armed force, and survey it. He took a deep breath and said firmly, "Come on out, son. Come out into the yard; we won't shoot. Come on out into the light. Don't rush. Just come out slowly." The guardsmen and the regular soldiers pointed their rifles. The lawmen leaned over their cars and pointed side arms, steady in both hands.

A long pause ensued. Nothing moved except for the writhing shadows that the trees made under a steady sea wind. Then the front door opened and a small, chunky figure appeared. Toby Yamoto raised his arms to shield his eyes from the glare. He stood for a time, blinking, looking about as if trying to orient himself. Hesitantly, he moved down the steps and into the yard with short, ponderous steps like some robot. He stopped and squinted into the light. "Please don't kill my daddy," he called. Suddenly the boy turned around with his back to all the firepower. "Dad - I'm coming back for you," he cried, his arms outstretched, reaching toward the house.

"For God's sake, no, Toby. Please don't," came an angry, frightened voice from within.

"Halt," shouted the man on the bullhorn.

"I'm going back," Toby screamed.

2

Events before the War had begun so simply, so innocently, it seemed. For Brick, his childhood closed and his manhood commenced that late spring of 1941, around the time they discovered the sea otters.

They were three friends who loved the sea, they and the shaggy gray mongrel that darted ahead, splashing through the rocky pools. Here at the edge of Uncle Burnie's Sea Ranch, they found treasures that delighted the heart of a boy. Now on a May afternoon as the tide ebbed, and the waves tossed choppy white under strong winds, the boys came to explore. Brick stumbled along behind, gasping, his eyes angry. "Wait up, you guys," he wheezed. Spud, his dog, yipped excitedly.

"Hurry up, yourself - you're always pokin' behind," Gerve shouted, bounding ahead to climb onto a small headland where the cypress hung gnarled above crashing waves. In the rocky cliffs were caves to explore and deer trails to follow that scaled the inlets so that one could stand dizzily above the rush of high water. Behind them on the bluffs rose twisted pine trees, spaced by grassy knolls, all riotous with blue lupine and yellow poppies. Farther along stretched a white beach backed by graceful sand dunes. The area was their favorite spot along the richly varied coastline of Northern California.

Gerve sprawled down at a cliff edge to peer over, his green eyes widening. Small, quick-moving, he looked clownish with his hatchet face and long pointed nose. Excitedly, he brushed a thatch of black hair from his face. "Hey, look, you guys. Quick."

Toby, the second boy, vaulted smoothly up beside Gerve. He was a chunky Japanese with a bright moon-face and dancing brown eyes. "Give him time," he said protectively, studying what Gerve had seen. "He'll get here." They waited as Brick, puffing and sagging, scrambled up the rocky side. Overly anxious, he misjudged the loose earth where high seas had gouged pockmarks. His footing crumbled and he began sliding back down.

Embarrassed, he managed a thin, "Help," his eyes widening. Immediately, Toby was to him with Gerve following. They grasped an arm, a shoulder, and then his belt, hauling him to safety where the rescuers collapsed in laughter, although it took Brick longer to find humor in the situation.

After they had calmed, Gerve said, "Look, that's what I wanted you to see." He pointed beyond the roily surf, where the water flattened in a wide eddy. A pair of seal-like animals bobbed, both lying on their backs, floating human-like, their arms crossed on their chests, their webbed toes pointing upward, their tails straight out. They peered curiously at the boys as they rode the waves gracefully, their white-faces striking with silver whiskers and button-eyes. "What are they?" asked Gerve. "Baby sea lions?" As he spoke, the animals stood straight up in the water, peering over the strands of floating seaweed to see the boys better.

"They look like little old men," said Toby, grinning.

"Hey!" Brick gasped, his face illuminated. "You know what?"

"What?" the others said as one.

"I think - I think - I know, they're sea otters. Rare sea otters!" Spud crawled up beside them and barked.

"Sea otters?" Skeptically, Gerve wrinkled his nose.

"They sure are," said Brick confidently. "I've seen pictures, and I've looked at lots of paintings of 'em. See, they got big whiskers and round faces that are white - real white. And they're not as big as a sea lion or a seal."

"Aaah," Toby scoffed, "Couldn't be. I heard the sea otters all got bumped off years ago. That the Russians and the Yankee sealers - they killed them all off."

Brick shook his head. "People thought so, 'til a couple of years ago. Then somebody found 'em alive, down around Monterey Bay. I never heard of them being this far north." Brick had read how the animals were hunted from kayaks, pursued until exhausted usually by experts - Alaska Aleuts with harpoons attached to leather floats. How the desperate creatures became cunning by hiding behind rocks or by diving and coming up behind the pursuers. But the hunters remained persistent, driven by a consuming greed. Often they caught a pup and hurt it, knifed or squeezed it - and when the mother heard its pitiful cries, she would come to its defense. Or if a parent were killed, the whimpering baby would swim right up to the boat to be lifted out of the water and clubbed. Thus, thousands were slaughtered for their beautiful furs, on and on, until they were believed extinct.

"Wow," said Toby.

"I read it," Brick said with final authority. "Finding them was a real big deal. That some had survived, gosh, that was something."

"Gee," Toby continued. "Now, we've found our own. Hope nobody else sees them. They're ours."

"Boy," said Gerve, extending his arms. "They're all ours. Maybe we could catch 'em, and sell them to a circus, and make a million bucks."

"Oh, yeah," said Brick, "and go to jail. They're protected. You can't touch them. It's against the law, not that we could catch them anyway."

"Guess we just better watch them," Gerve said, resigned. Gradually, the animals backed into the lunging waves and away, sculling their tails from side to side. One of them held an urchin on his chest, clutched firmly in his small paws.

"Wish my dad could see this," Toby said, beaming. "He'd get some darn good pictures." As a hobby, Mr. Yamoto specialized in seascapes, winning frequent recognition for his compositions and moody effects. Often he walked these shores looking for driftwood or wave-shaped sands that made interesting or unusual textures. "If he could get a picture of the otters - wouldn't that be great?"

"I'd like to bring Mike down here," said Gerve, his eyes twinkling. "He thinks he's seen everything."

"Well, if he brought Rose along, they'd never find time to look at otters," said Toby mischievously. The boys exploded with knowing giggles. Mike, Gerve's brother, a college man, was having a quiet affair with Toby's sister, a high school senior; the boys had known about it for some time; they had observed them holding hands and kissing; however, Brick had figured that his mother suspected as much, for Rose sometimes shared girl-talk with her. The fact that Mike was Caucasian and Rose was Oriental, and they were in love with each other, would have stirred gossipy, even vicious, tongues in the community, for they were defying local taboos. The boys liked and sympathized with the couple and wished them luck; the fact that the three had kept the secret had held them in an even closer bond, although rumors were leaking gradually.

For an instant, as the otters disappeared in some shoals, Brick wished his dad could share in their discovery. But Clarence was always busy, inland, trying to make a decent living on their apple ranch. Brick tried not to think about his parents. Recently they had separated after years of fights and worsening arguments. Now, Darlene, his mother, was talking seriously of divorce, especially since she had moved to an apartment in town where she worked as a secretary. Temporarily, he was living with Aunt Sathia and Uncle Burnie, a great uncle on his mother's side. The coastal air tended to soothe his bronchitis, which had become worse in the past months. Too, the ocean breezes eased his allergies - his suffering from the fruit pollens. The whole thing was bewildering, frustrating, so that he felt helpless and adrift much of the time.

"Hey, guys," Gerve said, sitting up. "I bet nobody else knows about the otters. I bet we're the only ones."

Toby looked seriously at his two friends. "I don't think we ought to tell anybody. I think we should keep it a secret - otherwise all the screwy people in the country will come down and scare them off, probably. Or somebody might shoot them."

"Not tell anybody?" Brick asked.

"Not anybody."

"Sounds good to me," Gerve said.

Brick figured that for a time, the otters were probably safe, here, along a wild stretch of beach and bluff which was seldom visited except by an occasional fisherman or a beachcomber; although of recent, the

Coast Guard was patrolling with small gunboats more frequently as war in Europe raged and the relationship between the U.S. and Japan deteriorated.

The boys consulted a moment longer and then shook hands. Disappointed, Brick wanted to tell Uncle Burnie, because Uncle was more like a friend than a relative - just a big kid, really. But, he wouldn't confide, tempting as it might be. After all, these were his buddies, especially Toby, more and more, even though the Japanese were becoming less popular under the increasing tension between nations.

The otters reappeared. Together the boys watched, stretched on their stomachs, their chins in their palms. "Man, can they swim," Toby said, as the little creatures threaded the outer waves, rolled and played, then nosed into the limpid pools below. Before being nearly driven to extinction, they had been long native to the area. "Sure good to find them," Toby beamed.

"What do they eat?" Gerve asked.

"Well, for sure, now, I'm going to learn everything I can find out about them." Brick's tone became authoritative then. "But I already know what they eat." He grew serious. "It's all down there." He pointed at the tidal pockets where the sea was clear, at the fantastic, feeding, fighting world of red crabs, purple urchins, yellow algae, and orange starfish. There were brown limpets and aqua anemones, their skirts waving flower-like. There were fan-shaped seaweeds, some leathery brown, some shimmery green. He explained how the pools fed all the little fish and animals and how they in turn fed the otters; how the pulsing life was a world in miniature, a perfect, harmonious little world.

"You're pretty smart, aren't you?" said Toby.

"Well, he reads everything," Gerve replied, unimpressed.

For a time they watched, absorbed, until the animals drifted south with the current. At last Toby said, "Well, I better get. Rose is having supper early. Dad's got some meeting in town."

"Wish we were going with you," said Gerve, smacking his lips and rolling his eyes.

Brick agreed. Supper at Toby's could be an adventure in food. Although Mr. Yamoto insisted that Rose, the now eighteen year old daughter, concentrate on American foods, she specialized in Oriental dishes: marinated fish, juicy pork patties, steamed rice generously stirred with pan-fried meat strips, bean sprouts, and water cress; or deep-fried shrimp and garden vegetables; sometimes grilled fish steaks - numerous goodies that filled her kitchen with savory aromas. Her minty tea and sweet cakes (the recipes a family secret) were the envy of the community.

Gracious and somewhat matronly, Rose had managed the household since their mother had died of pneumonia. Brick had never met Mrs. Yamoto, but, through Toby he felt as if he knew her. "It was old Doc Stone - it was his fault, and my dad has never forgiven him, even though he's dead now," Toby had confided once. "He was awful late in getting to our place. Dad called him, said Mom was in a terrible way. When he didn't get there, dad traced him down, found him by phone and threatened to sue him, if he didn't come soon. I guess they had words." Toby had swallowed hard. "When he did get to our place, Mom was dead. All I remember is Rose screaming, and, I saw the doc cover my mother with a blanket." A crushing despair had been mirrored in Toby's face and words. "All I really remember was that she looked like gray stone before he covered her. Dad went out in the living room and put his hands in his face and just sobbed and sobbed." Toby had looked evenly at Brick when he told of the incident. "Dad said later, she died because the doc didn't care - because we're Orientals, you understand." Brick had dismissed the supposed cause, but he had never forgotten the telling.

"Yep, wish we were going with you," Gerve hinted.

"Well, it may not be all that great - no matter what Rose has cooked."

"Why?"

"Dad was a bear this morning."

"Whatcha mean?" Gerve pursued.

"He charged out of the house, just boiling mad after some guys came to see him. Then, he took all his cameras and stuff, like he was gonna be gone for some time."

"What was he so mad about?"

"Something about selling our ranch. I never saw him so angry. We could hear him yelling in the front yard, something about he'd never sell the place, no matter how bad times get. Then, he walked away from them, got in his truck and drove off."

"I don't blame him," said Brick. "It's a great ranch you got."

Together they left the rocky point and headed across the dunes along the shore. For a time they laughed and chattered, stopping sometimes to draw their initials in the sand. Suddenly, far down the beach, a man appeared, carrying an elongated object over his shoulder. He bolted out of the dunes, his stride quick and familiar - his appearance startling in the vast emptiness of shore and sky. For a moment the boys watched, uncertain. "Look," Toby gasped, "it's my dad."

"Does look like your dad," said Gerve.

Toby whistled shrilly. But the man walked on. "Hey, Dad. Dad," Toby shouted. The man appeared to walk faster, turning then to vanish into the dunes as quickly as he had appeared. Toby began jogging after him, Gerve and Brick following, curious now. "Hey, Dad. Where are you going?" Toby called. He raced up to the crest of a small sand-rise, and cupped his hands like a megaphone. "Dad." But there was no one in sight, only rolling hills, the yellow-green rushes waving in the breeze. Gerve and Brick reached their friend's side. "He must have heard," said Toby, perplexed. "I know it was my dad. I just know it." Toby fidgeted his hands and spun around. "He was carrying his camera - you know - on the tripod, like he always does." The boy looked at his comrades for assurance. You saw him, didn't you?"

"Yeah, looked like him to me," Gerve assured.

"Sure did," said Brick.

"But if it was," Toby muttered, looking into the emptiness, "it's not like him to run off like that."

"Maybe he just didn't hear you," Brick offered. "Or maybe he's still upset."

Reluctantly, Brick left the boys and crossed the remaining strip of dunes; then he took a trail that rose gradually, skirting the edge of a hundred foot bluff of reddish clay to the moorlands above. Despite his growing exhaustion, he increased his pace until his body flushed warmly. Aunt Sathia would be waiting for the gathered eggs; daily she had to wash and ready them for market. She would be at the back gate with her arms crossed and her eyes narrowing. "Dang," Brick winced, hurrying. "Ugh, got to get the eggs and do all the chores," he told himself, shuddering with disgust. Gathering eggs, filling water troughs, feeding chickens, hoeing weeds - like the eighth grade, it was all routine and just boring. Admittedly, he didn't mind the work so much; it was having others tell him what to do, how to do it, and especially when to do it.

Defiantly, he thought of cutting out, maybe visiting with Ned, their hired hand in the cabin up in the redwoods. He would borrow one of Ned's poles and try for the big rainbow in Tannery Creek, the one that had eluded everyone for several years now. Except the creek would be gushing with spring runoff, making it difficult to entice the old fish. Besides, Ned would never tolerate it; he didn't want to invite Auntie's wrath anymore than Brick did, who knew that if he didn't show up, Sathia would shred him to pieces with her lashing tongue and her piercing eyes.

At sea a buoy moaned. Brick stopped to listen - it brought images of shipwrecks, of pirates, and of mysterious worlds hidden beneath the seas. He shielded his eyes against the ocean glare. Fishing trawlers strung across the bright water like white pearls, headed into port, bucking the wind, their prows dipping in spray. They followed the miles of sand beaches and wrinkled dunes, moving north along the orange cliffs toward Bodega Head, a dark peninsula that reminded him of a crouching she-lion. In the loop of the bay, where windows of the processing plants blazed in the sun, they would deposit their catch.

Puffing hard again, Brick reached the hill-crest to flop in the grass. Spud dropped beside him, his tongue wagging red, his tail slapping contentedly. For a moment, Brick watched the cotton-ball clouds sail by, darting shadows over the fields and the ranch buildings cradled below in a vale, all sunny and protected, yet high enough to view the sea. The whitewashed buildings: the two-story Victorian house, the barn, the sheds, and the corral, tied loosely by threads of fences and rows of blue gum trees, gave Brick a deep comfort, and a sense of belonging. A quarter of a mile to the north flowed the Stemple, a brackish river that fanned into acres of salt marshes. Beyond lay neighbor Raffetto's farm and more hills piling against the far mountains, somber and brooding. Somewhat revived, Brick hurried on.

In the shade of a mammoth gum tree, Uncle Burnie squatted, mending a mesh-wire fence for one of the six chicken houses that lined the slope. Spud zipped ahead and jumped against Uncle, yipping for attention.

"Hells bells, you guys startled me." Uncle grinned, his cheeks puffing. He removed his slouch hat and wiped his forearm across his head where the gray was balding. "Too bad man has to work to live." He grunted down to sit with his back against the tree, his belly bulging his overalls. He began stroking the loose skin behind Spud's ears. The dog closed his eyes and stretched out languidly. "How was your outing? You guys have fun? I know you always do."

"It was okay." Brick shifted his feet and thought about the otters, thought about telling him - yes, telling him just to watch the joy in his face. The two of them had become good buddies in the past years - fishing and observing the vast flights of wildfowl that swarmed the marshes each fall, filling the dawn and twilight with their beauty. Burnie knew a lot about birds and animals, about the mysterious way things worked in nature. Unlike with any other adult, Brick could confide in Uncle, yes, confide - confide almost as much as with Gerve and Toby. Well, certainly not about things like girls, nor about the strange forces changing his body, but about stuff that bothered him, like with his family or about what he saw or discovered on his nature outings. But the otters - well, that was a special secret now - one he had to keep, he told himself.

Burnie was a great uncle on his mother's side. His grandparents had immigrated from Scotland during the Gold Rush, where they had failed to hit it big. After a year of panning and sloshing about in the cold streams, friends had enticed them to settle along the north coast of California, because it was so like their native land. Here they had established the Sea Ranch, part of an Old Spanish Land Grant, a spectacular blend of beaches, rocky coastline, cliffs, estuaries, and rolling hills. Here, generations later, he and his two sisters were born. "Bein' born between two girls made me gun-shy," he would tease. He and his sisters had inherited the land, but only he had worked the Sea Ranch, building it into one of the finest dairy and cattle spreads along the coast. Ultimately, he had bought out his sisters' share, for they had other dreams to pursue and little interest in ranching. Now, semi-retired, he had given up the milking business because his heart was bad. He had turned to raising chickens and producing eggs and to leasing the rich grazing land to local ranchers who brought truckloads of heifers to pasture each year. Uncle fed and watered them, sometimes doctored and even sheltered them in bad weather. "You should charge more," Aunt Sathia often scolded, "for the time you give those creatures."

Burnie had built a solid reputation for helping others. He spent countless hours in assisting neighbors repair barns and machinery. "Good old Burnie," Auntie would mock, "just ask good old Burnie and he'll do it. But don't pay good old Burnie; ask him any time, any place, 'cause he just loves to help."

"Does a man good to help others," he would counter.

"And you'll die helpin' others," she would storm.

Brick sat down beside Burnie, grunting and spreading his feet like Uncle did. There's otters, he almost said, two of them playing in the ocean, not far from here. We discovered them. Instead he surprised himself, blurting, "Why do people get divorced?"

A little taken back, Burnie considered the question, his thick fingers rubbing thoughtfully over Spud. "Well, your mom and dad are not getting a divorce. They're just separated. I'm confident they'll patch things up. Right now, they've got to make ends meet on that apple ranch."

"You really think they'll patch things up?"

"Sure they will."

"How do you know?"

"Well, for one thing, they love each other."

"And for another?"

Uncle chose his words carefully. A sassy white hen clucked by and Spud watched it lazily. "Well, fruit prices are getting better with the war in Europe." The old man studied his great nephew. "And maybe most important - it often takes hurt to make people grow up."

"I don't understand."

Burnie tried again. "Your mom and dad will learn how much they need each other, that things aren't so bad after all. They're young and they got a long ways to go."

"What about Mr. McPeak payin' Mom so much attention?" Both the question, and the name hurt Brick to say. Mr. McPeak was Darlene's boss, a middle-aged widower who was bestowing her with gifts and much interest. In fact, he was planning to come to dinner at the Sea Ranch for her birthday.

"It's just flattery for her," said Burnie. "It will wear off. Just remember, we're going to have to let your parents work it out in their own time and in their own way." He smiled knowingly. "In the meantime, this old ocean air will clear your lungs good. And before school's out, you'll be playing baseball again."

"Think so?" Brick asked anxiously.

"I sure do."

Brick wanted to play, wanted to be part of the school softball team again. But his bronchitis, growing worse in the last year, congested him sometimes, making it hard to run and to breathe. After his parents had separated, he had gone with his mother to her apartment each weekend, but had suffered a few attacks there. During the week, he had stayed with his father, because it was too late to change to a new school, especially since the year was nearly over. His parents had agreed on that point. Besides, if problems could be worked out between the parents, Darlene would surely return to the apple ranch. But even on the ranch with his dad, his eyes had started watering, the sneezes had come, and his chest had tightened until at last he had gotten to the seaside; there always, he experienced some relief. He guessed that's why Dr. Thurlong had suggested he live for a time with his uncle and aunt near the ocean, where the cool and pure sea breezes were helping him breathe better, especially in the summer.

"Toby said he'd teach me to be a good batter, you know."

"Yes, and he'll be a good teacher, too."

"Maybe I won't make the team. It's the last game, anyway."

"You made it once. All you can do is try. Trying - that's what counts." Burnie had a look of amused tenderness.

"Brickford - Brickford Burton." Aunt Sathia's voice pounded up the slope. Spud pricked up his ears and wriggled out of Uncle's arms. "Brickford. I see you up there. You get down here right now!" Brick scooted lower in the grass. When Sathia called him, Brickford, she meant business.

"Better go, Boy," Burnie winked.

As Brick closed the upper gate, he saw Sathia emerge from the woodshed, her arms filled with chopped oak. Silently, he intercepted and removed her load. She brushed the splinters from her sleeves. "About time you got here, young man." Her eyes scowled through the thick glasses; her celery-thin neck throbbed, as she mumbled something under her breath. Obediently, Brick followed her, his face burdened. "You know you haven't gathered the eggs, or fed the chickens, or checked the water troughs."

"Yes, ma'am," Brick said, cowed some. There was a severity in her narrow face, in the gray hair pulled tightly into a bun.

"You still need to get your mother's birthday present - that was important to you," she continued. "And, after chores, you have to get your room cleaned up; remember Mr. McPeak's coming for dinner, and he will want to see the place."

"I haven't forgotten," Brick grumbled.

"You have to do your share. That's your responsibility. We can't let Burnie work much, you know, with his heart as it is. You have to help take care of him." To Sathia, life was a serious business and had been since her girlhood, when her mother died and her father - a lumberman - lost a leg from a falling timber. Proud, refusing charity, she had raised her younger sisters and a brother by taking in laundry. People who knew her, admired her, regarded her as a highly independent, self-contained woman, a kind of legendary type that didn't exist anymore. Well, Brick admired her, too, but why couldn't she relax some, let go once in a while, he wondered.

"I was talking to Uncle, 'bout mom and dad," he protested feebly.

"Well, let's hope they come to their senses and straighten things out. They might, if they ever grow up."

Brick didn't like it when Auntie talked that way about his parents, so he changed the subject. "Can I invite Toby and Gerve to dinner Saturday?" he asked, as they trudged toward the house.

Without looking at him, Sathia said, "I don't know. I don't know how your mother would feel. They're not part of the family."

"Neither is McPeak."

"Not yet, anyway. And it's, Mr. McPeak. If your Mom says okay, it's fine with me - you can phone her."

Silently Brick followed her into the kitchen, deposited the wood, spun around, and stalked toward the barn and chores. He wouldn't think about Uncle's heart, or about war, or about his parents - about anything unhappy, not for the rest of the evening, he decided. If only he had a job in Africa or in Alaska. He'd lead safaris for people wanting

16

to see lions and elephants and zebras. Or he'd photograph wild goats in the high mountains and brown bear catching salmon along the rivers like he'd seen in the outdoor magazines. The ideas elicited a happy whistle, the tune off key. He'd make lots of money. First thing, he'd buy a present for his Ma, so big it would outshow all the stuff her boss had given her. "Her boss," he grumbled to himself. "Mr. McPeak - no, McPeak," he said aloud! Brick scuffed the moist earth, sending it in a spray of dirt. When he reached the side of the barn away from the house, he chased a scrawny red rooster. It ran squawking in terror. That satisfied him some, but not enough. So he threw rocks at a black and white heifer. The animal bellowed and galloped awkwardly, slopping mud and scattering cattle at the feed trough.

3

Darlene and Brick sat on the front porch at the Sea Ranch, enjoying the mellow afternoon, as she read a letter from Aunt Ida. "Ida's coming for Christmas," she said.

"Gee, that's great." Brick smiled broadly, stretching luxuriously. He liked Aunt Ida, as she was Burnie's sister. She never forgot birthdays, or even holidays. Every visit, she lavished them with gifts, especially at Christmas. Now a retired nurse, volunteering if needed in Honolulu, Hawaii, she picked unique gifts like Macadamia nuts, coconut syrup, or even a ukulele. "Maybe sometime we can go visit her," Brick suggested, envisioning balmy beaches and hula girls.

"I hope we can." Darlene folded the letter and lounged against a pillar. "Ummm, smell the roses," she sighed, her hair stirring in the sea breeze. "I love it here, this time of year." A red-tailed hawk winged along the Stemple, its shadow bumping over the hills.

"I love it here all the time," said Brick, dreamily.

"Well, no matter what, I want you to invite Gerve and Toby this coming Saturday. Aunt Sathia wants to give me a birthday dinner." Darlene smiled warmly, her slender hands fluttering in a calm, consoling way. "It's important that you have your friends, too."

"Thanks," Brick gushed. "That's great - well, I kinda told them." Brick looked down, concentrated on some of Sathia's pansies flowering thickly. "I kinda hinted, but didn't say nothing for sure." His eyes came back to her, held on a reaction.

"Well, tell them for sure," she responded, leaning back against the railing, her eyes closed, to let the soft breeze caress her face and ruffle her hair.

"What do you want for your birthday?" Brick probed, knowing already that he would buy the box of candy in the country store he had seen; he'd pedal to the village and pay for it with money that he earned shortly - a job working for Uncle Burnie, who could always use help.

"Nothing, honey. Not a thing. Just you and your friends at dinner, that's all." Thoughtfully, she sat up partially, a little stiffly. "I will tell you, the best present of all would be coming to live with me at my apartment." She smiled sweetly.

Brick looked at her speechless, a little flustered. "This is my home, here," he said defensively.

Darlene sat up higher, her face soft and embracing. "Honey, you know what the doctor's tests mean?"

"Yes, I think so." But, his reply encompassed more. He wanted to cry out, protest all the injustices that life seemed to mete a young man. He wanted to blank out that physically painful day in San Francisco with his mother and dad. He remained grateful, that he was with his parents, united for the time, respectful of each other, but decidedly cool with one another.

Twenty-seven allergy tests! A young nurse had slid needles into his right arm, again and again, without end, it seemed. Afterwards his dad had taken them to lunch in a swank hotel with crystal chandeliers and white-coated men, while Brick, tense and nervous, had watched his mother for clues of which silver to use. Meanwhile, the allergy shots had reacted, some withering to pinpoints, some blistering, and others bloating red. Impatiently, he and his parents had waited through the long afternoon, until the specialist had appraised him, aloofly. "Your boy is allergic to pollen and dust," the doctor had stated.

"We guessed that already," Darlene had replied, "but, can you cure him?"

"Yes," he had said, "by moving him off your ranch." Those words haunted Brick. "The coastal air, where he lives with his uncle, will help for now," the doctor had explained, "but, he must be relieved of all that fruit pollen and the surrounding earth, furrowed as it is."

Brick stared at the rolling hills with shaggy Douglas Firs, crowning the rises. He waited, feeling empty, yet filled with conflicting emotions.

His mother said sympathetically, yet firmly, "It means we must get you off the ranch permanently. Most likely soon."

"But my friends are here," said Brick, defiantly. "Gerve and Toby. Toby especially. Can't I just stay on the coast?" His voice went high. "With Uncle Burnie and Aunt Sathia?"

"Doesn't matter where you go, you'll find friends. There'll be friends everywhere. Nice boys and girls."

"I don't care," Brick pouted, then tightened his lips in resistance. "There will be nobody like Toby. He's my buddy."

"Certainly, honey. He's a wonderful friend, and you know I love Rose," Darlene consoled. "Just as Toby is your friend, Mr. McPeak is my friend." Brick turned his head aside. "Honey," she probed. "You do like Mr. McPeak. Don't you?"

Trapped, Brick said, "He's okay."

"Do you enjoy being around him?"

"He's okay."

"He's a fine man. He's considerate and respected. He's a very successful accountant. And he has been good to us. All of us." Darlene smiled disarmingly. "Mr. McPeak likes us very much. You know that."

Brick's mouth twitched. "Does he love you?"

"Yes," she said with poise.

"Does he want to marry you?"

"He would, I think, depending upon what happens with your father and me."

Brick looked at his mother, as if she were far away.

"But, I could never accept," she added quickly. "Never ever without you agreeing. And he understands that." She toyed with her bracelet. "I'll never do anything without you wanting it, too. Otherwise it would fail."

"Do you want to marry him?"

Darlene hesitated and said carefully, "I'm not sure, honey. Sometimes I think I want to. Sometimes I don't know what I want. It's all so complex with you and your father and the ranch."

"What's wrong with dad?" Brick fired, with a tinge of meanness.

Darlene looked wounded. "Goodness knows your father and I have tried." Her voice was tender, almost childlike. "Maybe your father and I were too young. Really, we were just children when we married. Perhaps it was never meant to be." Brick felt empty, at a loss. Darlene continued as if she needed to. "Mr. McPeak could give us the security that we've never had. We could afford to live inland or in the mountains where you would get well."

Brick shifted away. Darlene pulled him around by the arm. "You don't understand," she said, her eyes fiery. "You can't understand. You think I'm wrong. But, is it wrong to be wanted, to be cared for? Some men can make a woman feel like a woman. You don't understand that now. But, I hope someday, when you're a man, you can be blessed with that gift."

Brick pulled away. "But, McPeak --."

"Mr. McPeak," she corrected.

"But, Mr. McPeak isn't like a dad. You know what I mean."

"No."

"Well, he's just not an all around guy. He's not like a dad, that's all." Darlene watched helplessly, as Brick moved off. "I'm going to go to Toby's."

"It won't go away. We will have to talk."

Brick loved and respected his mother, but, she filled him with conflicting, tormenting emotions at times. "A bright and beautiful princess," people had described her. An only child of a successful businessman and a fruit rancher, who was extremely strict with, "his little girl," forbidding her to attend University of California, "because women didn't need an education." Brick had heard again and again her complaints, the hostilities she felt for her father. In defiance, she had turned to secretarial studies, and in a spasm of rebellion, had married Clarence, at least according to Aunt Sathia. Darlene's mother (Uncle Burnie's younger sister), and her father had been killed in a tragic car accident, shortly afterwards. Grandparents, Brick was never to know. Burnie and his older sister, Ida, remained her only living relatives.

With her inheritance, Darlene had helped Clarence clear the financial burdens on the ranch, accumulated during the Depression. She and Clarence had not been compatible - things Brick could not understand, except that they argued much, and talked of separation, remaining together because of Brick, until now. He knew she was restless, wanting more in life, discovering something in the attention of her widowed boss - a man too old for her, Brick thought. She had taken that apartment in town, pushing to have Brick live with her, "Once on her feet."

"Calm down," said Toby. Brick had called his friend on the crank phone: one long wind, and two shorts, asking to meet at the Yamoto place.

"I'd like to go so far away, they'd never find me," Brick announced dramatically.

"Not even Uncle Burnie?"

"Well," Brick considered, "like your dad, he's okay. But, the rest of them, they're all the same."

"They're adults; that's why," Toby explained.

"All they want to do is push you around. They never listen to a guy. All because of that McPeak." He thought of his mother and stiffened, refusing to add a Mr.

"Maybe you can stay with us, or hide in the otter caves for a time," said Toby, his eyes dancing some.

"Where you running to?" Mr. Yamoto inquired, coming out the front door into the yard. Surprised, Brick held a flow of words. Toby looked suspiciously at his father. "I'm not spying on you," Mr. Yamoto laughed. "I just heard someone say that he wanted to run away."

"Well, I'd like to," Brick snapped.

"I don't blame you," said Mr. Yamoto, stooping over to tie a shoe lace. "Why not run away? We all feel like that some times. Every boy ought to run away once in his life."

Toby and Brick looked oddly at Mr. Yamoto, who confided, "Think how you'd worry them." Brick nodded in agreement.

"Dad - you feel okay?" Toby asked.

Brick's shoulders sagged in realization. "No, I can't run. I just can't. Dumb of me."

Mr. Yamoto crossed his arms and leaned back against the porch siding, a smile of understanding warming his face. "Not easy is it? Your family loves and needs you."

Enclosed with his thoughts, Brick continued. "Well, one thing I can do. I been plannin' for it. I can earn her a birthday present, something old McPeak can't give her - something from me."

"That's the spirit," said Mr. Yamoto.

"Uncle Burnie will have some work, I bet. It's a couple of days yet, before Mom's birthday." Brick hesitated and looked imploringly at Toby. "Would you help me? Together, we could cut the time short."

"Sure will."

"Maybe Gerve will, too."

Brick, Toby, Gerve, and Spud tramped businesslike through the upper pasture; they found Uncle tapping at a cracked board in the shadow of a brooder, where chicks are hatched. "Brought you a jug of cold water, and some fresh baked cookies - special from Auntie," Brick opened.

"Well, dandy," said Burnie, eyeing expectantly. "Mighty thoughtful of you." He took a long drink. "Mighty good," he sighed, then fingered open the napkin. "Oh, boy. Chocolate. Love chocolate cookies."

Brick shifted his feet, shouting gruffly at Spud for running in circles. He then became serious. "Need to talk."

"Figure I know what's on your mind." Uncle munched with pleasure.

Brick got fidgety, then straightened. "You said I could earn two dollars - you even kind of said that you might loan the money before I earned it."

Uncle frowned. "Well, now, two dollars is a lot of money. You gonna invest it?"

Brick reacted quickly. "The best investment I could make. You're teasing - you know - it's for Mom's birthday - a big box of candy."

"Good investment," said Burnie. "Will it still be there?"

"Lady said if it isn't, she could get another one." Brick wanted something special for his mother, something shiny and thoughtful, despite the hurt about Mr. McPeak. He had found it in the nearby village of Tomales, a silver box of chocolates with a swirly pink ribbon. To a guy broke, two dollars seemed as impossible as two hundred. When he got the money, he would bicycle to the country store, buy it, and Aunt Sathia would help him wrap it.

"For two dollars, that's a big box," said Burnie seriously.

"Auntie invited Ma for dinner, next week, and Toby, too, and Gerve here. She's going to have a cake and candles and everything." No doubt, Darlene would leave the office early and drive the twenty miles in her yellow coupe. Brick wanted to be at the gate, be the first to meet her, unless she came with McPeak.

"I know," said Burnie. "It's nice to do that for your mom. And you have time to earn it. That'll mean more to both you and mom. Right, Boy?"

"Yes, sir. I want to earn it. But, I need a job. You got one for me?"

"I'll work, too. I'll help him," Toby piped in, anxiously.

"Me, too," Gerve echoed.

Burnie wiped his face with a huge polka dot bandanna, folded it carefully, and said. "I don't have work for you right now. But, talk to Ned. Tell him why you want it. Sell him on why you need it. You boys get a job stacking wood for him. He's cutting trees downed this last winter for me. Probably could use help." Ned was a seasonal caretaker of Burnie's sprawling acreage, and who did miscellaneous jobs around the region as well as helping Burnie when needed. He lived, free of rent in a cabin in the upper redwoods.

"What if he says no?" Brick frowned.

Burnie chuckled. "You gotta sell yourself. Don't beg. Bargain. Compromise. That's the way life is, especially now - don't want to worry you boys - upset you - but, with the war in Europe and Asia -." Burnie hesitated.

Toby smiled with understanding. "I know, Mr. Burton. I know. Dad worries what the Japanese might be doing to us all."

From the pasture, a trail, the overgrown remains of an old wagon road, let through heavy stands of redwoods to skirt Tannery Creek and end at Ned's cabin beyond. Brick hated to ask favors. He was glad they might not have to cut wood. Fact was, he had never chopped wood - oh, kindling with a hatchet, but, not big hunks with an axe, like the lumberjacks did. He envisioned himself swinging, missing, losing a toe, or worse a foot. Grimacing, he stopped, "Got to think what to say to Ned."

"Just ask him," said Toby. For a pause, they crawled upon a split rail fence and plucked at the yellow lichen that streaked boards. They shaded their eyes and looked at the shimmering sea, while listening to some quarreling jays squalling in the brush.

"Not that easy," Brick said defensively. Spud circled wide through the red paint brush and the blue lupine, then bounced back to paw and whine at a post below them, pleading to be lifted. Brick sucked through his lips, squeaking a sound that made Spud point his ears and blur his tail. "You're awful ugly," Brick lamented, studying the floor-mop face and peekaboo eyes. "Hey, dumb mutt!" Spud wriggled loosely and dropped to the grass to roll belly-up. "Get up, dumb mutt. We got to get a job." Spud struggled up and charged after a butterfly in stiff-legged bounds. Brick shook his head. "You goofy hound."

They paralleled Tannery Creek. Here, under a fairyland of majestic redwoods, the lively little brook sang past mossy banks, danced down falls, and whirled in crystal pools where trout lurked. The watery wonder world produced Tanoak, the bark heavy in tannic acid, used in dyeing leather, an enterprising business years earlier.

Every spring, Ned Benucci returned from some far place to live through the summer and fall in the little cabin in the clearing, a place he loved, where he did odd jobs for Uncle Burnie, whom he always respected. "People don't behold the land anymore. They just want fast money or an easy job," he would say, shaking his head sadly.

Brick didn't understand, but, as Toby said, "Ned is sure a swell nut."

An outdoorsman all his life, he was lean and angular with iron gray eyes and a contemplative face, solemn like the hills. There was a leisurely grace in the way he swung an axe or hammered nails. He smelled of tobacco and nearly always wore patched pants and a blue shirt rolled at the sleeves. He was good at sewing - the boys had marveled at that.

To Brick, he was a Marco Polo, an Alexander the Great, rolled into one; he had tracked Brown bear in Alaska, for the Fish and Wildlife people, and had netted salmon in the Bering Sea. He had prospected for gold and silver in Nevada and in Arizona - even in the snowy wilds of the Yukon. He told tales of lost mines and buried treasure, spicing them with Indian legends. He described ghost towns, lonely and haunted and how their wooden bones rotted in the sun. He spoke of mud and blood in the war trenches of France. He told of cowpokes, of trail drives, of wild stallions high on a bluff, their manes silver and streaming.

Sometimes he described the Sea Ranch as he remembered - the days when coyotes and mountain lions filled the night with their wild cries. He recalled trapping foxes in the winter, and market-hunting geese and ducks when they blackened the sky. "It's good here," he sometimes said. "It's good here in the woods close to the sky and sea; that's the only life I could live now. I've seen too many men hate and kill, out there in that world they call civilization." Brick didn't grasp what he meant; it just all sounded good, although Toby confided that his dad sometimes talked like that. What intrigued Brick - there was a mysterious side of Ned, something secretive, and distant, something Brick would like to unravel.

Ned's cabin lay partially smothered under a blackberry bramble now riotous with bloom. In the yard, hanging from one of the gnarled pear trees, Brick found the man's cracked mirror for shaving. Carefully, he examined his chin, but, there wasn't even a good fuzz. Then, as always, he tried the rocking chair on the porch and found the contraption still creaked. Spud inspected the blackberries and growled at the bees.

Ned didn't answer the knock. Daringly, Brick opened the door and peeked. Fat white cups and tin plates littered the table. On the stand next to the narrow bed was a red coffee can forever present. "Now is the chance," said Brick half aloud, with Toby and Gerve close behind, "now I can see what's in it." Inside, he wrenched off the lid.

Toby's mouth opened with concern. "Should you do that?" Gerve stiffened, his eyes ferreting about, anticipating discovery.

"Now's my only chance - been wondering about this for years." An oval frame tumbled out of the tilted can, picturing an old-fashioned woman with high buttoned collar and hair drawn back in a pug like Aunt Sathia's. She was rather attractive with wide, patient eyes and a sad little smile. A wife? A sweetheart? Surely, here was a story that Ned hadn't told. There was a faded collection of more photos, the same woman sitting or standing elegantly in a long dress, and a starched, high buttoned blouse. Brick was disappointed, bitterly so. For many seasons he had looked at that can wondering, daring not ask, but knowing it contained gold nuggets, or Spanish doubloons; maybe emeralds or a treasure map.

A book lay open on the bed; it was leather bound, lovingly worn, something called, WALDEN. "Here comes Ned," Gerve shrieked in his thin voice.

"Do something," Toby's voice stabbed.

Brick fumbled the pictures back into the can and pushed the snooping dog aside, as he straightened and brushed his hands as if to clean them. He saw Ned rounding the cabin, and stepping onto the porch. Spud barked a greeting and bolted outside through the screen door. "He's an awful dumb mutt," Brick apologized, as the boys exited. Ned crouched down and drew the wagging animal close, his hands rubbing hard. Spud spraddled his legs and closed his eyes.

"Made yourself at home?" said Ned, tartly, enjoying the moment, for the boys looked uncomfortable. He laughed. "My house is always your house. You know that."

"We were looking for you," said Toby, quickly. "Sorry we came inside."

"Yes," Brick gulped, relieved that his friend was there for him. Obviously embarrassed, he hurried his words. "Didn't mean to come in on your place - just that we need to talk with you, Sir. We need help. We've been kind of in a hurry." Brick chose his words. "I want to buy Ma a birthday present, but, I don't have the money." He took a deep breath. "Uncle Burnie said I - Toby and Gerve - might be able to work for you, if you could use us or need us. Maybe stacking wood or chopping brush - anything. Could you use us? Uncle said he would loan it, til I earned it to pay back, but, I want - we want - to earn it now. Could you use us? It means a lot to me." Brick heard himself babbling.

Ned held a faint smile, his hands continuing over Spud. He nodded slowly, like a banker considering a deal. "What are you worth an hour?"

Brick drew back. "I don't know," he blinked, "enough for a candy box, I know."

"Ten, fifteen cents an hour?" Ned looked dead serious. Brick hesitated and shifted his feet.

"How about twenty-five? Thirty-five?" Toby interjected.

"Thirty-five?" Brick grasped.

"Okay," Ned said, with a twinkle, "we'll compromise at twenty cents. How much you need?"

"Two bucks."

"Figure a couple or three days not too much to kill yourselves off and you have it."

"Gotta have it by next week - Mom's special day, Saturday. Have to pedal to the village and pick it up. Toby, Gerve, and me, we'll start now."

"I have plenty of wood to stack," Ned studied the boys.

"We'll get it done quick," Toby said, "with no pay for Gerve and me."

"They must be real friends," said Ned, "to work for no pay." The man confronted the friends. "Not even a nickel or a dime an hour?"

Gerve and Toby shook their heads no. "They're my best friends," Brick boasted.

"All right, then, we've got a business deal." Ned rose from the dog and extended his hand. Brick found his arm loosely jaggled. Spud shook himself and turned in circles after his tail.

Through the late afternoon, the three friends stacked short logs in neat rows, finding it impossible to keep pace with the efficient woodsman as he sawed a pinnacle of timber into chunks with a snaggle-toothed blade. In addition, Ned trimmed small trees with an axe, working quietly, only his throbbing temples revealing the effort. The work wasn't half as bad as Brick had feared, although gradually his back pinched and his arms ached, until he wished he could rest. His pride took over, however, as he glimpsed his friends, especially Toby who moved steadily without a groan; while Gerve darted back and forth, unaware of how graceful his slight body.

At last, Ned said, "Come on, young friends, let's take a breather. We all need it." Gleefully, the boys followed him to the Tannery where the water silvered cool and sweet. Copying Ned's exact movements, they crawled belly down on the mossy rocks to cup their hands and drink deeply - satisfying gulps.

"Sure good," Brick said, splashing his face. Toby and Gerve agreed.

Ned slipped back to the bank, withdrew his pipe and lit it gravely; the wan light played across his cheekbones, giving his features a chiseled look. "I saw that big trout the other day." His eyes confiding, he waited.

A twinge of excitement swept through Brick. "Where?"

"In the same pool - the deep one down below us." Ned puffed seriously, his eyes heavy-lidded in pleasure.

Brick sat erect. "Are you going to catch him?"

"I'm waiting for you boys to do that."

"Wow, I want to. Is he still as big?"

"Biggest in the county. I'll swear on that. Still sleeps under the same log. He roams up and down the flow; breaks the surface now and then, like a whale in the ocean."

"I saw him once," Brick said breathlessly, "with you and Uncle. We crawled up on him. Remember? Boy. Boy, he's something. I been back lots of times since; but, I never see him. You called him something funny."

"Next time, sneak up over the pool, like we did. You just might glimpse him. He's smart and shy, that's why he's been around so long." Ned broke his solid features with a grin. "He's a wallopoloozer, that one."

Brick giggled. "A what? That's what you called him. A whopa-zooper?"

"No. Wallopoloozer. It means big. You know, big one - a wallo-poloozer. Haven't you ever heard of that?"

Brick shook his head. "Wallopoloozer." He sounded the name slowly, liking the way it rolled around his tongue and through his teeth.

4

"Ready, Lop Ears?" Clarence called, accelerating the motor to a rattling roar. Not minding the pet name, Brick nodded, pushed Spud away, and climbed into the cab. They wheeled backward to the weeping willows, scattering chickens from the shade. Then Clarence raked the gears, purposely lurching the truck past Aunt Sathia who knelt in the garden, pulling weeds. She looked up curiously and waved, her face rimmed by a straw coolly-hat. The truck rumbled over Tannery Creek bridge and down the cypress and gum-lined road. Quail darted before them, taking refuge in the cool shadows.

It was a grand morning. In the pastures, meadowlarks fluttered happily, their voices liquid, their bodies yellow against the glistening dew. A few Jersey cattle nosed dully through the fences, munching mechanically. On the hills, the fog retreated in long streamers, settling serpent-like on the Stemple River.

Clarence turned onto the county road, to whiz eastward along narrow shortcuts, past white dairy ranches that huddled in hilly cups. Brick looked for hawks or rabbits in the fields, or for a colt frolicking in the sun.

"Where we going first?"

"To see Toby and his Pa. Got business with the Mister," Clarence said, enjoying Brick's instant glow. "Then down to the Migrant Camp."

"To hire a family?"

"Yep. Need people shortly for picking cherries and then the apples."

"Can we take Toby?"

"Sure, why not."

Brick enjoyed being with his dad. Clarence, like Darlene, had been born to pioneer stock that had settled in the area during the Gold Rush. And, like Darlene's father, his father had purchased and cultivated a fruit ranch. The work and struggles, had resulted in a heart attack. Reluctantly, Clarence had taken over the property, while his sister, wanting nothing to do with, "digging in dirty ground," had gone her way - although she had suggested, if he succeeded, she would come back for her rightful share. Clarence's mother, depressed, sickly, had been confined to a nursing home, before dying - another pair of grandparents that Brick had never known.

Lonely, desiring company, Clarence had met Darlene at a dance and soon married her, according to family stories. Brick knew that he loved her much, that any separation was not his idea. Brick sensed his hurt, his bafflement, that he was determined somehow to get her back, even if it meant giving up the family ranch, which was his only livelihood. Clarence was interested in house designing, however, and had taken correspondence courses in the field. As a hobby, he was an excellent builder, and remodeler - known throughout the community for his cabinet making; ranching duties, however, did not permit him to pursue his first love.

Brick watched the sprawling dairy lands change into white rows of apple trees. Here, a few miles inland, was the famous Gravenstein apple country where Clarence and Darlene cultivated their fruit ranch. All was bursting bloom now - cherry trees in white plumes, peach trees laced with pink. And fresh-earth turned dark and pungent. Here, too, along the way was Toby's and Mr. Yamoto's orchard - an exquisitely tended showpiece in the county; although their land bordered the Sea Ranch, and, was but a short distance from the ocean, the wandering road did not connect the two places, but, swung wide in a circle to adjacent properties.

"Hope all this pollen doesn't knock you," Clarence said, "or your Mom will shoot me."

"It won't. I know it won't," said Brick, with bold confidence. "I'm going to play center field in the last game. Toby's coaching me and all the kids want me to." Brick licked his lips, gambling that all would go well. "The teacher said I will."

"Yeah, heard that - plan to be there." Clarence whistled a catchy tune, trilling nicely. On the hill ahead loomed the high gray roof and the fans of Mr. Yamoto's apple drier, an extensive building where Japanese crews peeled tons of local fruit each summer. A fun place smelling of sulphur, of wet wood, and of spicy warm apples. There were huge bins and large corridors where Brick, Toby, and Gerv had roller skated in winter; there were spooky furnaces and cellars for playing cops and robbers, and hide and seek. Brick sighed. Of course, all that was kid stuff now that he was older, graduating shortly. But, sometimes he longed for those good times when fantasy and imagination ran rampant.

They turned into the driveway that led up to the gray cottage, dwarfed by two shady oaks. The five-room home was simple and tidy. There was a small porch and white-trim windows with geranium boxes. A rock garden with sword fern and early blooming sweet peas embraced the house, giving it a toy-like quality.

Brick had always liked visiting the cottage. In addition to his photography, Mr. Yamoto loved ocean fishing and collected an intriguing array of hooks, lures and rigs, many of them original, constructed through trial and error. He had a variety of surf poles, several inexpensive stubby ones for youthful friends; there was a light 5 ½-foot bait casting outfit designed for one-handed flicks; next to it was a 6-foot surf rod for moderate casts from piers and river bars; a cumbersome 14-foot solid Calcutta pole; and several others, all with cork handles.

None so fascinated Brick as the one enshrined in a small, glass-fronted cabinet. The 7-foot split bamboo was brightly glossed and finely bound with a roller tip. The 30-inch butt had been hand carved with intricate patterns: curling waves, elongated fish, a sea hawk with spread wings. The black and silver drag reel was oiled and polished to a shine. Brick could never pass the case. It drew him like a magnet.

The handiwork reflected much love and patience beyond his experience. The beauty touched him, more, when he learned that Mr. Yamoto had created another art form.

"It is like no other - light and perfectly balanced," Mr. Yamoto had told the boys, once, removing it to let them, wide-eyed, run their fingers along the sculptured contours.

The truck scrunched agreeably on the white gravel as Clarence applied the brakes. Immediately, Toby slammed out of the screen door, followed by friend, Gerve. Smiling, Toby raised one hand high and drawled an exaggerated, "Howdy, Pard." Gerve waved both his thin, disjointed arms, his long teeth pearly in a broad grin.

"Where's your Pa?" said Clarence.

"Around, telling people what to do." Toby crawled into the truck bed to lean against the guardrail, his hands clasped behind his head.

"We're takin' you to the labor camp - the Okie Camp - with us," Brick said, joining him. "If you want to go, that is. Gerve can, too." The slender boy nodded in anticipation, hopping aboard to dangle his legs off the back, and listen.

"Man, yeah, that place is always interesting."

"Sure some goofy oddballs down there," said Brick.

"Aren't there everywhere?"

Mr. Yamoto walked out of a back door of the drier. He was a slight man with a moon-face and a generous smile that Toby had inherited. As a young man determined to build a new life, he had immigrated to California in 1915. According to Toby, Mr. Yamoto had struggled and saved to buy a small corner of their present ranch. He had tilled that section, planted it, hand-sprayed the young trees, mended the broken limbs. Alone, he had picked and hauled the fruit, year after year. With his growing profits, he had bought neighboring acreage from farmers who were less dedicated, and less talented. For seasons the cycle had continued until his orchards were geometric with bright green trees, their trunks whitewashed and sturdy.

Yamoto had spent his nights hunched over books, absorbing the wonders of American history and its democratic process. He had gathered the latest government brochures on botany and new farming techniques, excited always that he could contribute to a nation's growth.

He was a Republican, liked the Dodgers, horseshoes, and hamburgers with onions. He patronized both American and Japanese merchants and was active in organizations that promoted interracial business. In their home, unlike many Japanese-Americans, they never spoke or wrote their native tongue. "We're Americans," he would say, "and that's the way it will be."

Mr. Yamoto seldom mentioned the difficulties of those early years. It was from Uncle Burnie and from Toby that Brick learned that pressure groups had once tried to discourage and defeat him, claiming him unfair and unwanted competition. Real estate agents had hungrily eyed his ranch, had tried to persuade him to sell at unreasonably low prices.

In fact, Brick was surprised to learn that local newspapers had attacked all Japanese as undesirables; that local labor organizations had limited Japanese to working only for other Japanese; that stores and restaurants and zoning laws still discriminated, forcing them to live in their "little Tokyos" as their communities were called. Uncle Burnie once explained that much of the problem had intensified after 1924. That year, government officials legislated a bill that prohibited American citizenship for all Japanese. Brick could not understand why such measures were needed. He did know that most Japanese were bitter and restless.

Clarence slid from the truck seat and extended his hand, "Hi, Shiro."

Mr. Yamoto smiled graciously, "Will you stay for lunch?"

"No. No thanks," Clarence said. "We can't stay long."

"Well, you're surely welcome." Yamoto had an easy, accommodating manner. He and Clarence then talked about apple prices, and of how Yamoto would handle the summer's produce. As usual, the discussion bored the boys. Toby stretched out flat; his eyes followed the rushing clouds. Gerve imitated his friend and splayed out, too.

"I'd like to fly up there," Toby said dreamily. "It'd be fun to wrestle up there."

"In the clouds?"

"Sure. It'd be fun to roll around on that soft stuff."

"Think so?"

"Then I'd sit up there and look down at all you nutty people."

"Until you fell off," Gerve giggled.

Toby thought for a time. "Wonder if that's where a guy goes when he dies?"

The question startled Brick, disturbed him. It was unfitting. "No. He goes to Heaven."

Toby thought some more. "Wonder if a guy is the same guy in Heaven?"

"Whatcha mean?"

Toby looked intently at Brick. "Will I still be a Jap?" Gerve sat up to squirm uneasily.

"I'm afraid," said Mr. Yamoto. The boys stopped and listened, catching the futility in his voice.

"The U.S. will never get in war," said Clarence. "Oh, the big wheels will pound some drums and threaten Hitler some. Then apple prices 'll go up and help us both. But we'll never go to war."

"It'll get worse. I really think it will get worse," said Yamoto, his face crowded with sadness. Brick and Toby looked anxiously at one another. "Germany, the U.S. and Japan." He looked hard at Clarence. "Yes, Japan. We got to include Japan. They'll all find more and more to bicker over; just like little kids, they'll push and shove until somebody punches."

"Doesn't have to be," said Clarence weakly.

"I don't think we've seen anything yet." Mr. Yamoto crinkled the lines about his eyes and mouth. "And if there is war, the Japanese here are through."

"Think so?"

"We'll never be accepted. Not ever." He sat down on the tile-red steps and threaded his fingers. "Since I was a boy -- it's just gotten worse."

Brick had never heard Yamoto talk like this. Composed, readily cheerful, he seldom expressed deep emotions. Toby sat up, his eyes blinking uncomfortably.

Yamoto's face tightened again. "Now they're calling us un-American and treacherous and degenerate; and whatever else they can think of."

Clarence looked injured and a little pale. Yamoto continued: "Understand, Clarence, I'm not blaming you. You and your family -- you're wonderful friends. If everyone were like you, there'd be no wars."

Clarence nodded self-consciously, as Yamoto's eyes searched afar. "Makes a man boil, though. My land here is worth ten times what it was. I've never borrowed a cent in my life and never will. And I paid every bill on the spot for twenty years. You know that. I bet I know the history of this country better than many pioneer families around here. I love this nation. I love the American way of life. It's the wrongness that I hate."

Toby watched his father. A whiteness dotted his face.

Clarence sank against the fender and folded his arms. "Yes, it is bad times we're living in." He added clumsily, "Anyway, everyone I know sure likes you. And I wouldn't worry too much about this war hooey. Nothing short of an outright attack is going to get us into it. Believe me." Yamoto forced a smile. There followed an awkward silence. Suddenly Clarence smacked his hands and pounced into the truck. "Come on, kiddoes," he called, "we got to go." In giggling relief, the boys whooped into a roughhousing that sprawled them on the truck bed.

"We're off to the Okie camp, Okie camp," Toby sang, working headlocks on both Brick and Gerve. Yamoto winked permission as Clarence throttled the engine to a rusty whir. He geared the truck down the narrow curves, rattling and whipping it so that the boys rolled in delight. "Your dad is sure a crazy driver," Toby shouted, grinning in approval. Every few miles Clarence peered back through the rear window, his eyes glinting naughtily.

When they reached the outskirts of Sebastopol, Clarence turned onto a muddy road and wheeled down into the flood lands known as the lagoon. Here moss-hung oaks towered grotesquely above the black waters through which snakes and muskrats squirmed. On winter nights, mists curled from the marshes to smother the countryside. The murky fogs made people unsettled and superstitious. Some recalled the ghost tale of a man, drowned in a bog years back, whose spirit haunted the land and could be heard wailing and struggling at dark when the owls mourned and the bats darted blackly. Uncle Burnie had told of seeing a horse sink in quicksand here, so that the owner had to shoot it. "The Lagoon is full of dangers," he had said, "never go into that country alone."

Next to this inhospitable, mosquito-ridden area, was a county-run camp for migrant workers. Several times a season, Brick accompanied

Clarence here, liking to watch him hire because the people were interesting. The locals called them Okies -- a demeaning, even hostile label that classified them as subhuman. Most were sad, desolate people who had fled the Midwest because their land had turned barren and sterile. And California promised hope -- the land of honey and sunshine. They lived on salt pork, beans, and flapjacks. But most looked tattered and hungry. The ranchers distrusted them for they were apt to steal. They poured over the land with their countless kids, their battered cars heaped with meager belongings. Many drifted aimlessly. Most lived in government camps, but sometimes they squatted on federal land. When they could manage to purchase a small parcel, they built crude shacks. Having little pride, they often littered their front yards with old lumber, worn tires, junky auto frames, even household fixtures.

Clarence pulled up before the narrow gray office where a gaunt, bony-faced man sat crumpled in a wicker chair. He rose, tilted his hat and sauntered to them.

Toby stood up and looked about. "Gads," he managed.

"Something, huh?" Brick said.

The grounds were crowded for so early in the season. Smoky-white tents, brown tents, trailers, large and midget, lay wedged against each other and at odd angles under the trees. Dogs yipped and chased in quarrelsome play; dirty-nosed children with puffed stomachs and dusty feet, peeked from behind trees and tent flaps. A few emerged to stare silently with shy curiosity. Women with bulging fronts and scraggly hair worked over open hearths and steaming pots. Old men, smoking pipes, lounged sullenly on hard benches, their faces tight and unhealthy.

Toby wrinkled his nose. "I don't like this much, do you? Maybe we should have stayed at my place and practiced baseball. That would have been smarter."

"I don't like it either." Gerve stared, bigeyed.

"I'm used to it," Brick said flippantly.

"We should have practiced," Toby continued, looking uncomfortable. "I'm going to get you back on the team if it's the last thing I do. We'll make your dad and your uncle real proud." He appeared to be taking pleasure in changing the subject, but his eyes kept wavering over the campsite. Suddenly he said, "Boy, these people got faces like fists," and sat down.

Clarence talked to the bony-faced man who listened thoughtfully. "Hey, Brown. Pete Brown, come here," the man called to a slender fellow chopping wood. Brown strolled over. He was mild mannered, had a mustache and an apologetic face. As they talked, he kept grinding the ball of one foot into the ground and looking down. He frowned or sometimes smiled nervously. Brick knew Clarence was bargaining wages.

Four boys, shabby and dirty, emerged from the chaos of tents to watch. Brown tugged at his chin, then shoved a limp hand forward in submission. After shaking, he called his wife out of a tent. She came timidly, holding a blonde baby girl. The child buried its head in her neck and wailed. The woman was pretty, but tired and defeated.

"And these are my boys," Brown said, noting the four scarecrows. "They can work right hard, right 'long side me."

"Better keep them in school," Clarence advised.

"They'll go exceptin' when I need 'em," Brown added. The men walked back to the office to sign work forms. As the mother and child vanished into the tent, the four boys moved to the truck. The youngest, possibly seven, had a pinched face like a prune, Brick thought. The youth kept stopping, balancing nimbly to scratch one muddy leg with a horny toe. The two middle boys were eleven or twelve. One munched an over-ripe orange; the juice had smeared his face and eyebrows and had dripped to streak his chest. His hair hung over dark eyes, impersonal and bored. The other was husky with big front teeth that gave him a constant smile; he had stubby legs, so that he swaggered. His body pinnacled to a dull, freckled head with frizzled hair, unevenly clipped. The oldest was near Toby's and Brick's age, thirteen or fourteen. He reminded Brick of a young rooster -- scrawny with a pointed nose, receding chin, and a mass of bristling hair. He toyed with a huge slingshot. They were all naked to the waist, with patched Levi's shredded at the knees. They regarded Brick and Toby suspiciously.

There was a long silence. Toby looked at Brick and Gerve, rolled his eyes and shrugged. The oldest Brown fitted a flat rock in his slingshot and twanged it off the truck fender, then stood waiting. When no reaction followed, he fired a second at the back tire; it ricocheted crazily.

"We'd better get friendly fast," Toby suggested.

Cautiously, his neck prickling, Brick jumped off the truck and edged forward. The Browns' hunched, their eyes narrowing, their hands clenching.

"That's a pretty good slingshot you got there," Brick said, grinning so wide it hurt. The Brown with the sling stuck it behind his back. "I got a slingshot too," Brick confided. "But it's not as good as yours."

The boy brought his sling around and looked at it as if discovering it. Then a slow smile creased his face. "I made it," he boasted, surrendering the weapon to Brick, who admired it thoroughly. The frame was well-balanced, strong, built of choice willow. All the Browns encircled Brick.

"Hope he knows what he's doing," Toby muttered under his breath.

"Our Pop showed us how to make 'em," the littlest bubbled. "You want to see mine?" Without reply, he roared away, his tongue fluting a truck sound, his thin little arms pumping furiously.

"Come look," Brick called to Toby who eased off the truck. Gerve remained.

"No!" threatened the oldest Brown, jerking the slingshot out of Brick's hands. "Not him."

"What?" Brick wasn't certain he had heard right.

"He don't look at it."

"Why?"

The boy glared at Toby. "We don't want no yellow Jap touchin' our stuff."

Brick's throat collapsed. He stood paralyzed. After a moment, he turned to see Toby's face ashen. Silently he walked back to the truck.

5

Freshly bathed in new dress pants and shirt, Brick scuffed his way to the barn and climbed into the comfort of the hayloft to await the birthday party and the arrival of his friends. He gnawed a piece of hay and lay back carefully, to count the wasp nests clinging on the rafters. He would be in trouble if he entered the house with strands of hay sealed over him. The thought made him smile.

Despondently, he recalled the unexpected incident at the labor camp with the Brown boys and Toby. The situation had been troubling and scary. Brick didn't know what to say to Toby about the Brown brothers. They were intimidating like the Dallas twins, in Brick's estimation. The pair, Ray and Jay Dallas, were new to the school, moving from San Francisco after Christmas. Rumors circulated that they had gotten into trouble fighting in school, and stealing in the community, forcing their parents to move to the country to straighten them out.

They were fraternal twins, looking alike, but, not that much. Blond with butched hair and muscular torsos, they proved themselves excellent athletes, second to no one except maybe Toby, who was the softball pitcher. Most of the girls liked the twins because they were sure of themselves. Most of the boys feared them, because at recess, in the trees next to the playing field, and out of sight of teachers, they bullied, even challenged boys of any size. They had quickly reined as kings in charge, so to speak. Brick had not had any problems yet; apparently, the twins quickly learned that he was good at writing essays and figuring mathematic problems. It seemed they had decided they could use him to their benefit. So, he helped them when they asked, refraining from doing their homework for them. He wondered when they would confront him with that challenge.

A river of light poured through the hayloft door, flooding the walls, sparkling against a billion particles of dust. Brick raised a foot against the light and squeezed first one eye and then the other, so that it jerked like an old-time movie. Outside, Rodney, the bantam rooster chuckled to his ladies, and on the hill a heifer bawled. Brick wanted to bury himself in the stickery strands until they flaked miserably down his neck and into his shirt. He sulked once more, wondering how sorry people would be if he ran away. Vaguely, in his imagination, he heard Mr. McPeak - no, McPeak arrive followed by the liquid voice of his mother and the slam of a car door. The man had his arm around her, escorting her to the house.

Brick saw himself then in a sailboat drifting into the Pacific Ocean. The sun flamed bloody red, blotted by ugly black clouds that reached down. A heavy sea slammed the prow making the skimming form creak and lean precariously, turning it nearly over, until Brick swung the tiller up righting it. Now it was a schooner shattering the waves into a rainbow spray; its sails billowing magnificently under powerful trade winds. Spud sat beside him looking toward far islands, misty and green. Brick recognized Hawaii - the aromatic scent of hibiscus, intoxicating. Yes, he could see the swaying palms and hear the steel guitars. And beyond lay more islands in an aqua sea, all wreathed in clouds like ice-blue pearls. He visualized his mother, back on the California shore, crying, pleading with reaching arms. Uncle Burnie stood behind, his head bowed, while, Mr. McPeak ran aimlessly up and down the beach. He kept ringing his hands, looking silly in a dark, pinstriped suit while the foaming water rushed bubbling over his polished shoes.

Brick came alert with a start. He crawled to the hayloft window where he saw the green car turn into the driveway, its sleek body flashing through the lined trees. A streamer of dust trailed as it bounced over the Tannery Creek bridge, and ground to a stop by the side porch. He could see his mother in the passenger seat. He had expected her to arrive first in her tidy car. Why couldn't she have been alone with the family and his friends when he gave her the candy, he anguished.

Edward McPeak was San Francisco raised and college educated. Brick had decided there was something unmanly about him with his manicured nails and his tailored clothes. Darlene had admitted that he chose either dark or pale gray suits to emphasize his white temples. She had explained that he was a lonely widower, that he was highly respected as an accountant, especially for the Apple Growers' Association, and as a major in the National Guard and as a city mayor.

With practiced precision, Mr. McPeak rounded the parked car and assisted Darlene.

He stood vigorously erect, smiling, his eyes masked with sunglasses. Darlene emerged, sharply dressed, older somehow. Spud charged around the house, yapping and skipping, performing his duty too late. McPeak reached down and stroked the mutt's head. "Bite him," Brick growled. Instead, the dog rolled over on his back.

"Go away, hound," Sathia snapped, appearing at the screen door to emerge. Laughing gaily, Darlene and Mr. McPeak walked to her. He removed his dark glasses and enclosed Sathia's hands in greeting. Burnie waddled up behind her, hidden partially by the potted rubber plant. He won't win Burnie so easy, Brick thought. Spud got excited again and ran down the yard and back, and once around the car.

Before entering the house, Darlene waved, acknowledging Toby and Gerve standing in the shade of a locust tree, their presence unnoticed by Brick. Then Darlene stopped, shifted a black fur piece draped about her shoulders. Self-consciously, she toyed with the white-tipped tails, looked up to Auntie and said something. It's a present, thought Brick. And, only one person could afford it.

Suddenly, Darlene turned and looked around the yard and down toward the barn. "Honey?" Her voice rippled musically. "Your little friends are here." With boyish merriment, Uncle shrilled a whistle, the kind with two fingers pressed against his teeth and tongue. Brick ignored them, exhilarated, his being, aware only of the pull - of a tide withdrawing him, of his ship now unfurrowing fold after fold of sail.

"Honey?" Darlene called. Again came the spine jabbing whistle. Brick climbed down, dawdling, walking out nonchalantly, anxious to see Toby and Gerve, but, not the others. His Japanese friend stood to the side of the porch, the round face crinkling with smile, a small package clutched in one hand. Gerve was beside him, holding a card. Brick regretted not realizing that they, too, had just arrived.

"How's my best man?" Darlene cooed, stepping back off the porch to place a kiss on his cheek. She smelled pleasantly of perfume. "My goodness," she said, brushing bits of hay from his hair and shirt. "It's going to be embarrassing if you have to bathe again and change clothes."

"I'm fine."

"Didn't know you young men were out there," Sathia scolded lightly, scowling at Toby and Gerve. "You should have knocked - come on in now. All of you."

"This day means a lot to me, and, I want it to go right." Darlene slipped an arm through Brick's as they strolled to the front door.

"I'm glad you're here," Brick said, weakening. Slyly, his impish face dimpling, Uncle moved ahead of them in a rolling stride, his hands plunged deep into coverall pockets. Imitating him, Brick sank his hands into his jeans and swaggered a bit. He didn't look at Mr. McPeak, who smiled at him.

"Come in kids; come in Toby and Gerve," Darlene flitted her fingers, beckoning them. Inside, the house smelled of roasting meat, baked potatoes, garden vegetables, and of golden biscuits. Brick knew somewhere there was a cake, and an apple pie. Aunt Sathia lowered the heat in the immense black stove.

"Can I help?" Darlene offered.

"Nope," Sathia answered, sliding pots and adjusting lids. "Just go in and entertain your friend."

"Mom," Brick whispered, tugging her sleeve. "We haven't introduced Toby and Gerve."

"Oh."

"Yes, Toby and Gerve," Brick said angrily under his breath. "Toby and Gerve here."

Darlene glanced quickly at Mr. McPeak. "My boy has so many friends; two of them have joined us tonight."

"They're my two best friends," Brick interjected.

"I'm Edward McPeak," the man announced, leaning forward; his courtly manner breaking an awkward tension. He extended his hand to Toby who quickly received it.

"I'm Toby, Toby Yamoto."

Mr. McPeak reached to Gerve next, who offered a limp hand and fumbled his full name.

"Oh, I'm so sorry," Darlene hushed, "I'm a little flustered. I meant to introduce the boys."

On the dining room table, a candelabra glittered over Sathia's best china and silver. She had arranged a bouquet of pink gladiolus on the buffet under the dish cabinets, and another bowl of yellow daffodils on the big radio in the corner. "Sathia, it's lovely." Darlene clasped her hands.

Suddenly, Brick didn't want to go into the living room. He didn't want to give his mother her present in front of Mr. McPeak. "Ma!" The urgency in his voice stopped her. "Just a minute, Ma."

"I think he's got something for you." Burnie's voice came over, strikingly, - a command. As Uncle ushered Mr. McPeak toward the living room, Brick stalked into the big pantry, flipped open the bread drawer and pulled out a fat white box embraced in a pink-curled ribbon. Back he came, carrying it to her with stiff dignity. Sathia, cooking fork in hand, followed, smiling dutifully.

Again, Darlene cooed girlishly, took the box and gave Brick a squeeze. Carefully she undid the ribbon, the wrapper, and lifted the top. The thick creamy chocolates looked delectable.

"Toby's got something for you, too," Brick said rapidly, "and Gerve has a card." Gerve slid forward timidly and handed an envelope. Darlene embraced his head. Brick tipped his head at the Japanese boy.

Like a disciplined soldier, Toby marched a couple steps, bowed slightly, and handed her a neatly wrapped present. Darlene smiled graciously and parted the taped flaps. A green hand-knit potholder emerged. "My sister, Rose - she sewed it from start to finish," the boy said proudly.

Darlene held the present and the card to her breast. "I must thank Rose. She's so sweet. And, I Thank you three so much." She then moved briskly into the living room, lined her fur piece over a chair and said,

"Look what Brickie and his guests gave me." McPeak and Burnie turned from examining the clipper ship on the mantle - the one some old skipper had carved for Burnie.

"Ummm." Burnie sniffed the candy and smiled about the potholder and at the big card that Darlene opened to read.

Mr. McPeak took the gifts and admired them properly. "They're beautiful, guys."

"And, Brick earned the money himself," Burnie added.

"You did?" Darlene blinked with surprise, then patted her son's mutinous hair. "He's such a fine young man."

"Aw, Ma," Brick squirmed.

"This must have cost several dollars."

"Well, my best friends helped me."

"Your best friends?"

"Toby and Gerve! We stacked wood for Ned Benucci."

Burnie nodded. "They worked hard."

Darlene shrugged. "I'm afraid I'm losing touch with my son. So much happening - but, I am grateful for these lovely thoughts."

Brick moistened his lips and tried to look pleased. All he could manage was a solemn, "Yes, ma'am."

A strained silence followed. "You know," Mr. McPeak said uneasily, "I don't care what Darlene says, I like this room."

"Say that loud and clear when Sathia comes back," Burnie suggested.

"No, I really like it." McPeak studied the wagon wheel of lights that hung from the center ceiling. "Very original."

"That's a matter of opinion," Darlene said, for the room had always embarrassed her with its cowhide couches; its comfy leather chairs and Navajo rugs. Despite Auntie's nagging, Burnie had framed copies of his favorite Charley Russell paintings - a roundup, some Indian scouts, the chuck wagon at evening, the roping of a wild steer.

"I'll tell you," Burnie said, "it's been a thirty-year battle to make it this way. Here on the big radio, I listen to Seabiscuit win all the horse races, and, Joe Louis knock out all his opponents."

"Well, I like it. Makes a man feel at home." McPeak looked out the front windows at the Stemple River. "Beautiful view, too. One can even see the ocean."

Sathia strolled in. "Why don't you break out that vintage wine you have been saving so long, Burnie."

"Yes, let's celebrate." Darlene held out her hands so Mr. McPeak could take them.

He laughed. "I'd be delighted. We must make a toast. Especially to the cook. Sathia, the food smells wonderful."

"Oh, tut, tut," Sathia clucked.

"Well, then," said Mr. McPeak winking at Darlene, "it's time for something special on my part." He excused himself. And, with the gallantry of a cavalier, he swept from the room.

"I'll get the wine and glasses; but, first, let's see what the man's up to." Burnie relaxed on the sofa for a few minutes and stretched his feet to the fireplace. Darlene eased into a leather chair and stroked the fur piece with childlike delight. Outside the car door slammed.

"Such a charming man," Sathia sighed. She stood dreamily.

"Very nice," Uncle agreed.

Sathia stiffened and blinked. "Burnie, why don't you change to something decent beside those coveralls? Gracious goodness. A birthday dinner with guests and all."

"Yes, dear." Burnie rose with effort. "These coveralls are new, you know."

"And, your good shoes, too, not those loafers. And don't forget my best wine glasses."

"Yes, ma'am." Burnie slurred the last word. Auntie shot an accusing look. Mr. McPeak returned shortly carrying a small rectangular package.

"For you, little buddy." Brick looked to Darlene, then back at the package. "Go on, open it," McPeak said.

"Yeah, do." Toby beamed.

"Gosh," said Burnie, walking in from the kitchen with some wine glasses, "Like Christmas around here."

The paper wouldn't give, so Brick ripped at it.

"Honey!" Darlene admonished. "He's opened packages before, you know."

Brick flipped the box end up. A fat, five bladed, pearl-handled knife slid out. He held it, stared at it, tried to say something, but couldn't.

"Wow," Toby gasped.

"Gosh," Gerve echoed.

"And all yours," McPeak added.

"A beauty, Ed," Burnie said. "He'll sure get good use out of that."

"Well, honey?" Darlene prodded.

Brick avoided Mr. McPeak's eyes. "Thanks - thanks a lot, sir."

McPeak laughed in relief, reached over and punched Brick's shoulder. Then he walked back to the fireplace and cleared his throat. "How's the poultry business, Burnie?"

"War in Europe is helping prices. Irony, isn't it?"

"War's growing worse," said Mr. McPeak. "The nation I fear now is Japan." The man glanced at Toby, suddenly remembering his presence.

But Toby either didn't hear or was careful not to let on. "Sure a nifty knife," he said to Brick as they examined the various blades.

"Isn't he a nice man?" Darlene whispered.

A meanness filled Brick. He wanted to say, "Is dad joining us for dinner?"

Darlene caught his expression. Her face quickened with concern. "Are you all right?"

"Yes."

"You looked so funny at me." She recoiled and then found her composure. "Would you like some candy? I'm sure it won't hurt your dinner." The boys nodded.

As the friends chomped into crunchy chocolates sprinkled with nuts, Mr. McPeak said politely, "May I have one?" Darlene passed him the box, then tucked her arm in his. "Aren't you going to have one?" he asked.

"No," she said. "I've got to watch my figure."

"Looks okay to me," McPeak smiled. Darlene stuck her tongue out. She picked up her fur piece, flung it over her shoulders, then twirled so that her skirt billowed.

"Like my birthday present, Burnie?"

"Uh huh. Fox."

"Silver fox."

"I gotta go change, boss's orders," Burnie said softly.

After dinner, Brick tucked the knife in his coat pocket; he, Gerve, and Toby walked outside. Early evening shadows streaked the yard. The wind whished through the cypress trees and the air smelled of threatening fog. After they reached the barn, they could see the misty rolls moving darkly across Bodega Head. Eventually a fine drizzle would blanket them in murky cold so that the trees and buildings would loom formidably, and by the morning the trees would patter wetness like rain.

In the potato field, between the barn and the river, hundreds of blackbirds roiled restlessly, feeding in the furrows of new turned earth. Beyond, a blue heron lumbered up from the Stemple, its spidery legs trailing. Shivering with cold, Brick slid back the barn door and crawled hurriedly into the loft with his comrades behind. Impulsively, he buried the knife under the hay. He stood tense and still for a time, listening to the beat of his heart. No one spoke.

Silently they walked up the yard then along the row of stately gum and cypress, past the white feed houses and the shelter pens. They puffed up the incline through the chicken yard, through the vale to the hill above that ended abruptly in one hundred foot cliffs; below, the sea thundered in its high tide rush, forming scallops along the upper beach. The water hurled shoreward in foam lines, became trapped behind the shallow bars, piling up inside while flowing laterally until breaking free. The excess rushed seaward to erode a channel of its own making. Called a riptide, the force ran in opposition to the natural flow of the sea. The waves clashed violently, creating an undertow that could easily drown a swimmer and carry the body out to sea, likely never to be found. Everyone native to the coast knew about such dangers. At the cliff's edge, the boys could look directly down and see clearly the turbulence - the crosscurrents.

"I don't understand this man-woman thing too well," Toby said. "My Sis and Mike Hamilton - I know they love each other, but, everyone is against it. My dad, my folks, the neighbors - everyone."

"That's true," said Gerve.

Back of the cliff dome, a stunted wall of cypress enclosed the last chicken house, abandoned now in a lonely, windy spot that commanded a fine view of the bay and the beaches, with the otter point to the south; from there one could see the Stemple and the marshes and all the rugged headlands to the north. The boys found protection against the siding where they sat thoughtfully.

"It's Mom." Brick wagged his head. "I just can't talk to her."

"Well, maybe you should be thankful that you have a mom."

Brick pondered the thought. "You think I wasn't pleased enough for the knife?"

"I understand."

"Me, too," Gerve added.

"I'll probably use it someday."

"Probably will."

"Meantime, we won't worry about it."

"No use even thinking about it." Toby slid a hand of dismissal, palm down.

Brick looked into four earnest eyes and sealed a bargain.

6

Strange, yet, not so strange, Brick would recall, how something so wonderful - the baseball catch, and the celebration afterwards could turn so sour with the fight.

"Up and at 'em, Boy. If you're going with me, that is." Uncle slapped his hand on the bedroom wall.

Brick wormed sluggishly from the blankets to sit up in the morning sunlight. "Couldn't sleep all night expecting today - just dozed off."

"We'll bundle you up good," Burnie advised, "until we get there, so your Auntie and Mom won't worry." Brick skinned off his pajamas and grabbed his clothes from the leather rocker. Burnie strolled to the window. "Great day for baseball." The ocean rolled strong and friendly in the curve of bluffs at the river mouth. A marsh hawk tilted on the wind, dropping in graceful swoops.

Excitedly, Brick ate only half of his grapefruit, the yolk of a fried egg, and the center of his toast. "You must be plannin' a homer," Burnie said, an eyebrow raised. He pawed into the cereal box. "Should be something down here; box top said so." His hand crunched through the flakes until he grinned. "There you are, Boy, a present." He spun a miniature Mickey Mouse across the table. Brick watched, mildly amused. A weighted base wobbled it upright. Auntie walked out of the pantry, her face dark and

50

set. Defensively, Burnie said pointedly, "The game won't hurt him if he keeps bundled afterwards. He'll go for a few hits, and play center field."

"Then when he coughs all night, you going to get up and care for him?" Sathia scowled. "Well, are you? You know his mother is worried."

Burnie pouted slightly; rubbed his nose and then his chin. "Well, a boy needs to be a boy at times."

"I'll be okay," Brick assured.

"You don't know," Sathia snapped, walking from them, into the living room with Burnie and Brick trailing. "You been getting a cold, Brickford. And, you, Burnie, you don't know either." She pulled a feather duster from her apron, patted it brusquely over the mantel, then down the bookcase and over the sofa. "When he's with us here, he's our responsibility."

"But, it's only a softball game."

"Yeah, just a game." Brick was bubbly, bright-eyed.

"My two children," Auntie sighed, shaking her head. She confronted them; glowered at them. "I warn you both; if Brickford gets a bronchial attack; if he gets sick and misses school - then you, Burnie - you face the parents - Darlene especially."

"So? Clarence is coming - he's attending the game. He helped coach."

"Humph. Men!" Sathia turned back to dusting. In her own way, she was submitting. Burnie looked at Brick, and communicated a victory sign by curling his mouth and lifting his eyebrows.

The car hummed down the road toward Springhill Grammar School, site of their final game. "Shiro Yamoto and your dad will meet us there. Dad will bring the truck and most of the team and equipment." Burnie measured the curves ahead, tooting the horn now and then to warn drivers of his approach.

"I know," said Brick, pounding a fist into his mitt. "Wow, everything's going great." He reached back and tickled Spud's ears. The pooch bounced happily around the rear seat. Mr. Yamoto and his dad had coached the players, when time permitted, with Mrs. Applebee, their teacher supervising; she didn't know much about baseball, beyond what she had read. But, she was sporting and enthusiastic. Uncle Burnie had showed up to give support, when he could get away.

"OK, Brick babe, like I showed you," Toby chortled. The Springhill nine shifted; the shortstop moved up; the right fielder dropped back, not knowing Brick, anticipating a trick.

"Go go, Brick babe, go go," the kids in the bleachers chanted. The team rose from their bench. The Dallas twins twisted their visors up cockily. Gerve beamed with pride as Brick raised the bat, angling it the way Toby had trained him. The pitcher measured, tilted a shoulder forward, whipped his arm back, then windmilled the softball over. Brick swung, nearly losing his balance.

"Stee-rike."

"Don't chop them," Toby yelped. Uncle Burnie crowded in with the kids. The Springhill team smiled with confidence and crept forward. Brick wetted his lips and tapped the plate. Whiz came the ball.

"Strike."

Brick felt a sinking feeling. He so wanted a hit, not a homer, just a hit. Uncle had said it didn't matter, except to those joyful in seeing him play, that he was well enough. The pitcher readied and wound out a fast one. With half-closed eyes, Brick swung. Kwump! The ball zipped at the shortstop, scooted up his arm and over his head. There was confused scurrying in the outfield as the ball bounced beyond a reaching glove and then between a pair of pursuing feet. Brick thudded across first. The Gold Ridge kids jumped up, to cheer as one. Toby sprang high and threw his hat.

Ila May moved to bat, the only girl on the team. Daringly Brick sneaked toward second. From the corner of his eye, he saw Toby clutch his cap and crush it. Splat - the first baseman snatched the ball from the pitcher, as Brick slid back - safe. Sobered, he watched Ila May wrap the bat around her for three strikes, closing the inning.

The game passed tensely. Bottom of the ninth inning, Gold Ridge Grammar School ahead two to one, with Springhill members up to bat. Toby remained as pitcher, Ray Dallas at first; Jay commanding second; Gerve the shortstop. Brick stood deep at center field waiting anxiously. He could see Burnie, Mr. Yamoto, and his dad together in the stands. Rose & Mike had arrived late.

Deftly, Toby windmilled three perfect pitches over the home plate, as a Springhill batter swung out. One player remained on first following a bunt. Glancing over his shoulder to observe the runner, Toby wound a pitch, lower than intended. The batter swung upward, smacking it, sailing it high outward, the crowd gasping audibly. Brick saw the ball coming, like a big black comet against the western sun, approaching, growing enormously. Brick readied himself, concentrated, lifted his glove and felt the smack as he enclosed the priceless gem, his right hand trapping it. Instinctively, he heaved the ball to Jay Dallas at second, as the remaining runner rounded the base toward third, halted, tried to return and became flustered, dancing one way and the other. Jay started to throw the ball to the third baseman, until he saw Toby charging in to intercede. He tossed the ball to the young Japanese, who caught the hapless runner, tagging him, ending the game. A Gold Ridge victory.

Everybody patted and hugged everybody else. His teacher, Mrs. Applebee, his dad, Mr. Yamoto, and all the kids squeezed and pumped Brick's hand. Toby said, "You looked darn near professional." Rose and Mike embraced everyone.

Uncle Burnie stood back, luxuriating in Brick's glory. When the fervor subsided, he announced, "I'll take everybody for milkshakes, at Paluzzi's place on the bay."

"Hooray," the kids shouted. At all the parents' insistence, the two teams joined, shaking hands and punching each other in good sportsmanship, although the Springhill nine each slumped in obvious depression. Then, heaped with bats and mitts, the Gold Ridge gang pushed and piled into Mr. Yamoto's spacious station wagon; others onto the bed of Clarence's truck.

"You go with the other kids, I'll follow," said Burnie to his grandson.

Toby pressed forward. "Why can't we go with you, Mr. Burton? Brick, Gerve and Me?" Gerve nodded, supporting the request.

Obviously pleased, Burnie shrugged submission. "Whatever you wish." The boys swayed tightly clasping each other's arms.

With whomever he went, Brick was elated. Since the sixth grade he had been on the team as a regular, but, often missing games when bronchitis attacks hit him, which had plagued him from the first grade on.

"Brick is going to play at least once, hopefully more, this year," Burnie had told Mrs. Applebee. That was shortly after he had discovered Brick crouched under the bleachers, watching, as Ray Dallas rounded out a homer. "I don't care what my wife thinks, or what his mother says," he had talked grimly. "His father and I agree, the boy is going to play. He'll practice easy, and people don't have to know."

In secret, Toby had assisted, coaching Brick after school and on weekends, usually in the pasture above the Sea Ranch. Toby had taught him how to hold a bat, free and ready from one's shoulder; how to lean into a pitched ball, with one's weight; how to place the feet for perfect balance, and for greatest flexibility. For hours, sometimes, he and Brick played catch, strengthening their arms, and perfecting their timing, which was not easy, for Brick often got his feet crossed, or his arms entwined, so that he dropped the ball or even fell. Toby had tried not to react, tried not to show his frustration. But, his frequently closed eyes and his squinched face distracted, sometimes unnerved the overly sensitive Brick. Toby, however, remained patient. Happily, he caught or chased the balls that Brick hit.

The Buick hummed down the road toward Tomales Bay and the village of Marshall. Spud yapped joyously until everyone scolded him. Tomales, a 12 mile inlet, lay bordered by woodlands and rolling dairy land, a sportsmen's paradise with salmon and halibut in the channels and wildfowl in the tide flats. Here in the spring, racing enthusiasts leaned sailboats against the wind. Here, archaeologists explored the graceful sand dunes for Indian burial grounds, uncovering pottery and beads, and sometimes human bones. Here Russians, Spaniards, and Yankees had vied for control. Later, ranchers, Scotch and Swiss Italians, made it rich and productive.

Brick and his family loved exploring the area. Just strolling the shores, Brick could be wisped back into history: Russians vigilant in the towers silhouetted against the bay; their guns aimed threateningly from the fort. Red-coated Spaniards approaching on prancing white steeds, their lines fanning before the redwood gates, now opening. Words. White angry faces. More words. A brandished knife, flashing. Brick wanting to cry out. Too late. Gunfire. Collapsing horses screaming to earth. Shouts. Returned fire. A fur-garbed Russian plunging headlong over the wall. The command, "Charge." Blazing muskets, anguished cries, creaking leather, thunderous hooves, mingled in the spattering mud.

Burnie eased the car around the curves, the sun sparkly bright on the bay. They skirted a cove where threads of water laced between beds of pickle weed. Shorebirds played in jittery flight, their white and black wings fluttering. A white egret stood regal like a statue against the sand glare. The boys observed without seeing. "Our best game this season," Toby gushed, happier than Brick had seen him for some time. "This is great - no war talk for a change. That will be good for dad." The words rolled awkwardly for Toby.

"Yeah," Burnie assured. "I was so glad your dad and Clarence were there for you guys - especially Rose and Mike. That was great seeing them show - late- but, they got there."

"Surprised me," said Toby. "They've been showing up more in public all the time."

Gerve's brown eyes glimmered with pleasure. "Mike must have missed class to get here. He's a great guy, except my dad just doesn't think that Mike and Rose should be so close - boy and girl, you know."

"My dad is the same," Toby lamented. "It isn't right."

"No, it isn't," Burnie agreed.

"It's all about hating Japanese."

"Well, it's complicated, a lot of Japanese came to America as Japan was becoming more powerful. I guess it was to escape what they saw in their home country. But, people, here, looked at it as an invasion. The leaders and the military in Japan have sided with Hitler. That's why much of the hard feelings here now; lot of locals think they might figure in sabotage or guerrila warfare, or something like that." Burnie squirmed uncomfortably, wishing he had not spouted history and crushing reactions. "I shouldn't have opened my mouth," he uttered, his lips tight and gray.

"But, Mr. Yamoto would never do that," Brick said.

"He hates Hitler and he hates Emperor Tojo," Toby said in frustration.

"Your father is a very sensible man."

"He even said he doesn't understand his old country anymore."

"He's a good American, your father." Burnie looked back at the boy in the rearview mirror. "Trouble is, if people are scared or hatin', they don't see individuals. They just feel hate or fear."

On an infrequent straightaway, nearing Marshall, Clarence passed the Buick with the team members hooting and waving from the truck bed, followed by Shiro Yamoto and the rest of the team, hollering and thumbing their noses from the station wagon. "This subject is too heavy," Burnie cautioned. "We got some serious celebrating to do."

Marshall, a slumbering colony with the buildings clinging like mussels to the bay edge, hung gray and salt bitten from years of sea wind and winter storms. Burnie pulled in front of Paluzzi's store, its faded yellow front bordered with hand-carved gingerbread, shades of a forgotten era. Old men, gray and forlorn, sat sunken in chairs on the long porch. They regarded the boys and Burnie with impassive curiosity. Clarence and Mr. Yamoto's machines were lined outside, the team all inside. On Paluzzi's extended wharf, four boys threw rocks at a mewing gull. Their zeal contagious. They looked familiar to Brick. "Don't you recognize them?" Toby said coolly.

"Yes," said Gerve. "The Browns."

"By golly, it is." At that moment, Brick and his friends recognized Mr. Brown, casting a fishing pole from an adjoining longer wharf. The line and sinker plopped into the shallow water.

Spud frisked out the car door to sniff canes and shoes. From off the wharf, where the four boys frolicked in mischievous play, a muscular bulldog trotted, his hackles stiffening. Spud backed into the building, his eyes apprehensive, his ears back. With a flurry of fur and teeth, the bulldog charged. Hunched old men bounced to life and departed with amazing swiftness. Spud yowled and vanished under the porch; there, the big dog pawed at the dust like an enraged bull. People poked heads out of the grocery store; more filed out of an adjoining bar; others meandered out of a barber shop; a few strolled over from the garage. The four Brown boys, to Brick's surprise, ran from their wharf and hauled the snorting dog back. They stood about, dull and clumsy, staring at where Spud was hiding. It angered Brick, infuriated him, they and their bully hound. He wanted to walk up and punch one or two of them.

Of course, there were four, but, with so many adults around, the fight couldn't go long he reasoned.

Brick saw himself, like in the movies, sending the first Brown reeling up the porch through the saloon doors and over a table, him pushing in, the other Browns following. Brick turns, catches the second Brown, spinning him against the bar; the first Brown rolls up, swings wildly, a smashing cuff to the jaw, downing Brick to scoot along the floor. With the swift ease of a Jujitsu expert, he bounces to his feet. A third Brown swings a chair. Brick backhands him, slamming him crazily, brokenly, as he thunders against a wall to collapse. The first Brown reeling dizzily, stunned by Brick's power, reaches for his gun; too fast for him, Brick, with perfect precision, knocks the gun aside and cross hooks a left. The Brown, his arms flailing, crashes through a window and splashes into the bay. The fourth Brown, the little one, begs for mercy; and Spud, ferociously chases the bulldog up the street.

Uncle grunted to his knees, stretched out on his pillowy stomach and peeked under the porch. "Here, Spud, old boy. Come here, old boy." Spud hid his nose in his paws and bellied deeper. "Come here, you little devil," he commanded. "Come on, you crazy mutt." A couple of mechanics stretched down too, and peered under. Brick joined to see Spud, bigeyed, quivering in the darkness. Burnie called and whistled. The mechanics called and whistled.

Brick coaxed, "Come on boy, it's okay." Whimpering, Spud slid out at last, his eyes sorrowful, his ears droopy.

"Roll down the windows and get that dog back in the car," Burnie ordered, worming himself up. Brick tossed Spud into the Buick, as everyone watching laughed. The Browns tugged their struggling hound down the wharf.

Once inside Paluzzi's store, Brick felt great, so terribly glad. Everyone, his dad, Mr. Yamoto, the team sat happily congested in a corner window overlooking the wharf. It was pleasant in the warm sun, although, outside, afternoon winds stirred the bay into churning-white breakers.

"Hip, hip hooray," they all cried, their voices resounding through the building.

"Well, buddy, we did it," Toby said, punching Brick lightly.

The Dallas twins rose with set legs, their cap visors tipped up. Ray raised a water glass toward Brick and sang, "For he's a jolly good fellow, for he's a jolly good fellow." Everyone joined in a rousing song. Burnie got coy, loving the attention on his grandson.

"Speech, speech," somebody yelled. Ila May whistled, others clapped. Some men at the counter laughed.

"Nope, no speech," Brick blushed, embarrassed.

"I got a speech, then," Toby piped. He lifted a fist. "To us buddies; we'll be buddies forever and ever, even with Ila May."

"Hooray!" everybody whooped and some whistled. Ila May, crazy looking with her cap backwards over a pony tail, her little fingers pressed against her teeth, whistled loudest, so that customers flinched.

"Hello, Burnie," a group of men chimed, playing cards, and sitting lazily around a table. "How's the dog catcher?" one teased. Grinning, Burnie slid into a booth, with Brick, Gerve, and Toby at his sides. "Want a cigar, Burnie?" another offered.

"No, got to watch my old ticker, I guess."

"Must be a big celebration," said Paluzzi, serving the team a second platter of sodas and shakes. "What do you boys want?" He concentrated on the three buddies and especially on Burnie. His clownish face beamed with enjoyment.

"Whatever they want," Burnie giggled with joy. "It sure is a celebration. All these boys here are baseball men and they deserve the best." Brick was glad, so terribly glad. He drew noisily through a straw, consuming the rich sweetness of a vanilla shake. He liked Mr. Paluzzi, and loved the store; the side nearest the wharf was a combination fountain bar that offered sandwiches, milkshakes, sundaes, and tap beer. Back of the beer fountains, on the dingy walls, hung outdated calendars of pinup girls, sweet-faced, full-mouthed and shapely. Brick could never resist looking; what embarrassed him were the people seeing him look, especially at the one back of the cash register. On a beach, behind a rock, the girl was changing her clothes, looking painfully frustrated as a little golden spaniel carried away what she needed.

The place was like a wildlife museum. Many-tined deer heads adorned the walls. On a shelf above the mirrors stood mounted geese, a snarling wildcat, and a slinking fox. A bald eagle filled a corner ceiling with its stretching wings. Above the windows on sculptured plaques, hung thick salmon, all winners from local derbies.

The second half of Paluzzi's Palace (as locals liked to call it), was devoted to rows of general merchandise and wall shelves that extended to the high ceiling, filled with everything imaginable. To reach goods, Mr. Paluzzi had a ladder on runners which he scooted about. Jokers frequently asked him for objects on the highest shelf, just to watch him climb, for he was chunky with a belly that shook. He grunted and puffed much, grumbling the while. He had bushy black hair and a mustache that wriggled as he talked. His glasses magnified the dark eyes, making them owlish and penetrating.

In addition to running the store, he harvested oysters from the shallows beyond his wharves. There, in a tightly picketed enclosure, they lay thick in pearly clusters, protected from starfish and other crawly creatures that might devour them. When not serving his customers, Paluzzi cleaned oysters at a side counter, where there were hoses and drainage pipes. With hands gloved in black rubber, he'd slip an ice pick between the clamped shells, snapping them apart; then with an experienced scoop, he'd slice out the pale white meat. He delighted in entertaining children by sometimes swallowing a raw oyster in one juicy gulp. "You gonna gag-down some oysters for us?" Ila May called out, grinning broadly, her freckles arranging themselves in a devilish manner.

"No, when you kids are through, go enjoy yourselves." The teammates finished up quickly, many racing out, the Dallas twins swaggering like old-time lawmen into the street, Ray tossing a baseball up and down in his mitt.

Brick did not join them just yet. "Gee, thanks, Unc. It's been a swell day." He accompanied the old man to the cash register with his dad and Mr. Yamoto trailing.

"Don't mention it, Boy."

"Guess I better see what's going on." Brick left, his steps jaunty.

"Let me help pay," said Mr. Yamoto.

"And I want to help, too," Clarence reached for a billfold.

"No, I invited you. This is on me. You two go out and help the boys celebrate. Seems the Dallas twins still have their mitts and a ball - may want to play catch." He watched Shiro Yamoto and his nephew-in-law nudge shoulders and exit.

Paluzzi took the tag and money and rang it up. He leaned across the counter, looking back and forth for anyone hearing, his eyes big through the thick glasses, his face red. "The two Japs, I take it, are with you."

Burnie looked up curiously. "Yeah. Why? You know Shiro Yamoto. He owns that big drier inland. He's one of our coaches and his son is our star pitcher." Burnie's voice grew thick and sultry.

Paluzzi stiffened. "No offense, Burnie. It's just that some of the stores are putting up signs. They're not serving Japs - I mean Japanese anymore, that's all." He looked into an unsympathetic face. "Now, you know I'd never do that. I'd never really turn Japs - I mean Japanese away." He laughed self-consciously. "Except, you know that they are going to push us into war - you know, I know, everyone knows."

"Probably true," said Burnie checking his change. "But, we can't beat up our neighbors and friends, for what a few idiots are doing across the world." Burnie raised his eyes to connect with Mr. Paluzzi.

The storekeeper could not hold the connection. He looked down and admitted. "You're probably right, Burnie. Pains me, but, I think you are right."

Outside, the team scattered in happy disarray. Clarence and Shiro Yamoto walked away west into the strong winds, invigorating and ruffling, to share ranching talk. The Dallas boys tossed the fat baseball to each other. "Hey, guys, we won; some more ball?" Ray called. The team members, including Toby, hung back, waiting, not sure. "Hey, we're out of school, no jail 'til Monday. And our old brain beater, Applebee, she ain't here, probably couldn't take men talk, I guess. Whole front street here is ours. All ours. Like it used to be in Frisco. We cleaned all the streets up of bad guys; then it became San Francisco." He and his brother, husky, with square faces, their short noses freckled, made them look pugnacious.

"Hey, Brick, old partner. Come on, let's pitch a couple."

"Let's go, Brickie," Jay chuckled, "You won us the game." He took a ball tossed back from his brother and whipped it upward.

Ray broke into a racing charge, judged, and jumped high to bring the ball down in a perfect enclosure, swivel-hipping over an imaginary base. He jumped and danced. "Scored," he shouted, skipping and dancing again. "You ready, Brick? Here comes the winning catch again."

"Back off. Don't get sucked in," Toby called.

Frantically, Brick tried to think of an excuse - a sprained ankle, a cracked rib. Ray retreated for the throw, his right arm cocked, his left pointing. He heaved the ball bullet-like. Halfheartedly, Brick reached; the missile twanged against his naked thumb. "Eeeeeouch," he wailed, grimacing, thinking it broken. Gallantly, he pursued the wayward ball, booting it instead, slamming it against a porch to ricochet back into the street.

"Eeee gads," Jay spouted, grasping the loose ball with one hand and flipping it over his back as a floater. With desperation, Brick lunged; somehow, impossibly, it dropped between his hands, conking his head. Furiously he sprawled over it. "Looks like you're after a greased pig," Jay taunted.

Suddenly, the Brown boys were standing to the side, watching in rapt concentration. Their bulldog, tied on the outer wharf, barked in a frenzy. "Better stay out of this," Toby said solemnly, extending his arms to press his teammates back.

The littlest Brown giggled, nervously. All their expressions were growing more elated. Ray sensed a threat. "Go on," he shouted, "this is our game - no one allowed." Everyone froze. Toby held his arms extended, the team members rigid. Brick remained face down on the street, to watch and wait. At school, the two families had disliked each other from the start, fighting once, until Mrs. Applebee separated them. The Browns had entered school, recently, so late in the year, that they could not fulfill requirements necessary for passing onto a higher grade. "You hear?" Ray said again. "Go on, Get. Put an egg in your shoe and beat it." He looked around, impressed with his wit. "Make like a tree and leave," he tried again. "We don't like Okies who stink." The air was electric then. Brick got to his feet, his heart pounding. "Go on," Ray said, advancing, his face tough. Deep down, a meanness jolted through Brick, exhilarating him. Suddenly then, he wanted the Browns to twist with hurt, the way they had hurt Toby.

Ray, seeing his brother and Brick backing him, yelled, "You guys are asking for it. We're going to beat you up, Okies." The Browns crouched like animals, defensively, their eyes darting. The littlest one started whimpering.

Like the strike of a cobra, Ray lashed a right into the oldest Brown, which landed with a squishing sound, so that he staggered and grasped his face. Blood squirmed between his fingers and down the faded sweater. He uttered a wild cry and burst away to the wharf, his brothers following, frantic-eyed and loose-mouthed. The Dallases bolted after them.

Jay, his eyes glowing, shouted, "Let's get 'em good."

"Hey, babies. Hey, babies," The twins sang in disharmony.

"Hey, run Okies," Ray yelled.

Jay liked that, too, so he yelled, "Hey, run stinky Okie babies."

"Okie babies," Brick ripped out, surprising himself, but feeling better as he, too, went into the street. The oldest Brown sank against the railing, his legs buckling. Blood streamed around his receding chin and trickled down his throat. He sniffed and wiped his pointed nose with a red-smeared arm. The Brown with the buck teeth, clenched his hands and cowered slightly waiting. The little Brown dug his fists into his eyes and sobbed.

"Come on," Ray teased, his voice venomously sweet. "Come on. Show us what big tough guys you are." He held out his hands and gestured them to him. "Come on and fight, all of you. Take me on," he screamed, when no one budged. "All of you. Take me on."

Clarence and Shiro Yamoto were rushing up the street. Burnie came out of the restaurant. Clarence shouted, "Stop it. Stop it you kids. And, you, Shiro. Stay out of this. Don't want you involved. I'll handle it." He strode forth. "You kids stop it, knock it off," he growled, pushing in between the Browns and the Dallases. He saw Brick had been involved. "What the devil you doing in this?" His eyes snapped at his son, more angry than Brick could ever remember.

Mr. Brown came jogging off the wharf, pole bobbing in his hand, his face strained, his mustache twisting. "Don't know what happened here.

Sorry," he apologized, clutching the two older boys by their collars and marching them away, their bulldog yanking on his leash. The waters reflected slivers of painful light. Brick shaded his face, ignoring his father, for he felt incredibly small. At the mouth of the bay, crashing the sand bar, the growling waves sounded and resounded, their pounding fury would remain with him, he knew.

7

Grammar school was over, at last, and Brick was a high school freshman. Miserable with a stuffy head and a hacking cough - caused by his dramatic involvement with the baseball game and the Dallas/Brown fight. He kept wondering why he had vented such hate. The exciting baseball catch, suddenly didn't seem so important.

Following a phone call from Darlene, Dr. Thurlong had come to the Sea Ranch, since he was in the area checking a woman with child and a crippled old man. "Well, so our boy got a relapse, huh?" Dr. Thurlong said that evening, his Mississippi voice deep and rolling. "Been winning baseball and refereeing dog fights, I understand." He looked devilishly at Burnie, who glanced down and squirmed uncomfortably. Sathia and Darlene crowded around Brick, who, lay back in a comfy rocker, a thermometer stuck in his mouth.

"A shame," said Sathia, raising her nose in disdain. "When he returned from that - that -," she tried to think of something disparaging - after hesitation, she just finished with, "game, he got sick - all congested up, and coughing something fierce." She looked accusingly at Burnie. "I especially told him not to take the boys to that Paluzzi place."

"Doggone it, woman, the boy was a hero in that game. A hero. And, the kid-squabble afterwards, just happened." Burnie had puffed his whole body. "Things happen like that around boys and dogs."

"It was my fault," Darlene lamented. "I should have gotten leave these last few days, been here for my boy. I should have gone to the game, although I feared this would happen." She patted her son's arm.

"Nonsense," said Dr. Thurlong, "Why feel guilty? You have to stand aside a little; so the boy gets sick, he'll outgrow it, and there's new medicines appearing." He removed the thermometer and read it. "Yeah, it's the old bronchial problem." He pulled a stethoscope from the mysterious black bag. "Okay, Babe Ruth, the usual." Brick inhaled deeply while the cold instrument explored his chest. Dr. Thurlong listened intently. "Now breathe out." He slid the knob around Brick's back. The doctor reminded Brick of a bantam rooster with his quick jerky steps and his red hair combed forward, partly back, and some sideways to conceal an expanding bald spot. His freckles quivered in amusement, as he replaced his gear, and shook his patient's hand. "You been shot out of the saddle, cowboy, but not for long."

Sathia suddenly blurted, "Doctor, you should check Burnie. He's having heartburn a lot - I hope it's not my cooking."

"Sathia, this is not the time or place," Burnie huffed.

"Little indigestion?" Thurlong inquired.

"A little, maybe," Burnie conceded.

"Best you call my office for an appointment. Things like that need checking. Things I can't do here."

"Some coffee, Doctor, I have a fresh pot on the stove," Sathia offered.

"Just a spot, I've got other patients waiting." Brusquely, Thurlong led the family in a procession out of the room into the kitchen.

"Does he need to go back to the allergy specialist?" Darlene asked.

Brick cocked his head to hear better.

"He'll just say the same thing, dust and pollen are the big cause. Possibly a drier climate could help. We know the ocean has been helpful for him. Good coffee, Sathia, wish I had time for more." He set his cup down. "Before I go, I'll say this, Darlene. The best medicine in the world would be a reconciliation between you and Clarence." There was silence.

"A recon --- what?" Brick strained to hear.

"You're saying it's psychosomatic?" Darlene's voice rose.

"I'm saying the boy is at a trying age. Any stability you two could afford him would sure help. If you two could work something out. That is my opinion, for what it is worth."

"Psycho -- what?" Brick muttered. It infuriated him when doctors didn't talk English.

"So long, Doc," Burnie called.

Miserable, with a stuffy head and a hacking cough, Brick stayed indoors for the needed period to recover. They were shiny days of cold sunlight and wind that rustled the doors and windows, that brought spices of seaweed and decaying marsh, mingling wild and free, that made him hunger for the far country, where ocean and sky and mountain blended; to go with Spud at his heels, a pole on his shoulder, when and where he wished; to go where the tide called.

In the evenings, Darlene visited. Together, with Sathia, they listened to radio dramas and comedies. Mr. McPeak sent Brick a new copy of one of his favorite stories: TREASURE ISLAND. Brick loved the tale, as his mother had read it to him, when he was young. He identified with Jack Hawkins, admired Squire Trelawney; and, try as he might, he could not dislike that shrewd, but, lovable, Long John Silver, and his memorable parrot. It was fun listening, for her voice speeded at the attack, tensed at a crisis, and saddened at touching moments.

Clarence visited, too, bringing hunting and fishing magazines. Fortunately, to Brick's relief, he did not mention the Dallas/Brown incident. Although Brick knew eventually, he would have to confront his father - about feelings he could not grasp. The parents dropped in at different time slots, apparently avoiding each other; if they did meet, it was amiable, although a few contacts ended in bickering, which angered Brick.

Being "under the weather" for a while had its advantages. Sathia fixed custard puddings and played cards, or listened to her soap operas with him, while polishing eggs for market. When cleaning house or baking bread, she often sang. Her voice drifted high and surprisingly sweet as she lost herself in work. Somehow Brick could not reconcile her serious nature with happy and romantic songs; yet, old-timers told about her at camp meetings, as a girl, playing the piano and harmonizing with her sisters.

Burnie came in from work frequently to see how his boy was doing, usually announcing, "I'm letting the pooch in to visit."

"That dog better be good, then," Sathia would say, sounding her old self, as Spud romped through the house and wriggled up to the big chair, to kiss Brick with a slurp.

Brick would wipe his face, rub the dog's ears, and invariably say, "Down, dumb hound."

For Brick, early summer was both pleasurable and painful. He was excited about high school, but, he sensed that momentous forces were happening around the world, that he did not understand - that disturbed him. On the positive side, Clarence and Mr. Yamoto chaperoned the graduation picnic and led the pony ride through back trails of the redwoods. Brick was grateful that his father had taken the time, that he was sharing more with the kids, as did Burnie and Mr. Yamoto.

Because he was allergic to pollens and dust, Brick could not work for his dad. Instead, he helped Burnie and Sathia, feeding chickens, gathering eggs; carrying tools for his uncle, which he enjoyed, feeling good that he could assist. He did not see Gerve, who was working on his father's ranch, or, Toby who was working in his dad's drier; nor had he seen the Brown boys and their father, now gathering apples for Clarence.

Frequently, in the afternoons, he and Sathia picked blackberries up in the redwood glades. Brick loved Auntie's succulent pies and cobblers, which were rich and sweet, the crust flaky. In addition, she fixed his favorites: thick beef stews, creamy clam chowders, and date-nut cakes. And sometimes in the early evenings, he and Burnie fished for perch where the Stemple met the sea. With weighted lines, they cast far into the rumpled waters, sitting afterwards to watch the wet sand flush with color. Burnie, then, in a contemplative mood would remove his harmonica from a pocket, close his eyes, and let the melodious strains of "Annie Laurie," or "Home on the Range" drift across the marshes.

Darlene had become a puzzle and a pain to the family, anguishing and frustrating Clarence. Apparently, she had consulted a lawyer about divorce, but could not commit herself to such, although still dating Mr. McPeak. She had said nothing about it to Brick; however, the thin walls told secrets and he had overheard the family. She continued renting her apartment, while visiting the Sea Ranch regularly. Burnie and Sathia remained gracious and receptive always, although Brick knew they were hurting inside.

The morning of July Fourth was bright warm; the Pacific blue and glassy. The cattle moved from the hill to the deep shade of the gum trees. Chickens fluffed lazily in the dust under the weeping willow. Uncle Burnie walked from the mailbox with its daily paper and handed Brick the funnies. They settled in the wicker chairs on the long front porch. First, Brick tried reading Prince Valiant; then Blondie, but, the excitement was too great. Clarence was taking them to Joy Woods - a popular park in the redwoods - there would be a carnival, games for the little kids, a log rolling contest, an arm wrestling competition, with dancing and eventual fireworks at night. There'd be potluck food, and Sathia's fried chicken and corn bread. Waiting was unbearable.

Restless, Brick tossed the paper down and wandered through Sathia's rose garden, down the road, to the white fence and crawled onto the high gate. By leaning back and forth, he swung the gate, riding it lazily; soon growing bored. Exasperated, he stared down the road, bathed in shadows of mammoth walnut trees. "Doggone it, Dad, where are you?" he cried aloud.

At last, Clarence drove up. Brick rushed to meet him; but, as he approached the truck, a strange sense of guilt engulfed him. Clarence looked tired, thin, his face leathery from sun, as he had been working long hours on the ranch, supervising crews in the early harvest - necessary numbers beyond what the Brown family could accomplish. Brick knew that Toby and Gerve had been helping their dads; that they had assumed responsibility by working side by side with mature men; the sight of his father, alone, giving precious time to the family now, made him hesitate. I'm letting you down, he thought uncomfortably.

"Hi ya, Lop Ears," Clarence greeted, sporting a Hawaiian shirt with green palm fronds. "Learned to pick yourself up by the seat of the pants, yet?" With calloused fingers, he squeezed Brick's neck.

"Aw," said Brick, "that's getting old." They walked toward the house.

Clarence laughed softly, "You're growing up. Hard to believe. You can still do it, someday, if you're a good man." That was an old joke, dating back before the time Brick had ripped a good pair of slacks trying.

"Howdy," said Burnie handing the sports page to Clarence. "Sathia's getting her chicken and stuff together. She has a light breakfast ready shortly."

"It's fritters," Brick said happily, "with maple syrup."

"Well, let's go in and snitch some," Clarence suggested with a wink.

"Not me anymore," said Brick.

"Last time he did, Sathia socked him with a spatula," Burnie chuckled. Sathia specialized in small, finger-shaped pancakes called fritters - so golden and slightly crisp that Brick and Clarence delighted in scooping them hot from the skillet before Sathia could serve them, which both flattered and irritated her.

"Yes, my hands are still stinging from the last time she whacked me," Clarence added in mock concern. They sat quietly reading, Brick returning to the funnies. The hills, bleached and shimmering, lay hushed. A dove cooed. Bees hummed drowsily in the climbing roses. Brick tried to enjoy the moment, but, it was no use; he thought of his mother. What was she doing now? Who was she with? Was she alone on a holiday? How could she be happy without her loved ones, where she belonged? He wished that she might be present, so the day could be a real family outing.

Uncle rattled the paper, sat taller, and leaned forward as if to see better. He read seriously, his mouth moving silently. "You hear about this?"

"No. What?" said Clarence.

Burnie read on, paused thoughtfully, then passed the sheet to Clarence. "This little article here." Burnie pointed, and frowned, as Clarence's eyes snapped across the lines.

"What about it?" asked Clarence.

"Hitler decorated some Nazi boy for turning his father in as a resistance fighter, claiming he's a spy. Now they could execute the man. That's a report that comes out of the Belgium underground. It says so right there."

"Too bad," said Clarence taking the paper.

"But, to make a hero out of the kid?"

"Whether for us or for them, I don't much hold for spies; guess they're necessary, though," Clarence said in his practical way.

"Yet, to turn his own father in," Burnie mulled. "That I can't understand. And to accept an award and think he's done right. That's terrible."

"The Nazis encourage that sort of thing," said Clarence.

Burnie was lost in his thoughts. "Okay, the militant Germans are bad. I just don't understand how a child can be so twisted," he said, shaking his head. "Just no character or no decency. And to turn his own father in." He clicked his tongue. "It's the times we're living in."

By noon, they arrived in the flatlands below Joy Woods. A glum-faced boy directed them to park in a car-crowded field. Scraping fiddles and thumping guitars sounded from the picnic area. There came a mingling of shrieks and laughter, and the barking of a bingo caller.

Brick raced ahead toward the redwood grove, now alive with activity. Firecrackers popped everywhere. Under the great trees, barbecue smoke hung savory over long tables laden with salads, casseroles, beans, cakes, pies, platters of cooked beef, and baskets of fried chicken. People sat munching in jovial groups, the elders talking, not moving much. Young parents shouted and chased and paddled children, who continuously broke into happy riot, screaming, grabbing caps, throwing them, sliding, pushing. Toddlers wandered off, falling, wailing. To the side, in a snug circle, dozens of affectionate young couples clapped hands to a radio song.

Auntie distributed her chicken and cornbread among the foods. Two small boys came over to watch appreciatively. "Dig in, fellows," she said. Instantly, brown hands shot into the bowl to clutch drumsticks. Clarence, Burnie, and Brick took paper plates and fell behind a short line. "Hello, Maud," Sathia called, as Mr. and Mrs. Raffetto waved from a table under a tall redwood.

"Come on over," Mrs. Raffetto called back, her face round and smiling. She was an enormous woman with arms as big as Brick's waist. Mr. Raffetto ambled over, dressed in his usual striped coveralls.

"Can I help you, Sathia?" he drawled.

"My, how nice of you," Sathia said, "but, no."

"How you doing?" Burnie asked.

"Not bad, not really bad. But that's what I was going to ask you." He ushered Burnie aside. Raffetto's face had a rough, unfinished look, his eyes blood streaked from days of sun and wind. Stoop-shouldered, looking older than his age, he moved slowly and spoke so deliberately, Brick could hardly handle it. Mr. Raffetto was a kind man, a good neighbor, Brick knew - if only the man could talk faster, get his words out.

"Been thinking about you lots of late," Brick heard him say to Burnie in confidence. "Sure been worried about you."

"I'm fine. Just fine." Burnie held up a hand as if to silence Raffetto.

"Your ticker again, huh? The ticker kicking up again?" He rambled on, oblivious to Burnie who glanced furtively about.

When Uncle saw Brick listening, he said abruptly, "I'm fine. Never felt better. Little indigestion, that was all. Just a little indigestion."

Brick understood the concern. Burnie and Mr. Raffetto had gone fishing on the bay. They had just launched Raffetto's small boat, when Burnie complained of feeling ill. "Indigestion," he had told Sathia later, as Raffetto delivered him to the door.

"Is it your heart?" she had asked, the words like an electric shock. "Dr. Thurlong just checked you out - cleared you."

"Just a little stomach cramp," he had assured her. The fright on Raffetto's face had made Brick wonder. Sathia had kept Uncle in the house for one day, while he scoffed at her sputtering. The next day he had puttered in the toolshed, and by the third he had fixed a leaky trough on the hill.

"What are you proving?" Sathia had raged. "Don't you have any good sense?"

"Choose your partners for an old-fashioned hoedown," called the man from the dance pavilion; his hands worked softly over his guitar. Dancers bounced up, tugging, giggling, to swarm onto a platform gaily festooned with paper streamers interlacing red, white, and blue. Band members, fancy in cowboy gear, took up their instruments. Again, came the thumping, squawking music. "Swing your ladies and do-se-do. Join hands and away we go," the man chanted. All was a frenzied blur - people clapping, prancing side by side; then around - laughing, stomping, crossing, backing, whirling. "Aw haw!," someone yowled.

"Damn," Clarence crunched the words under his breath, his eyes blinking. "Darlene - so many Fourth's - we danced here." Brick felt heavy inside for a moment, thinking he saw his dad's eyes, watery. He wished his father and mother were together again, shaking the dance floor apart, with their whirls, and snapping claps, and their thundering feet.

Several teenagers galloped horses by on the trail below, clouding dust over the picnickers and dancers. A wave of protest followed; a burly man rose and shook his fist. Two speckled dogs yelped from under a table and chased the horses, nipping their hooves. Everyone laughed, for it was all part of the chaotic fourth, a time of joyful oneness.

After a filling lunch, Brick and his dad joined the milling crowd to watch the fun. They circled first to the log rolling contest in a mill pond where skilled lumberjacks dumped one another splashing into the murky water. They visited a compact carnival with a shooting gallery, ring and penny tosses, dart throwing at balloons, and more - winners to receive rosy-faced kewpie dolls, teddy bears, and other stuffed animals. There were turkey and ham raffles; horseshoe games; pony rides for the tiny tots; barbershop singing quartets, and the busy preparation for the night fireworks and the big dance. There would be sparklers, bursting flares, rainbows of colors; there would be glowing Chinese lanterns across the pavilion; pretty girls laughing, and couples slipping secretly into the shadows. Everything smelled of summer, of weedy fields, and of sprouting branches. Brick was content within, momentarily at peace with the world. He left his dad then, to wander ahead by himself.

Ned Benucci sat playing cards with some old-timers all hunched around a table. "Hi," Brick said. "I - we - my buddies and family are going to miss you."

Ned looked up and smiled; slapped a card down. "I'll miss you kids, too - and your family, especially Burnie." Brick had just learned that Ned was leaving the cabin for a time, packing out. He had taken a good paying job in the Bay Area at a ship building center called Mare Island. "Hopefully, I'll be back after all the problems in the world settle down." He readied another card.

"Mr. Benucci." Brick's voice rose with a secret urgency, that surprised himself. He faltered.

Ned leaned toward Brick, his rough hands folding his cards with a clumsy gentleness. "What, son?"

"My friend, Toby, he and I, and Gerve, too, we think we saw otters - rare sea otters, up along the rocky coast. Could that be? You know everything about the coast - everything." Brick's eyes had dilated, even in the summer sun.

Ned Benucci turned a back to his card partners, studied Brick, his gaze addressing, focusing, and then melting with an embracing enclosure. "You boys are smart - you notice things."

"They're sea otters - real sea otters?" Brick exploded. "Real sea otters. Do you know?"

"Well, let's not get too excited."

"Meaning what?" Brick probed.

"Best to let things like that alone. Don't want harm to come."

Ned Benucci seemed to sink into himself; he studied and fanned out his cards, smiled reflectively back at Brick and pivoted around to his impatient partners.

Brick did not understand what Ned meant. Vaguely, something felt good - that maybe - just maybe he and his friends had discovered something significant - or, maybe not. He didn't know how to tell Toby or Gerve, the latter, who wasn't seeming to care anymore.

"What's troubling you?" a card partner whipped at Benucci. "Let's play."

Ned Benucci scowled at his cards; at the table, his lips twisting. "Everything's troubling me. I don't know why the Italians would side with Hitler."

Ugh, Brick thought, war talk. A beautiful day, and war talk. How boring. He left, indulged in an ice cream cone from a vender and walked further up the old road, savoring the sweet, peachy taste, thick against the roof of his mouth.

"Hey, buddy." Toby and his father came happily up a side trail, both guzzling cokes. "We're tryin' to escape all the crowds. Whatcha doin'?"

"Crazy day, but fun down there," said Brick, crunching the last of the cone. Together, they sat on a log and watched the throngs of people.

Sathia, Burnie, and Clarence trudged up the trail to join them. "We could see you up here - why?" Clarence's clear blue eyes locked into Brick. Then he nodded toward the Yamoto's, "Welcome, Shiro, Toby."

"Just wanted to get away for a time." Brick looked off, for he could not cope with his father's intensity.

"Sure not as young as I used to be," Burnie complained, puffing up with difficulty.

"Walking up this hill is not very smart of you," said Sathia.

"I think you look good. Got good color," said Mr. Yamoto.

"Now there's an observant man," said Burnie, dropping heavily to a stump.

Six teenage boys strolled by, smoking, while carelessly tossing cans into the brush and talking loudly, making Brick nervous the way they looked back and snickered. He was sure the empties were illegal beer.

"I hate to see people throw stuff like that," Mr. Yamoto said. "There's plenty of waste barrels around."

The teenagers sauntered up the trail; stopped, conferred, then came back to loiter nearby. Brick sensed trouble, for the youths kept shifting and looking at their feet; then glancing up hotly at Mr. Yamoto, as if building up courage to act. "Hey, Japs, why don't you leave those people alone?" one, the largest, hissed at last. There was an icy silence. Blood jolted through Brick. "You heard us, we don't want Japs - this is a white man's picnic." The young man speaking was tall, cruel-faced, taking pleasure in his act. Casually, he flipped a cigarette and twisted it out with his foot. The other boys waited expectantly. Brick held his breath. The youth advanced and repeated coldly, "We don't like Japs around." He slurred his words slightly, struggling possibly from the effects of alcohol.

"Who do you smart alecks think you're talking to?" Sathia exploded. "You impudent smart alecks."

"You kids better move on," said Clarence, his eyes dark, his voice filled with anger.

"Oh - Jap lovers," the youth said. His friends snickered again. In Brick, the horror broke to madness; he wanted to kill them. Beat them bloody. Hoods threatening, name-calling his friends, his family. A red hatred raged through him - more furious than that which had consumed him against the Brown boys.

"You give us any trouble," Clarence said with suppressed emotion, "we'll throw every law in the book at you. Now just go, and we'll forget it."

The leader retained his image by calling, "Jap lovers."

Mr. Yamoto said calmly, "It's all right, Clarence, we'll leave." He backed away, his face sad. "Come," he said, touching Toby's arm.

"No," said Clarence, putting out a hand to restrain them. "We're not going to be pushed around by punks. You got as much right here as they have."

"But they're Japs," the youth cried, not so confident of his position.

"They're as much American as you boys," Burnie chimed.

"Now, Burnie, don't get your heart stirred up," Sathia cautioned.

"Try something," Clarence warned, "and we'll see you go to jail for assault and battery. That's a felony, you know."

"Let's go, Bill," one of the boys urged.

"They're still Japs," the youth protested.

"Come on," another tugged at his jacket. The leader stepped back, then wiped his mouth with a sleeve, gave a haughty toss of his head and swaggered down the path, his buddies following, no longer imitating his sway. "We don't want trouble," the last boy called back, the one who had tugged the jacket.

At first, Brick felt intense relief, then a welling sickness. He wanted to go home. He looked at Toby standing silent and unmoving, very close to his father.

"I think we'd best go," Yamoto said quietly, his lips drawn.

"No need to now," said Clarence. "They won't bother us again."

"You want to come home with us, later, for supper?" Sathia asked.

"No - we'd best go. But, thank you." Yamoto looked at all of them. "Thank you." The family watched them depart through the trees, back down the side trail. Mr. Yamoto placed his arm over Toby's shoulder. They looked small under the redwoods.

8

Brick and his friends anticipated high school. Brick tried to ready himself. Now, nearly six feet tall, he wished he had a mustache, except that his upper lip looked limp with spindly hairs. He swelled his chest, flexed his biceps, turned each arm at an angle to accentuate the magnificence of his perfect body, as he envisioned it. Trouble was, he didn't look like the musclemen in the advertisements. His biceps lay limp and stretched too lengthy, needing work. His chest seemed scrunched, far too narrow. Maybe it was the bedroom mirror distorting him, not reflecting his true form. He stood taller on his toes, and swiveled a V'd torso, as did those massive body builders in the photos and sketches. Again, he couldn't see a V'd chest. For a time it was fun - for a time. Soon, he fell into a dizzy depression, realizing, that he really looked scrawny, despite his height; he sighed in resignation, "I look like some of those young roosters here on the ranch."

There had been some painful and disturbing incidents that occurred in the late summer. His father had called him aside after conversing first with Burnie and Sathia. Clarence had been earnest with a solid confidence. He had clasped Brick's right shoulder and looked at him, his light blue eyes assuring. "I had to fire Mr. Brown this week," he said, his words slow and even.

"Fire Mr. Brown?" Brick's face tightened, perplexed. He hushed the word, "Why?"

"He was stealing gas from our ranch tank."

"Stealing? Why?"

Clarence considered his answer. "With the war in Europe. With the Japanese all over Asia and more now in the Pacific, gasoline has become expensive. I'm sure it's going to be rationed, except to ranchers and farmers, who must produce food."

"How do you know he was stealing?"

Clarence kept his eyes leveled on his son. "I suspected it. He drives that old truck of his, which gulps lots of gas. I noticed the gage on our tower tank has been coming down, more than it should."

"So, how did you catch him?"

"I told him, I was going into town. I hid our big truck down in the walnut grove and came back to the house and watched out the back window, until I saw him drive around to the tractor shed."

"What did he say?"

"What could he say? I just paid him off. Now, I'll have to find someone for our remaining season." Clarence patted Brick on the back, turned to leave, and looked back. "Sorry."

Brick tilted his head aside. The Brown boys, soiled and tattered, and somehow so alone. Where would they drift now, he wondered, remembering himself delirious with revenge, and the Dallas twins, their faces contorted with savage delight. He thought of the older Brown, streaming blood and the little one whimpering like an injured puppy. He wanted to push it all from his memory, blot it out forever. But, he knew he could not, that it would haunt him.

As early fall touched gently, with long shadows and fading sunlight, other problems emerged. Mike Hamilton surprised the family one morning, knocking quietly, but, firmly. Sathia answered. Brick stood in the alcove sipping a fluffy malt. Sleepy-eyed, having stayed the night, Darlene stirred a cup of coffee. Primly dressed after a bubble bath, she was leaving for work when the unexpected guest arrived.

"Mike," Sathia's voice cracked.

"Sorry to disturb you. Is Burnie here?"

"I am." Burnie appeared in the kitchen behind Brick and walked passed him. "What can I do for you?"

The tall young man, his face pleasant, the brown hair groomed as always, contemplated them, his hazel eyes serious and concerned. "This is in confidence," he said, with suppressed emotion, and waited. The family members all nodded in total assurance. "You are wonderful friends and neighbors." Mike's lips trembled slightly, "I have to share with you, in confidence."

"What is it?" Darlene asked with alarm. She pressed forward, her hands touching her throat.

Mike smiled boyishly. "First, you probably heard, I've decided to join the Army."

"Yes, we had heard that." Burnie stood taller. "Didn't know whether it was a rumor or not."

"No, it isn't." Mike locked his hands in front of him. "Since I have some college, and following basic training, they - the government promised, or, at least claimed they will send me to officer's training school. It would be better than just being drafted outright, as will happen, you know."

Darlene, Burnie, and Sathia responded in a supportive clapping of hands. "Wow, an officer." Burnie whistled. Standing even taller, he added, "We're so proud of you."

"An Army officer, isn't that wonderful," Darlene gushed. Brick was grinning widely.

Mike Hamilton thought his words out and swallowed with control. "I'm here to tell you more than that," his eyes canvassed the family, reaching to Brick, who waited well back, fearing what to expect.

"I know my mother either wrote or phoned you - inviting you to our home for a casual supper - salads and sandwiches, mom's special desserts - a neighborhood get-together."

"Yes, we received them," Sathia said. "In fact, your Mom phoned me personally - said it was to celebrate a new job you were taking - that you were leaving college for a time."

"That's what it said in mine and Clarence's," Darlene interjected.

"Well, the new job is my joining the service - that's the celebration."

"We're proud of you, being so patriotic," Burnie added again, curling his fingers in the shoulder straps of his coveralls.

Mike licked his lips. "Actually, I wish it had been an engagement party." Silence engulfed the listeners for a moment.

"We kind of expected such, or hoped for it," Darlene said, readily in support.

"Rose is afraid." Mike's words were not apologetic - simply matter-of-fact. "There's so much fear and hatred now in the world." He grimaced and shifted his feet. He said tenderly, "I looked at some rings. Rose knows it, but she's scared to tell anyone."

Darlene's eyes lit. "I'm happy for you two."

"She wants to wait - doesn't want to stir things. She's taken that secretarial job in San Rafael. The one in the big apartment store. She'll have to find a rental there."

"She'll be good. She was such an excellent student," Darlene beamed. "A good secretary runs things, believe me."

Burnie cleared his throat. "Must be more reason why you're here." His low voice rolled, knowingly.

Mike smiled in a self-conscious, but relieved way. "There is, it's gotten to a serious decision. We may elope, to Reno."

"Sometimes that's the only way, if things don't work out," Darlene said quickly.

"I agree." Burnie said slowly. He had a resigned, slightly sad look.

Mike squared his features. "We understand Ned Benucci has left that cute little cabin of yours in the redwoods above - to work in ship construction - at least, temporarily."

"He has."

"Rose and I, we'd like to rent the place for a honeymoon. I'll have a leave after my basic training."

"Of course," said Sathia.

Burnie grew a big smile. "We'd be delighted - but, you couldn't rent. That would be our gift to you."

"And I'll help Rose prepare the place - probably needs plenty of cleaning. You know how bachelors are who do pretty much their own thing." Darlene spun slightly, whirling her dress, almost girlishly.

Relieved, Mike clapped his hands. "Wow, I can't thank you folks enough; this, of course, is amongst us - it has to be a secret, for now, until we know more." His eyes sought those of Brick's, who nodded in immediate agreement. "I must go now." Mike bowed slightly. "I will be in contact with you. I'll let you know everything."

Darlene approached the young man and embraced him. Sathia handed him a plate of mints; and, Burnie shook his free hand. Brick stepped closer and waved an approving hand.

Brick sensed that events had progressed somehow beyond control of his family and of the world. He knew, felt, realized, from some deep part, that momentous events were developing - exploding in confusing and unexplainable ways. Uncle kept big continental maps on the kitchen wall; there, he moved thumbtacks as incidents in the news changed daily. He also had a packet of miniature flags representing various German and allied forces, which he pinned according to the advance or retreat of armies. Mostly now, it was retreat for the allies, as the Nazis swarmed over the continent. Sathia shook her head, "Beats me," she decried, "a grown man playin' little general."

Brick wondered if Uncle Burnie's indigestion was more than indigestion. Was it the result of all the negative news that permeated the airwaves; that slashed across the headlines; that dominated every morning, noon, and night? Uncle Burnie was restless, for the daily news depressed him and made him fretful. In Asia, in Europe, in Africa, forces were alive and threatening peace everywhere. A raving, ranting maniac named Hitler was dominating all the news with banners and marching soldiers, their black helmets and dark uniforms thundering across the news films; the enormous tanks with thrusting cannons all backing the unlimited platoons of military force; their propaganda dominating airwaves.

In ways, Burnie had moved inside himself to work casually on the Sea Ranch, not doing much, really, except to fulfill his daily duties with the chickens - sometimes strolling aimlessly along the seashore. Brick wanted to help, somehow, but was at a loss. A year earlier - Hitler had conquered most of Europe, absorbing the lowlands of Holland and Belgium, then overflowing France, forcing the nation to surrender; crushing the defensive British units into a tragic defeat to be rescued by small boats, volunteer fishermen, and random heroes in something called Dunkerque.

Brick didn't understand - it all was boring, confusing. He hated it all, just wanting to be a freshman in high school where he could meet some pretty girls. Then, had come the onslaught of England, known as the Battle of Britain, where the Germans attempted to destroy the proud people with constant air raids, bombardments, pulverizing, engulfing the cities in flames and death - mostly London. The English, however, had prevailed, making all of Brick's family, especially Burnie, proud of their British heritage.

People began protesting the freight trains of scrap metal rolling through their towns, steel and iron that they perceived as being sent to Japan. "The Japs are going to fire all that back at us in bombs," people shouted, making noise in the streets and writing their newspapers and their congressmen. The big manufacturing corporations launched into action, producing guns and tanks, planes, ships, and munitions for the allies. Words like patriotism and espionage were on everyone's lips. Signs on the city streets, and in the store windows, and even on the country billboards, exhibited an Uncle Sam, scowling, pointing a finger, demanding action. Germany broke its nonaggressive pact with Russia and invaded the massive country.

Then, Japan had moved warships into the Pacific, and invaded French Indochina. President Roosevelt froze total Japanese assets, cutting off all oil supplies. "The Nips will attack the U.S.," a reactive headline read. In the nearby town of Sebastopol, hoodlums raided the Japanese section, stoning windows and hospitalizing two elderly men. The following day, an editorial in the local newspaper described all Orientals as treacherous.

Brick, Toby, and Gerve sat in the shadows of a side steps at the Hamilton's, waiting for the food to be arranged - a delectable presentation on the tables in the open living room and on the back screened porch. People were arriving, the women bringing salads, casseroles, meats, cheeses, and desserts. People had quietly gossiped, questioning whether Ezra Hamilton and Shiro Yamoto would attend. As a result of Myrtle Hamilton's intimidation, Ezra was waiting in the dining room, watching. Shiro Yamoto had sent a bouquet of summer flowers. People then surmised that he would not be present. He arrived quietly, and was greeted outside by Burnie, who had waited patiently, confidently.

The boys watched them shake hands and talk. Then Mr. Yamoto produced two tin cups from his truck and removed a small bottle. He poured something in both and handed one cup to Burnie. "What's that?" Brick asked.

"It's Saki, a Japanese liquor or wine, I don't know - made from rice, with a real kick," Toby explained.

"Holy cow." Brick's eyes went wide. "If Auntie learns about it."

Toby snickered, "They're just celebrating." The boys watched as the two men swigged with one gulp, licked their lips, pounded on each other, and proceeded into the house after Mr. Yamoto hid the cups back of a seat. "Wow, I never saw Uncle Burnie do that." Brick laughed to himself.

"They're just preparin' for the party," said Toby. "Probably both need it."

"Wish I could try some of that," Gerve said.

"Don't think you'd like it," Toby giggled. "You got to get used to that stuff. Any alcohol. Nothing tastes like it looks. I remember sneaking one of dad's beers - boy, it bubbled up, all golden and white, like you see in all the movies. I could hardly wait. Gulped a lot at the first try."

"How was it?" Gerve's face was concentrated, his nose, cheeks, and jaw pointing, waiting.

"It tasted like hell. I spat it all out. God awful."

The boys sat in contemplation. A small car arrived, a coupe, and parked in the shadows. "That's Mike," Toby acknowledged. "My Sis must be with him." In the enclosing twilight, the lights from the house reached the cab, revealing a couple - Rose and Mike. The boys waited, wondering what might happen, enjoying their secret proximity, feeling a mixture of guilt and excitement, that they were involved in the forbidden, as Peeping Toms. Suddenly, Mike took Rose in his arms and kissed her.

"Good gosh, my brother, smooching with a woman?" Gerve gurgled his words.

"Of course, you dummy, she's my sister and she's pretty," Toby said with pride.

The threesome waited, impatiently, nervously, anticipating something that only young adults might do. They saw the couple in the car embrace; saw them clutch arms, to draw closely; saw Mike kiss her neck; saw her eyes roll up distinct even in the faint light. "Best we get into the house now," said Brick, feeling strange stirrings in his body.

"Me, too," said Gerve, "but, maybe I'll stay."

"Gotta see this out," said Toby, nodding seriously.

The man and woman sought each others lips - softly, tenderly, then hungrily. They squirmed, working against each other, their mouths holding. Mike kissed her throat again, down to her upper cleavage, revealed partially in the white blouse. Rose laid her hands on Mike's chest, with-straining him, but, without force. She then turned aside, flipping her hair up, as if welcoming a gush of relieving air. The two sat for a time, looking ahead, until Mike took her hand and lifted it firmly to his lips.

"You know, she has a good body, I've seen it through a keyhole," said Toby.

"Well, that's it." Gerve spat with disgust. "My big brother doesn't do things like that."

"Let's get out of here," Brick said, sounding dislocated. "We're supposed to be in the house, anyway."

"Yeah," Gerve soared back. His eyes alight. "There's gonna be cake and ice cream."

The small crowd rumbled in friendly conversation, sharing local problems, but, obviously ignoring the big issues of the world - and, especially about the rumored engagement between Rose and Mike. Nobody dared suggest that - it was Mike's joining the service, and his probability of becoming an Army officer, that monopolized every discussion, for his joining was no longer a secret announcement. Myrtle Hamilton's two story ranch house had been arranged to accommodate the guests, with even the upstairs bathroom arrayed in decorations, and tables now with bounteous food. Her floor lamps had been turned low to give a romantic aura.

"Where have you boys been?" Darlene asked, standing next to Clarence, but, neither touching each other.

"Oh, just sitting around outside." Uncomfortable, Brick avoided a direct look at her or his father.

"You boys see Burnie?" Sathia asked. "He should be here with me."

"No. No." Brick assured. "Haven't seen anybody."

"No, we haven't seen anybody really," Toby added, and Gerve agreed in his toothy manner.

Then, Burnie and Mr. Yamoto appeared, seeming happier than usual, and everyone in the room clapped a welcome. Burnie shook Ezra Hamilton's hand vigorously. The man stood back some, scowling slightly, performing his expected routine as a host, a controlled graciousness that his wife, Myrtle, had threatened him to do or else.

The doorbell rang. The guest of honor walked in, his lovely lady, Rose, in advance of him. Everyone awed and gasped, and someone whistled. Rose bowed her head, blushing in shyness. "Our hero, the man of the hour," someone shouted. Another led a chant of, "He's a jolly good fellow." A few champagne bottles were popped, for those who wanted more than punch.

"Supper is ready," Mrs. Hamilton announced. "Please help yourself."

People began milling, but, eyes could not stray from Mike and Rose, the latter standing apart from her date. Were they serious? Were they secretly engaged? A White and an Oriental? The whispers reverberated. A few with genuine affection approached the couple, hugged them, welcomed them, told Mike over and over how proud they were that he was serving the military forces.

Burnie and Shiro Yamoto stood side by side, nudging one another occasionally. "You all right?" Sathia snapped at Uncle.

Burnie saluted her, "Never felt better in my life."

Mr. Yamoto also saluted her. "We're great. Love it all."

"Well, I hope so." Sathia slumped some, deciding she was too stiff. "It is a nice party," she nodded in concurrence.

Brick and Gerve joined others at the elongated tables, spread with delicacies: food so varied that the boys didn't know how to start. They piled their plates with open-faced sandwiches and cake. "Wonder where Toby is?" Brick screwed his face up, concerned.

"Oh, he's still sitting out there in the dark - can't get over Mike and his sister."

"What do you mean?"

Gerve licked some frosting from a cake, yet uncut, from which he had broken a piece. "They're Japs, that's what I mean."

"They're our friends," Brick said defensively.

"The Japs?"

"No. The Yamoto's. Toby."

Gerve shrugged, finished the bite of cake and licked his fingers. "They're still Japs."

"The three of us, aren't we good friends?" Brick pursued, disheartened. "What about the otters?"

"Otters?"

"Remember? Our secret?" A heat of anger was building in Brick.

"Well, maybe he's still your friend," said Gerve gravely, "I'm not sure he's mine anymore."

"What does that mean?" Brick raged. "What does that mean?"

Gerve dug into some potato salad. "Maybe the otters aren't real otters."

"Ned kinda suspected they might be."

"Don't mean nothin'." Gerve added slices of ham and beef to his plate; then juicy pickles.

"I just don't understand what you're sayin'."

Gerve avoided facing his old buddy. "When I saw my brother hugging that woman - not even a White girl." Frail, but, resilient, his narrow shoulders rose. The boy labored his words. "Maybe like the otters, my brother isn't real. Maybe he's not a brother anymore."

Brick looked at his friend with disbelief, feeling hollow, not knowing how to cope.

The phone rang early. Burnie answered. "Mike?" He paused. "Darlene here? Yes, she's in the kitchen. You sound upset."

Hearing the words, Darlene left the percolating coffee and took the phone. She listened, frowning. "She what?" Sathia entered the room. Brick, reading the comics, perked up and followed. "How long does she want to wait?" Darlene pursed her lips. "What did you decide?"

Sathia looked imploringly at Burnie, as if seeking to help her. He shook his head no, and slid his hand sideways, palm down, signaling - stay out.

"Maybe I can talk with her. I could phone her. We know she trusts me." Darlene listened openly, for a time. "Well, you hang in, and keep us informed." She set the phone back slowly. Curious eyes focused upon her. "Rose wants to wait. She needs more time, before getting so serious. She wants to think it over, I assume. Mike's upset, as you can expect." She shook her head. "I'm not sure what to do, exactly, except listen."

"My advice is to stay out of it," Burnie said.

"He needed to talk," Darlene replied flatly, "and, he'll need to again, I'm certain. He mentioned that Rose respects me, might listen to me."

"They're not breaking up?" Sathia sputtered.

"Oh, no, it's a delay, until they can work things out. You know, with family - then Mike joining the service."

"Well, with all the problems building here and abroad, it may not be so easy," Burnie sighed, and turned toward the kitchen. "Need some stiff coffee."

Rose returned a few days later, after staying with a friend near the City, Brick learned upon contacting Toby. The friends sat together at the base of a big apple tree overlooking the Yamoto buildings. Following a contemplative quiet, Toby said, "She wants to hold off any serious stuff with Mike. She said she had to get away to think."

"Meaning what?"

"Meaning she's going to work at her new job. Get an apartment there."

"So?"

"She figures that if they get engaged now, he'll get hurt."

"How?"

"I heard her tell dad, that she loves Mike too much. With all the bad feelings here on the coast, she fears he'll become a 'White Jap.'"

"Wow."

"Not sure of what all that means."

"Did my mother ever call Rose?"

"Not that I know of."

"Don't understand where things are going." Brick's voice trailed away. The apple leaves were tinting yellow, fluttering some in a softening fall.

Through the next days, concerned and not knowing, the family anticipated a phone ring, or a visitor, who might inform them of a tentative decision by the couple. At last, Mike called Darlene in the evening. He would work for his father on the ranch in the next three weeks or so, before reporting to Fort Ord, she informed the family after the short conversation. She answered the inquiring looks. "Things are a little shaky for now. Rose and he are not back together, yet, but I feel certain things will work out."

"We heard you say you were pleased," Sathia probed.

"He's writing Ed McPeak a thank you note. Fort Ord is primarily a draftee camp, but Ed used his military influence to get Mike in there. I told him I was pleased for thanking Ed."

"I'll thank Ed, too," Burnie added. "That means the young man will remain close to home and his loved ones, at least for the time being." Ford Ord was on the coast south of San Francisco.

9

Brick felt like an outsider in the early painful weeks of his freshman year with Toby his only real friend, the two of them a minority lost in a new teenage world of sports, hot rods, dating and sophisticated conduct. After a grammar school graduating class of six boys and one girl, high school was overwhelming: ringing bells, classes here and there with a different teacher for each, split lunches, wisecracking seniors, everybody looking bigger and older, and some girls seemingly as mature as his mother.

Never would he forget the nightmare that had been his first day on campus. Twice he had gotten lost, so that he had stumbled in late to class. Even at lunch, the cafeteria with its long lines and banging trays and yelling kids had bewildered him. Timidly, he had hidden alone in a corner, reluctant to nibble at Sathia's packed food - a hand-carried lunch seemed too much like grammar school stuff. He had had trouble with the combination on his new locker, fearing, too, that he would forget or lose the numbers.

Then late and alone after gym class, he had searched desperately for the gate through a high wire fence separating the gymnasium from the main building. In frustration, he had climbed the fence, but half way over, he had ripped a hole on the inside of his trousers. Three passing girls had hooted and waved. Humiliated, he had crawled down and had run back around the gym to the columned front of the main entrance, which he should have found in the first place. Two students, leaning out an upper window, had observed his headlong flight. "Must be a freshman," he had heard one shout.

As the hectic days flowed into fall, Brick grudgingly resigned himself to school. Spanish was dull and the teacher ancient, remembering his mother as a good student. Algebra was hard. In mixed glee, Brick found his voice cracking and high, so that the teacher placed him in front of the girls' section, along with a few other boys, who had screechy voices worse than his. Every session was torture, with him paralyzed, looking straight ahead, trying to follow the musical notes, a redness creeping around his ears. In addition, Brick found himself growing distressingly awkward with feet that wouldn't manipulate, that slammed into doorjambs and that hooked around desk legs. However, he was shooting up in height, towering over his fellow freshmen; the one good feeling, despite his sense of looking like a scrawny young rooster.

Each morning, as the bus pulled away, he would look longingly at the Sea Ranch, at the ocean of dancing whitecaps, at Spud frolicking. He envied Spud, envied the free hours in the familiar surroundings. Many times Brick wished he could quit school, savoring a hostile fantasy. The long tiring bus trip forced him up before six o'clock, and got him home at five-thirty. After chores and dinner, he could hardly keep his eyes open to study. He lived in two worlds: one of darkness and homework, one of daylight and school.

He had made no new friends yet, although a slender brunette with almond blue eyes and a pretty face, smiled at him sweetly in art class daily. Neither Toby nor Gerve were in any of his classes. Gerve concerned Brick. Something had changed him. Unlike most kids, who were sprouting from their clothes, he remained elfish and retiring. He didn't mix, but often prowled the halls or the campus alone. Back home, he had picked up with some tough eighth graders who lived with their itinerant family in a shack near the Stemple. Together, they bicycled about the countryside after school or on weekends until darkness. Then Gerve began cutting school, and missing assignments. One morning, the basketball coach caught him smoking a cigarette behind the gym and he was suspended for a week.

Everyone blamed their problems and frustrations on the fighting in Europe and on the world uncertainties. Yet, because of the conflict, a number of people were prospering. The war scare, resulting in a rising economy, was bringing thousands of people to California, thus giving the apples a new price boom and making Clarence happier and more confident. Then Darlene received a sizable raise. Immediately she bought Brick a glossy brown jacket with slacks, beige, tan, gray, and varied dark, all with matching socks. Brick preferred his Levi's, but, went along with Darlene's wishes. Admittedly, it made Brick a little better dressed than most of his classmates, a fact he momentarily enjoyed, especially when some girls started calling him, "The Jacket." That's when the Dallas twins started commenting.

"Hey, pretty boy." That's the way it commenced. "Hey, pretty boy," the Dallases smirked, their faces superior, as they faced Brick in the high school corridor. Ray mussed Brick's hair. "Ooooh, pretty curls. Why don't you butch it like everybody else?"

Jay swaggered up and said, "Oooooh, isn't he cute, Mr. Jacket," and ran a teasing finger over a new sweater. Finding a loose string, he jerked out a loop. Brick with clenched fists, snapped the thread away. He heard the Dallases laugh as other students gathered, waiting. They are still my friends, Brick told himself, not wanting trouble; especially, if they got into a fight, since he and the twins would be kicked out of school. He could not understand the twin's growing hostility.

The problem had begun in English where old Mrs. Hoyle remembered Darlene as a fine student, which left Brick self-conscious and unnecessarily pressured. The Dallases sat in the back, talking football plays with their buddies. They had made first string junior varsity, which added a sureness to their stride, and much boasting about their own importance. Constantly, they disrupted class with clever comments, or by throwing spit wads, or by hiding the girls' purses. Mrs. Hoyle would scowl at them over the rim of her glasses, and reprimand them, but, the effect was only momentary. Once, during a quiz, the twins lighted a cigar. Mrs. Hoyle, who could hardly see the last row because of nearsightedness, did smell smoke, which startled her into calling a fire alarm. The brief test was abandoned to everyone's pleasure.

Then one day, during discussion, Brick made an unforgivable mistake. He said openly, and honestly, that he liked the assigned horse story about a country veterinarian, who had saved it. He then proceeded to support his opinion: it was colorful, action-packed, and well described. With conviction, he concluded, the horse seemed just a little too human.

"My, that was most perceptive," said Mrs. Hoyle. "The word for giving animals human qualities is called anthropomorphism, which is not good writing. Yes, the author failed at this point." She puffed with pride. "Thank you, Brickford, we all learned something new today." Deliberately, she pulled her glasses down to the end of her nose. "I know that some of you didn't even read the story, let alone think about it."

Sensing the silent, stabbing looks of his classmates, Brick shrank low in his seat. After class, in the hallway, Ray mimicked in a falsetto voice, "My, how perceptive." Brick tried to ignore him.

Twin Jay sucked on the coil of a clenched hand, making wet squeaky sounds. "Kissy, kissy, kissy," he muttered, his face gloating.

"Some apple polishing," Ray spat.

"Well, she assigned it, why not do it right?" Brick countered, knowing his argument weak, but at a loss for any other.

"That ain't any excuse," Ray taunted.

"I hate English, and I don't like Mrs. Hoyle much better," Brick said defiantly.

"Who you kidding?" Ray said meanly.

"It's boring," Brick responded, unconvincingly. He would never admit, not in a thousand years, that he sometimes liked it. Not the stupid grammar, nor the dumb essays, but the worlds to explore - all the grand books where a guy could conquer jungles, or land on planets, or fight pirates.

Mr. Yamoto met Toby and Brick to take home. Grateful, Brick joined his friend in the back seat, knowing that the bus ride home would seem torturously long. Silently, he stared unseeing out the window at a passing flow of fields and orchards.

Toby said softly, so that his father wouldn't hear. "Sooner or later, Pal, you're going to have to fight them. I'll help what I can. But, someday you're going to have to punch them." Brick nodded. It seemed to him that hatred and hurt and misery infiltrated life everywhere and with everyone. There could be no escape and he felt depressingly alone.

"Nice time of year for pictures," Mr. Yamoto said, apparently sensing the quiet tenseness. "Think I'll look around this weekend for some photos."

"I'm going to go into politics," Toby announced. "When I grow up, that is."

"Politics?" Brick came out of his lethargy for the moment.

"Sure, I'm going to be the first Jap senator."

"It's Japanese not Jap," Mr. Yamoto corrected, looking at the boys in the rearview mirror.

"Whatever."

"I'm going to be a game warden someday and write about nature," Brick said, watching some brush rabbits jitter off the road. He and Toby sprawled in the back seat, relaxing some.

"You write a lot of good hooey about me, and I'll help you."

"Really? Will you help me protect things? You know. Will you make parks and refuges? And save all the wildlife?"

"Sure I will." Toby looked serious. "You're my best friend, now. Even more than Gerve." Toby seemed at a loss for words, but Brick understood. He, too, felt the deepening bond between them. And, he knew what Toby meant about Gerve, who was withdrawing more within himself. Toby was aware and concerned. "And the Dallases," he continued, returning to a painful subject. "They think they're pretty hot stuff. They and the other kids put up with me 'cause I'm on the football team, and they find me hard to tackle - I move quicker. That makes the difference, I think. But, with you, you're not an athlete. Instead, you're smart. Do good in school. The girls like you. The twins don't like any of that."

The car rattled over the bridge spanning the Stemple. Below dozens of mud hens played in the ripples. Fingers of fog reached over the hills. Uncle Burnie was repairing a gate latch. "Your Uncle looks exhausted," Yamoto said, sympathy in his voice, as he pulled up. The boys piled out.

"How's Rose doing?"

"Worrying me." Yamoto wormed from his seat.

"Well, it's a difficult time for Rose and Mike."

"She's real independent. Used to listen to me, for what it's worth." Yamoto reached out to the fence, supporting himself as if weary. "I just don't know how to help her. The two kids are overwhelmed by all the pressures. I've tried to tell her to stand back for awhile. That's apparently what she's doing."

"She's a bright young woman; she'll decide what's best. Just give her some rein," Burnie suggested.

"Maybe in America we give them too much rein," Yamoto lamented.

"Here in America we encourage them to be independent." Burnie chuckled softly. "Even though when they are, it makes us mad."

"Yes, but we teach them they're American and free, with wonderful opportunities. Everyone is born with equal rights. She's quoted that to me, I don't know how many times. Now, I don't know if she and Mike will ever get together, or if she can hold her job down along the way."

Toby and Brick looked uncomfortable, shifting their feet restlessly. "We'd like to go into the house or down by the creek," Toby said.

"No," Yamoto said somewhat sharply. "We're leaving shortly. Chores to do."

"We're kinda bored," Toby grumbled.

"I'll put you to work - that won't bore you."

Toby rolled his eyes. "Gee."

"Get your stuff done; then come over tomorrow with your homework," Brick suggested.

Toby looked at his dad for permission. Yamoto nodded. "Get done and you can."

"There's a good low tide Saturday," Burnie tossed. "Could be some good rock fishing."

"Wow. Really?" the boys reacted.

"Wish I could get Rose and Mike here for fishing. Might relax them and take their minds off everything, except each other." Burnie laughed and twisted a screw into a latch.

"Rose is beside herself right now, over Mike and pressures, and her job, she's growing uncertain about it." Yamoto had a pained look.

"Why? I know she's a darn good secretary. Was best in her class."

"She's Japanese." Yamoto focused straight at Burnie. "That and Nazis are scary words now."

"It's the times we live in," Burnie said. "Things have to get better."

"I wonder," said Yamoto, his voice dreary. "I wonder. For us Japanese, it's getting worse. Everywhere, all over, from everyone. Unions, tax collectors, people in the street, even women's bridge clubs are protesting us."

"Jumpin freckles," said Burnie, almost as a curse.

"Guess they figure we might do something unpatriotic. Have you heard about the Loyalists for a Safer Democracy?"

"The what?"

"It's a new organization, but growing," said Yamoto, with an edge of bitterness. "It recruits white citizens to 'investigate all people of Japanese ancestry.' You know, to see if they're un-American."

"Terrible," Burnie gasped. "Haven't heard of 'em."

"It's happening. In Southern California, and even in the Bay Area, I understand they have their own patrols. They send out ultimatums telling Japanese where to live, and what areas are off-limits. Those who don't listen could get burned out, or even hospitalized."

"Hard to believe such wrongs happen in America," said Burnie. "Papers just don't publish things like that."

"Funny," said Yamoto, wistfully. "Guess I'm an incurable dreamer, but I still have faith. I just know Uncle Sam won't turn his back on us. Eventually, he'll protect us."

"Put your books away, boys," Burnie said to Brick and Toby Saturday morning. They sat suffering over piles of school books at the dining room table. "You fellas deserve a break. So, I'm taking you fishing."

Gleefully, they slammed their algebra books. "When do we go?" said Brick.

"Right now," said Uncle, rubbing his hands vigorously. "Maybe for a little poke-poling on the rocks, huh?"

"Poke-poling?" Toby asked, his eyes excited. "Dad does it sometimes, while taking pictures, in all those wild rocks. I've gone with him. But. he prefers casting a line from the shore. He's better at that."

"Your dad is a connoisseur." The boys blinked. "That means someone who is an artist at what he does." Burnie bulged with pride at his knowing insight. "Well, young friends, you have a treat in store," Burnie declared. "The tides are real low. You, Toby, will have to borrow some of Brick's sneakers. Don't want you to ruin your shoes on the rocks."

"Sure, anything would be better'n this crummy algebra," said Toby, tossing his pencil down.

Poke-poling was a unique and popular sport on the north coast. Brick's family had indulged in it for years - an assured meat supply. The equipment was simple: a long bamboo pole, a three-foot wire taped to one end, a six inch string and hook gobbed with bait. At low tide, the fisherman then worked about the rocks and the tidal pools, poking the wired contraption into crevices and deep holes; sometimes one enticed a perch or a rock cod; sometimes a blue-fleshed cabezone - an ugly bullhead like fish that was good eating, the meat turning white upon cooking. Sometimes one snagged a wriggly eel - good eating, too, if one ignored its snakish look.

Uncle removed strips of frozen clam necks from the refrigerator. "This is the best bait in the world," he told the curious Toby, as he thawed the white pieces under a faucet. Hurriedly, they selected three poles from the woodshed, took a sack for the fish, and three tobacco cans for the bait and the hooks. Jabbering happily, they hiked through the potato field, down the cliff to the river, then across the sandbar, where they waded the shallow waters of the mouth. Now, the river flowed evenly into the ebbing sea. Spud floundered in the shallows, there to whine for help, until Brick hoisted him under one arm.

"Laziest dumb hound in the county," Brick remarked, as they approached the ragged coastline beyond. The black rocks lay silky with kelp, the pools crystal-clear and peaceful in the low tide. The trio sloshed and slipped over the rocks, each balancing or propelling himself with a fish pole. Spud squirmed from Brick's arm to flop about the rocks and skitter into the water as they worked seaward toward the deeper pools. Frustrated, the hound whimpered to be carried again. Ignored, he plunged into the pools to wade and swim, determined to be with them. At last, he crawled up beside Burnie on a large rock and sat shivering, his back to the sea, for he much preferred the shore.

"You're a wonderful dog," Burnie said, caressing the animal. He turned to the boys. "Put on your bait, fellows, and start fishing. It's good anywhere along here." Burnie's breath had a gaspy, sharp sound.

Brick, picking his way carefully, looked up from the precarious rocks. Uncle was sitting hunched, his face bluish.

Brick felt an instant chill, not knowing exactly why, except Burnie didn't look right. Auntie had said he was tired and overweight. Burnie took a deep breath, and rose with effort. Noticing both Brick and Toby watching, he said, "What's the matter with you guys? Get to fishin'!"

After loading their hooks with clam hunks, they explored the submerged crevices with their poles, sinking them deeply. Tensely, Brick waited for the take, for the tug that meant a fish. Momentarily he dismissed any thought of his uncle. How good the sea, he thought, the air tangy, the sun warm and sparkly. All so distant from school and schoolwork. Brick lost himself in the moment.

Burnie crawled across a high rock, then waded to a reef where the waves eddied. He caught Brick's stare, and again Brick reacted, for Uncle looked old, his eyes watery and his face puffy, with a sickly shine. Brick hadn't noticed before, enwrapped as he was with school and mostly with himself.

Just beyond the reef, two otters popped to the surface, sharing the wave fun. They seemed larger than Brick remembered. For an instant he doubted his skill in identification. They were rare otters, of that he was certain, for he had seen pictures. Toby, recognizing them, winked at Brick. Uncle, on the other hand, glanced at them and showed no surprise. Brick wanted to call out, "Look, Uncle Burnie. They're sea otters. Real sea otters." But he held back, for the secret was not his to tell. It troubled him, for he was drifting from Uncle, which saddened him in ways, but he could not help it. These last months had opened new horizons, brought new friends, introduced new worlds beyond Uncle. Brick was still proud of Darlene, and even Clarence, because they were young and good-looking. But, secretly, he didn't want the kids at school to see Burnie. "He's just an old farmer," Brick mumbled to himself now. The one time Burnie had picked Brick up at school had been mortifying, with Uncle waiting in his shabby Model-T, directly in front of the main entrance. Brick was certain that every kid in school had seen, had laughed at Uncle, and at him, too, and he was deeply ashamed.

"Say, fellas, look. Widgeon." Uncle pointed to a ribbon of ducks, high over the ocean. "They're heading south." The three of them watched in silence. It had been a long year, and now it was good seeing the wildfowl return. Once it had been a game between Burnie and himself, naming the species, and Brick knew them by heart: the delicate cinnamon teal, the green-headed mallard, the swift goldeneye, the flashy redhead. He had taken pride in his knowing. And Brick chuckled now, remembering a day long ago when he and Burnie had spotted a flock of canvasbacks playing in the bay. "Yep, they're canvasbacks," he had told Burnie. "See their white backs." Burnie, strangely silent, had propelled their motorboat toward the spreading birds. To Brick's horror, the canvasbacks had turned out to be swimming harbor seals, their heads sleek and wet, catching the light, so that they looked black and white like bobbing ducks. Brick's self-image had been destroyed.

Afterwards, whenever Brick had spotted a flight of ducks, Burnie had gazed into the sky and had said, "Sure they're not seals, Boy?" Brick smiled inwardly now, the goodness of forgotten times lingering momentarily.

Suddenly, Uncle bent over. "Jumping freckles, I got one." He raised the pole and jerked out a tumbling eel.

"Yippee," cried Toby.

Uncle swung the writhing fish toward his sack, stretched open on a rock. The eel shimmied loose, however, splatted across some spungy kelp and slithered into a crack. "Doggone it," Uncle wailed, and jumped into the water to scramble for it. Instead, he faltered, groped for a rock to brace himself, and stood there with the water clutching at his legs.

"Uncle Burnie?" Brick's throat constricted.

Burnie looked slowly around, glassy-eyed, and stunned, his face deathly white. He began wading toward shore. His movements stiff, unseeing. "Help him," Toby shouted, hurdling several rocks in an attempt to reach him. Brick stood frozen, not comprehending, until Toby was beside Uncle, assisting him. Then Brick found himself next to them, his hands clutching Burnie, supporting his wavery steps toward shore. When they reached the beach, Burnie sank to his knees; collapsing, he rolled to his back. His thick hands moved heavily to his chest. His breath came short and hard through bluish lips. Brick looked into the dilated eyes.

"Phone - Ra - Raffetto," he managed. "Have him help you get Ezra and Mike, too, if he can."

Terrified, Brick cried, "Go for help. I'll stay." Toby raced up the bluff, stumbling and plunging, his arms pumping.

10

"A mild coronary," Dr. Thurlong told the family at the Palm Drive Hospital. "A clot in a coronary artery," he clarified. Seeing the stricken faces he added, "We've given injections to relieve the pain. It's not bad. . .not as heart attacks go."

"But how is he?" Sathia demanded, her eyes red. Darlene put her arm around Auntie; and, Clarence, his face harried, put his arms around them both. Brick stood behind, near the emergency entrance. He watched silently, his features desolate.

"He's resting," the doctor said evasively. "We've given him oxygen and drugs to dissolve the clotting."

"He's worked too much," Sathia said. "And, he worries too much. It's my fault."

"We're all to blame," Darlene said.

"I figure at least three weeks in the hospital. Hopefully less," Dr. Thurlong said with his usual drawl.

Sathia blew her nose. "He will be all right, though?"

"He will. It's serious, but not terribly bad - this time." He emphasized the last words. "From now on you must be cheerful and give him lots of help. He's been so doggone active all his life. It will be hard for him, at first. He'll have to learn that someone else is going to have to fix the windmills and dig the wells. And he's going to have to learn to sit and watch. And you'll have to keep your worries and problems from him, as much as possible." Dr. Thurlong looked at Sathia. "No more heavy foods, no more greases, or pastries, or creams or cheeses. I know he loves 'em, but he's going to have to live a new role. And it will be hard, but we can all help - make him feel needed and important."

Sathia stood taller. "Burnie can do it."

"You can all do it," said Dr. Thurlong.

A held-in cry was building in Brick. He wanted to hurry home, to feed the chickens and gather the eggs. He would cut the wood fast, all night if necessary - so much nobody would ever need to cut it again. He would fill the water troughs and pull weeds in the garden and clean the barn, too.

Outside in a small anteroom, Toby sat alone in a corner, waiting, his hands folded. Nearby, Mr. Raffetto, Ezra Hamilton and his son, Mike, kept pacing, stopping often to look anxiously through the door's narrow window. It was Mr. Raffetto who had phoned for the ambulance; he, Ezra, and Mike Hamilton who had returned with Toby, to a frightened Brick on the beach; they, who carried Burnie on a folding cot up the steep trail, with Burnie assuring them, apologizing for the inconvenience all the while. Deeply grateful to them, Brick would never forget their assurance and their total commitment.

"Everything will be fine," Dr. Thurlong reassured them. "Go home and get some rest."

"I insist on seeing him," said Sathia.

"He's resting, but if you want to step this way --." The doctor swung wide the doors and a medicinal smell engulfed them. A husky nurse swished by and several more popped in and out of rooms. For Brick, the corridor was unmercifully long and doom-shadowed. At last, the doctor motioned them into a room at the far end. Brick's heart jolted to his throat. Burnie lay still, his feet propped up. He heard them, and cocked his head slightly trying to smile, but his lips barely moved. His face was clayish-gray, swollen and black about the eyes, looking so ghastly and unnatural that it was not the Burnie that Brick knew and loved. Sathia emitted a tight sob. Brick closed his eyes and turned away to lean against the wall.

In the days that followed, telegrams, letters, and flowers poured in from all over the north counties. Aunt Ida telegraphed flowers from Hawaii: anthuriums, bird of paradise and hibiscus. Next, local florists brought in several baskets of red roses and white carnations, entwined in luxuriant ferns and wide ribbons with "Get Well" cards from groups of neighbors. Then came bouquets from various local organizations, and from dairy and poultry feed stores, all wishing Burnie quick recovery. "So many people," said Sathia, wonderingly. "So many I don't even remember."

"But they remembered," said Darlene.

Each evening, Mr. Raffetto, Ezra Hamilton, and Clarence often did those chores too demanding for Brick, arranging by phone who would do what and when. They mixed chicken feeds for the proper blends; they crated eggs for shipping, and they repaired faulty equipment. Daily, Mr. Yamoto phoned Sathia to ask how she was, to offer assistance, and to give assurance that Burnie would recover shortly. Toby and Gerve came by to see what they could do. Mrs. Raffetto sent casseroles and fruit cobblers. And, Ezra and Mike Hamilton offered to drive Sathia anywhere, at any time. "People are so good," said Sathia. "I just didn't know they could be so nice." Rose drove home from the Bay Area as often as possible to console Burnie and his family. She and Mike were seeing each other, first running into one another at the hospital.

Once the dangerous hours had passed, Burnie improved quickly. The pale color gave way to his normal rosiness; the bloating decreased; soon a twinkle lighted his eyes, and he sat up, braced against pillows. Although he talked slowly, seemingly with difficulty, his old self was returning, for he inquired about the menus, far in advance of each meal, and he constantly tossed barbs of fun at the nurses.

"I'm so grateful," said Sathia, as she, Darlene, and Brick confronted Dr. Thurlong in the hospital office. He looked highly dignified, as they waited in anticipation of their daily report.

"You can't keep an old fire horse down," he opened. "He keeps wanting to smoke cigars."

"Bless him." Sathia wiped her nose with a hanky.

"In all fairness, I must tell you, there'll be no more heavy labor or lifting for Burnie, not for the rest of his life," he explained, in his drawling, intimate way. "It will be necessary that he retire."

"Retire?" Auntie exclaimed. "I don't know if he can ever retire. The Sea Ranch is his life."

"It'll be tough on him, I know," Dr. Thurlong said gently. "I haven't told him yet, because it'll be hard for the old fire horse to take a back seat. That's why he'll need understanding, not pity."

"Sathia needs understanding and help too," Darlene interjected, nodding toward the woman.

"That she does," said the doctor.

"That's why I'm leaving my old job," Darlene announced, squaring her shoulders, "at least temporarily."

"You are?" Dr. Thurlong looked surprised. Brick smiled broadly, happy to hear the words again.

"Yes," said Darlene. "I'm going to help Sathia and live at the ranch as needed, not be away from my family, any more than I have to be. Although, I won't give up my apartment just yet." She smiled happily. "I belong at the Sea Ranch now. Sathia and I have discussed it."

"Can you afford it, though? You had such a good job," Dr. Thurlong inquired.

"I'm going to be the new bookkeeper - for the local Dairy Association," Darlene beamed with pride. "That way I can remain at home and set my own working hours."

"How wonderful," said Dr. Thurlong. "How did you manage that?"

"My former boss, Edward McPeak. He arranged it for me."

"Mighty good ex-boss, I'd say. Yes," Dr. Thurlong assured, "that will be wonderful for everyone concerned." And he looked directly at Brick.

"I want to see Burnie, now." Sathia insisted.

"Certainly."

"Go ahead, you go alone," Darlene urged, patting Auntie's arm. "We'll come later - in a few minutes."

As they watched Sathia follow the doctor up the hall, Brick said, "I didn't know Auntie could be so nice."

Darlene looked tenderly at him. "Of course she's nice. She loves Burnie very much. She loves us all - especially you."

"Me?" Brick exclaimed.

"You're really like a son to her." Darlene paused. "I've never told you before, but you see, she could never have children of her own."

The days flowed. The pastels of fall streaked into the dark twists of clouds as early winter teased and sometimes battered the seacoast. Burnie grew stronger, more positive. Mike left for basic training. He and Rose promised to write each other daily. Fortunately, the Dallases had let up bullying, let up on their tormenting comments, although sneering and glaring often at Brick. Doubtless, Burnie's health problems known to all in the area, and the concern and love of neighbors and friends throughout the county, had intimidated them for the time being.

Perhaps more suppressing, the twins had suffered setbacks in their football aspirations. The junior football team had consistent losses in their mid games, including two total shutouts. Jay had suffered an injury from a clip, forcing him out of play for the season. Then, Ray had fumbled the ball on several key plays near the enemy goal line - the recovery changing the course of the win. That happened in two important contests. For the Homecoming Game, Ray was relegated to the bench. Brick had to admit that he took a satisfactory pleasure in watching the bigger twin sitting the full 60 minutes with his head down. That's when problems started over.

"I'm awful ugly," Brick thought again, glancing into the mirror in the boys' room at school. First, he combed his hair to one side; then he swept it to the other side, but it all sprang impudently in varied directions. Hopelessly, he shook his head. His nose, he figured, was too long, and his chin too receding. Red pimples blotted his forehead, spreading worse each day. And his voice - in glee club, he squeaked one moment and croaked the next, and sometimes in simple conversation his voice cracked, making listeners smile. It's no use, he thought, all the swanky clothes Darlene had bought - none made him dashing, nor miraculously confident. When he walked, his lengthening feet still hooked around desk legs to clump loudly. His arms and chest remained lean, not broad and tight-muscled like in the senior boys. Brick thought seriously of saving his lunch money, then buying barbells and stretchable bodybuilders. He could hide them in the hayloft, work out there, he figured, until he emerged one day, a powerful, massive brute.

"Hey, hey, Mama's pretty boy." Jay Dallas swung open the door. "Ooooooh, looky at the pretty clothes."

Brick felt sick. "What's eating you guys? What's the matter with you, anyway?"

"Oooooh, what's the matter with us?" Ray said from behind. Four football players ambled in with them, waiting for Brick to prove himself. Well, he'd fool them, he thought heatedly, because he didn't want to fight. Not here. Alone, against two? They could push him back and forth between them, batter him against the tile walls. Chances were that no teacher would appear, and the football boys might block the exit, might keep anyone from entering until too late, and he lay bloodied.

Jay slapped Brick's binder and books off the shelf; with resounding impact, materials parted, flittering papers over the room. "This end of the hall is off-limits to you, sissy boy," Ray leered, his head tilted arrogantly.

Jay warned, "Stay with your Jap friends down at the other end."

Coolly as possible, Brick picked up his books and papers. He sensed the disdainful eyes, waiting. He knew now how a trapped animal felt: alone, frightened, tormented for no apparent reason, with escape dependent upon his cunning. Vigorously, Ray mussed Brick's hair in frustration, then pushed him. "You goin' to do something about it, pretty boy?"

Brick stood erect. He looked into fiery eyes; then looked down. "Not now." It was the hardest words he had ever mustered. He understood, deep within, that the twins were struggling with their own devils: the football embarrassment; some problems in classes, where they were failing. Most darkly - their father, erratic in work; drinking beer in a pub; many afternoons the sheriff arriving at their home. Rumors that neighbors relished and that would not go away - their pressures were beyond Brick - not his. Painfully, he knew, however, everything was enclosing, forcing him to face the inevitable.

Next day, Mrs. Hoyle led a discussion on Charles Dickens' <u>Great Expectations</u>. "Describe the character of Pip, someone," she began. No one responded. Her eyes hardened. "I said, will someone describe the character of Pip." She surveyed the class. Some students stared into their open texts, a few at the ceiling, a couple at the floor. All squirmed uncomfortably. "Well," said Mrs. Hoyle, "we've been discussing the novel for a month now." She took a deep breath, and controlled herself. A small girl, sitting in the front, raised a timid hand. "Yes, Milly Mae," she said, relieved.

"He's a very nice boy." When Mrs. Hoyle showed no enthusiasm, Millie Mae qualified with, "He's nicer than the other boys. Really nicer."

"Now what kind of a description is that?" Her eyes settled on Brick, who shrank lower in his seat. "Now you, Brickford. You understand this story. You tell us." She smiled softly in anticipation. In the back of the room, someone made loud smacking sounds on the back of his hands.

Brick liked Pip. Sometimes he felt orphaned like Pip. It was a good tale, with adventure and escape. And, although he had read the many pages, devoured most of them, he said, "I don't know, I haven't been reading." Again, he sensed the calculating eyes, behind, waiting.

Mrs. Hoyle gasped. "Really, Brickford, I'm surprised. This isn't like you." Someone scoffed. Brick wanted to burrow into the woodwork.

At class end, after an interminable hour, the teacher asked for homework. To his horror, Brick discovered his binder gone. It had been lying at his feet and now someone had stolen it. It didn't take much imagination to know who. Biting his lips, he waited for students to file out; and, glancing, he saw the Dallas twins, and their friends look at him, expectantly. As feared, he found the binder in the corner of the room, open, his notepaper ripped, his pencils and assignment stolen - a descriptive essay of the ocean, and the otter point under sunset. "Worth hours of work, and a darn good grade," Brick muttered.

Dejected, he walked out, his head lowered. But, Mrs. Hoyle challenged him. "Brickford, don't you have a paper - the descriptive one?"

"I did," he tried.

"What does that mean?"

"I had one."

"Well, do you have a paper, or don't you?" she insisted.

"No."

"Why?" she hushed.

At a loss, he shrugged.

"Your mother is certainly not going to be happy about this." She gave him a severe, condemning look. "Do you know what you are?"

"No."

"You're becoming an underachiever." She punctuated the word with a sharp nod. "You have the ability when and if you want." Then she added an unexpected comment that clutched Brick's heart. "I know you're having problems with some fellow students here."

"Yes, ma'am," Brick said politely and walked out.

Down the hall, Toby was waiting, his face dark. "The Dallases are out to get you. You know that?"

"I know," Brick agreed, resigned.

"They're calling you sissy. Say they're goin' to bloody you up, then tie your pants on a telephone pole."

"What's the matter with them?" Brick asked, his words electric with emotion.

"Mixed up, I guess - don't know who their friends are and who they aren't."

Brick was hurt. "I just don't want trouble."

"Well," Toby considered, "sooner or later, you're going to have to fight. I think my dad's going to have to fight, too, - eventually."

"I don't understand."

"Never mind."

In the days after Burnie arrived home from the hospital, the family clustered around, catering to him. They served him meals in bed, opened mail for him, and read him any newsy letters. They surrounded him with floral arrangements from friends and neighbors; and Sathia added roses from her garden - all high-stemmed in long-necked vases. The phone rang constantly with inquiries as to his well-being and offers to help in anyway. Mrs. Hamilton brought a beef stew for everyone one night; the Raffeto's brought a tuna casserole the next night; and Rose Yamoto brought a large dish of custard pudding. "Gosh," said Burnie that evening, his eyes twinkling. "Maybe it was worth shakin' up the old ticker."

The doctors did not anticipate any more heart attacks, but, they warned that Burnie should not be too active for a time, or that he not be subjected to any unnecessary stress. That's why Sathia sputtered and scolded when he read the newspaper or listened to the news with all its depressing happenings throughout the world. "Man can't bury his head like an ostrich," Burnie fumed at her concern.

Brick longed to confide in his Uncle, to pour out his anguish and his frustrations, but he couldn't lay those burdens on him, he knew. He would have to be his own man and shoulder them himself. But, sometimes, especially in the dark of afternoon, he feared going to the bathroom at school. He wanted to cry out to Uncle - that he hated the place more each day; now even the pals of the Dallas twins were taunting him, calling him Curly and Kissy. In a restroom, a big kid he had never seen before, told him that the place was for "white kids" only. Then a day later, a Dallas friend called him a Jap lover. The act stunned and hurt him. Brick could no longer concentrate on his studies; the constant tension left him exhausted; usually he fell asleep after supper. "Your father has to see the Principal about those Dallases," Darlene had said one evening, suspecting the growing abuse.

"No," Brick had answered firmly, "that will only make it worse."

"I don't care. Something has to be done." Darlene had been determined. "When I see your father tonight, I'm going to insist that he does. Trouble with you, you keep too much bottled up inside."

Exasperated, Brick cringed at her words. It was true; it seemed he had been locked up forever with his fears. But to have his parents fight his battles was not the way to go, he assured himself. And so, after much consideration, he approached his uncle cautiously, not wanting to upset him in any way; but, knowing that the old man would have some good words. Burnie lay quietly in bed, looking out his window toward the hill. Upon hearing Brick, he glanced at the boy and smiled, then turned back to the hill. "The gum trees are pretty aren't they? Never noticed how pretty they can be in the coming winter."

"How you feeling?" Brick's words were burdened.

With calm, receptive eyes, Burnie observed his nephew. "I'm fine. But what about you? You look troubled, Boy."

Brick sat on the foot of the bed; his eyes roved over the dark-paneled bureau with its oval mirror, then over the head of the bed with its intricate leaf-carvings heavy and somehow depressing. "It's everything, I guess. The Dallases mostly," he admitted.

"Still givin' you a hard time, are they?"

"Yeah, both Toby and me. Not so much Toby - he plays football."
Brick looked perplexed. "How did you know?"

"Not surprising. I figured it'd come."

"You did?"

"Sure, they're the type that likes to bully. Remember the Okie kids
down at the bay? How they pushed them into a fight?"

"Yes - and beat them up," said Brick, solemnly.

"Well?"

"I just don't want trouble."

"Sometimes trouble follows us whether we want it or not."

Nervously, Brick moistened his lips. "Ma is afraid I'd bother you
about this. You won't tell, will you?"

"Hells bells, this kid gloves stuff sickens me." Burnie squirmed
himself up to a half-sitting position. "Your troubles are my troubles.
Besides, what she and Auntie don't know won't hurt 'em."

Brick relaxed some. "Toby says I'm going to have to fight them."

"Toby's probably right."

"The name calling - sure it hurts, but I can take it. It's the other
things."

"Like what?"

"Well, once at lunch my books were sneaked out of my pack. Some
kids found them tossed under some stairs. And now an assignment in
English was stolen. Hopefully, Mrs. Hoyle will let me turn it in, late. I
think she suspects what happened to it. But, I can only hope."

"You know for sure the twins did it?"

"I can't prove it, but who else, except them or one of their friends?"

"You can't tolerate that. Can't you talk to the Principal?"

"That would only make things worse. If I just knew why they're
doing this. We got along pretty good in grammar school. Now in high
school, it's different - they hate me." Brick's voice was heavy.

"Some people can't feel tall, unless they're putting others down,"
Burnie said simply. "And they may be jealous."

"Jealous? Of me?"

"Sure," Burnie said, without hesitation. "Ever think of that?" Brick
wagged his head. "You're doing well in school; you've made new friends;
you're getting big and good-looking; and, you have beautiful parents
that make a decent living - even if they are having their problems. Old

man Dallas has drunk up every nickel he ever made, I bet. And his wife looks twenty years older than she should."

"Never thought of it that way." Brick had an inward look.

Burnie continued, "Probably down deep, they're scared. Scared you'll be somebody some day. That you'll be somebody worthwhile."

"I hope I am."

"And then, too, you keep befriending those Japanese kids."

Brick looked curiously at his uncle. "Yes, they're still friends, especially Toby."

"In times like this, that could anger some people. Especially kids like the Dallases, who look for any excuse; and, that would be all they need to go after you."

"I just don't want trouble," Brick shrugged. "I don't expect them to be friends ever again, I just want them to leave me alone."

Burnie looked searchingly at his great nephew. "So you've put up with their guff. Well, Boy, their kind see that as a weakness. Only thing their type understands is a punch in the nose. And the sooner the better." He worked himself even higher on his pillows. "Wait 'till this evening when your dad gets here, we're going to have a men's conference."

"The next time those twins call you a name, you call 'em pig bristles," Clarence urged. "That's what those crew cuts they wear look like. At least on them." Brick chuckled; he liked that. Clarence kept pacing back and forth, his fists clenched, his jaw set.

"And I say punch the smart alecks," Burnie swung an arm. "Take one out and then go after the other."

"But I'd have to catch one of them alone," Brick said. "And they're always together."

"Two against one is not fair, for certain, so don't let them get you off the school grounds. Take 'em in the hallway or even in a classroom where a teacher can stop it," Clarence advised.

Brick looked at his father with disbelief. "Inside? And get kicked out of school? That's one rule old Principal Huff holds by. Get in a fight and out you go."

Clarence looked at his son in frustration. "If a man's to be a man, he's got to stand up for his rights and take chances."

"But is fighting right?"

Clarence opened and closed his hands. "If it stops what's wrong."

"Evil ways get worse, unless they're stopped," said Burnie. "Don't forget it, Boy."

Brick considered the advice and asked, "But if I manage to hurt one of them, won't they just gang up on me later?"

Burnie flashed a look at Clarence, then at Brick. "What you mean is, will violence stop violence?" Looking squarely at his nephew, he said. "I can't rightly say, except if the world had have stood up to Hitler a few years ago, Europe wouldn't be in the blood bath it is today."

"You're talkin' nonsense, Kid," Clarence scoffed. "If a guy picks on you, and you kick his teeth down his throat - chances are he'll quit pickin'. Your uncle is absolutely right, if the free world hadn't been so pussyfooted with Hitler and with the Japs, maybe the world wouldn't be in all the hell it is now." He looked around to see if Sathia could hear and said seriously, "Tonight in the barn, I'll fix up some sort of punching bag. That's the first place to start. You and me, Kid, we'll make some excuse to get out there alone."

Brick nodded in resignation.

"Good," Burnie said. "Teach him something for me."

"With a bag he can learn timing, combinations, the feel of hitting someone." Clarence looked at Brick intently. "No son of mine is going to be labeled a coward, not if I can help it. It would be better to get licked than be thought a coward."

11

Darlene took a room upstairs at the Sea Ranch, across from Brick, still retaining her apartment. Mr. McPeak called frequently, inquiring how she was doing. Brick heard them talking softly, always for a long time, although she never hinted again about any serious commitment to the man. She was pleased with her job at the Dairy Association, not far from the ranch, so that she could return to assist Sathia as needed. She and Clarence talked much, seriously, not fighting as usual, apparently realizing that there were bigger problems than their personal differences. They cooperated in all the family needs, yet, Brick rarely saw them touch, or whisper, or hopefully, hug. Doctors continued optimistic about Burnie's complete recovery.

Brick rewrote the "missing" essay from memory for Mrs. Hoyle. As a descriptive assignment, he attempted to bring alive the setting of the Sea Ranch with its sweep of shear cliffs, its rolling dunes, and the long angle of white beach. He had attempted to impart the presence of Coast Guard boats and military personnel seen more each day. In honesty, he had written from the heart while sitting on a bluff overlooking the ocean; he had tried to capture every impression. Touched by Uncle Burnie's plight, he had concluded with a flourish, that the beauty and the power of a watery expanse made him feel better about things.

He had stood waiting before her desk, as Mrs. Hoyle read. He could see her face registering pleasure, surprise, and a quiet contentment, off and on. Brick didn't trust his impressions, for, he had learned - or at least heard - that teachers could be devious, reacting one way and then acting another in the security of their offices.

Finally, she set his creation before her and poised a red pen, "It's very sensitive. Very well done. I don't know what happened with you and the original." She looked up at him, with an asking look, but, without asking. "It is late, of course. I will accept it for credit, with a penalty." She wrote down an, "A", crossed it out and labeled the paper with a, "C", and handed it back. She nodded his dismissal and picked up a pile of schoolwork.

"Thank you," said Brick, his voice hoarse. He left, relieved.

Brick continued punching the boxing bag in the barn. Clarence had stuffed pieces of tire strips, broken cardboard, and crunched wrapping paper in a big apple sack. He had hung the bag from a beam, secured it at the bottom, and painted a mock face with a stencil pen at the upper end. Brick found his arms tightening, the muscle tonus building. Clarence bought him some boxing gloves, so that he could pound hard without chaffing his knuckles.

More young men were joining the services without waiting for a draft. Rose continued to return home on the weekends. Brick recalled warmly, the day Mike had left for basic training. He and his parents, the Yamoto's, Mr. and Mrs. Hamilton, and Mr. Raffetto had met at the train station in Santa Rosa. Everyone shook Mike's hand, hugged him, and clapped when Rose kissed and held him tightly.

The Dallases seemed preoccupied with their own problems for the time. In one incident, Ray said something to Brick that he couldn't hear, but the twin's face was contorted with hostility. Brick stood up from his school desk and clenched both fists, facing the boy - not flinching. Ray blinked with uncertainty and backed off.

Brick felt less fearful about Burnie and a relapse as the days passed. Uncle remained resolute, determined. When not rubbing Spud's ears and spoiling him, he assisted in minor chores, like folding clothes and cleaning eggs. With the ending of fruit season in mid-November,

Clarence took time to assist in Burnie's poultry enterprise: egg gathering, feeding, repairing equipment, and checking facilities.

Most satisfying for Brick, Clarence devoted more time to his son, accompanying him to the last football games (where the Dallases were no longer involved), and to high school basketball games, where Mary Ann from the nearby stands contacted him with her almond blue eyes, and, he her; later, Clarence took him to Friday night dances in a downtown hall rented by the school for the weekly highlight. His dad would drop him off, giving him money for entrance, cokes, and whatever, although most cookies and candies were included in the price of admission. Faithfully, Clarence picked him up at twelve midnight, where he usually stayed at the ranch in the old house, appreciating his abandoned room and bed. Toby chose not to attend, and Brick understood that he felt no part of the white teenagers. Gerve, sadly, had retreated further into another world, backward, into the grammar school ways still, with kids from their old school - some who had gotten themselves in trouble with the ranchers, and later, the authorities, by vandalizing gates and isolated buildings. The Dallases never appeared either, although some of the athletes did. As one kid commented, "Them twins are home licking their wounds."

Most fulfilling for Brick at the dances, were the new friends he met - both boys and girls. He had never learned to dance, but, had a natural rhythm and sense for steps that came quickly to him. He found himself uncertain and awkward at first, enjoying holding a girl and swirling around, while prancing here and there. He especially appreciated Mary Ann, who appeared one Friday and thereafter. She readily accepted his asking her to dance. Brick tramped on her toes a couple of times; soon, however, they were jigging, twirling, and laughing. It was great, giddy, a little frightening, but exciting, opening a new world yet unborn.

When Clarence drove him back to the ranch, he asked, "You're pretty quiet. Everything okay?"

"Just thinking." Inside, Brick floated, his emotions mingling - some soaring, some colliding.

On Saturday, Toby phoned Brick to ask about Burnie; then said more urgently, "I got to get away from here - it's my dad, Rose, everything. Maybe we can walk to the otter cove - just talk, you know?"

"Sure, I'm here. Come on down. Let's talk."

"I'll be there after chores, probably in the afternoon."

Brick heard the steady, firm, knock and let Toby in. They stood, grinning sheepishly, feeling uncomfortable for a moment, evasive; then reaching each other quickly as old friends. "Don't know what to do, yet." Toby shifted his legs.

"Let's go down to the caves," Brick suggested.

"Let's."

They left the Sea Ranch, hiked the moorlands to the crest. Like the wind, they raced down the greening slope, toward the sea where eerie coils of fog writhed inland, hanging low, enshrouding the shoreline. Breakers boomed, shattering violence against the headland. "Sounds like a cannon," Toby shouted. They ran daringly along the narrow paths of the cliff edge, and down through an aisle of moss-hung cypress, black and shadowy. At last they reached a bluff overlooking the caves. They sprawled down and peeked over. Back of a bordering reef, the water eddied deeply in what became a snug, natural harbor of old. Decades before, small cargo schooners had anchored in the protected inlet. By winch and cable, crates of cheeses, potatoes, and meat had been hauled from shore to ship, all for San Francisco; and, later, great logs of fir and redwoods to build the city. Brick had been reading much about it; also, again, much about the sea otters and their terrible destruction for the precious fur. He liked using study hall in the library to learn so much about the family territory.

"Sure a great spot," said Toby, his words not really with the idea.

"Lot of stuff went on here." Brick was waiting for Toby to open. The cove had been an illegal hideaway for "booze runners," during a time called prohibition, when liquor consumption was outlawed. Presently, local fishing boats caught in sudden storms often used the place for quick refuge. Yet, the spot had not always been a sanctuary. Untold eons ago, geologically, when the headlands lay partially sunken, mighty seas had pounded the ancient cliffs, gouging out the soil, leaving many caves, some fifteen to twenty feet deep, and high enough for a man to stand. To a boy, they had proven wonderful worlds to pretend he and his friends were pirates and swashbuckling buccaneers; the hidden rises were little known to visitors, as they faced the sea, just above tide line, and could not be seen except from a ship. Or were they easily approachable, except at a minus tide, like the one Brick, Toby, and Burnie had attempted, before the heart attack. Some climbers scaled the cliffs above, dropping to them from ropes, a dangerous undertaking.

"I don't see any," Toby shouted. "The otters aren't there."

"They have to be," Brick assured, as they squinted through the enclosing mist; but, the sea rolled empty, and the deep waters rose and fell with no sign of animal life.

"Wonder why your uncle didn't recognize otters?" Toby asked, his voice depressed. "They sure don't look like seals."

"Oh, I think he did. I saw his eyes light up. I just think he didn't want to excite us too much. We know that Ned all but admitted to seeing them."

"Hope so."

Brick waited, "What all you want to talk about?"

At last, Toby spoke. "I think sometime soon, I'm going to have to leave school."

"How come?" Brick said, upset.

"I can't say. I just feel it."

"Tell me."

"Well, first of all, it's Rose. She's driving us nuts. I guess it's because Mike's away in the service. I don't understand." Toby gulped, thought about how to explain. "Sometimes she laughs and giggles for no reason at all; sometimes she starts crying - the tears not stopping. She comes home and cleans our house over and over. She keeps thinking something is going to happen to Mike." Toby looked vacantly at his friend. "Dad says we got to get away."

"You mean move?"

"I can't say now." Something deeper troubled Toby.

Brick felt sick at the thought. "Boy, I sure hope not." He pondered a moment. "You mean your dad would sell the ranch? Everything?"

"He might have to."

"But, why?"

"It all has something to do with Japan. And the way people are treating us. Then, there's been these Japanese coming to our house." Toby hesitated.

"What?"

115

"I can't say for sure," said Toby, his voice troubled. "They were having coffee in our kitchen. I heard them tell dad not to sell, that salesmen were coming to see him, wanting to buy our ranch. I don't understand."

"Uncle Burnie says we got to help you folks," Brick tossed in, quickly.

"What's that mean?"

"He says people are responsible to each other."

Toby gnawed the back of his wrist and stared at the otter-less waters. The wind rose, swirling the dark fog. "Dad's out there now, taking some pictures. It's the weather and the clouds all black and gray, too. Good for pictures, I guess. He read about it happening - was preparing for it."

"Well, that's good."

"Not really. He's more angry than serious. He was going to have an exhibit of his photos in Sebastopol's town hall, you remember."

"I know."

"Well, some big wigs are having second thoughts. Someone said that enlarged pictures of our coastline may not be good for security sake. Whatever that means. I'm just telling you what I learned."

"You've lost me."

"I guess, if an enemy country, like Japan, decided to attack us, our whole north coastline is there for the seeing - because of my dad's pictures. That's all I know."

"That's dumb."

"Sure it's dumb. But that's what's happening."

Brick said nervously, "I don't feel good here, now. I know Uncle saw the otters. I know he'll tell us he did."

Suddenly a light flashed at sea. "Am I seeing things?" Brick gasped. "Am I seeing things?" Again it flashed, weirdly through the ragged fog. "There's someone or something out there," Brick said, with mounting excitement. He flattened his eyes as if to see better.

"Maybe somebody needs help. Kinda spooky, huh?" Toby said, shuddering. Stiff-legged sandpipers flitted about the protruding rocks, their cries piercing and wild. The boys waited.

"The only thing around are those birds," said Brick, catching Toby's uncertainty. With the ending of day, the clouds became unreal, luminous, a silver brightness below the fog, with the water purling, then silent. Came a purling again, then the strange quiet, followed gradually by the rhythmic crumble of wave. The boys lay flat on the cold earth.

Entranced, they listened, hardly breathing. Never before could Brick remember such a moment, so weird, like something from another world. The fog lingered, sunset pink, turning gloomy-purple with the dying sun. The waves spread on the far sand, whispered, and retreated.

"Guess this is what dad wants to get pictures of."

From below them, a bright light punctuated the dimness, piercing outward, then withdrew. A wan blinking lit the cove like quick lightening. "What is it?" Brick's voice cracked.

"I - I don't know," said Toby. "Somebody is signaling somebody, maybe."

"Must be s-someone down there," Brick stuttered, peering over.

The wind rustled the dry seaweed; the sea lisped in retreat. Again, a light flashed at sea, once, twice, rapidly. From ashore, where the fog now reached like claws, there came a repeat. Brick's neck and head prickled icily. Toby, highly disturbed, said, "Let's get out of here. Just hope my dad's not down there anymore."

Mike Hamilton was dead. Shock numbed the community after a telegram reached his family informing them that he had been on a special training mission. Killed by a faulty hand grenade, or by a premature explosion, perhaps by a mistiming among the participants - no one knew. Then a day later two officers arrived with Mike's personal belongings and to extend their condolences. They had praised him highly, claiming he had the potential to be a demolition expert - a specialist in defusing time bombs and booby traps, as well as planting them. He was destined to become a leader. The family believed the latter, but could not readily imagine their sensitive son, capable of involving himself in such dangerous work. He was a teacher by nature, not a tinker with his hands. The officers spoke of him as a brave young man, who had volunteered to string wire across a field to blow up a designated radio shack. In the simulated battle, machine guns had spat real bullets fanning some two feet above his flattened form. Soldiers crawling behind him had tossed real hand grenades against mock enemies when something went wrong. Possibly a poorly thrown grenade had reached Mike. A witness had reported that he had attempted to heave it away. The Army men would not give exact details, considering the secrecy of such operations, except to state that an investigation was in order. But, it didn't matter, Mike Hamilton's Army adventure had ended.

Mrs. Hamilton took to her bed and Mr. Hamilton retreated even more. He lost himself in the orchard and in the fields. He rose before sunrise and worked until long after dark. The daughters, Delores and Gay, cried a lot, even after they returned to school. Gerve remained out longer, and when he did come back, he wouldn't talk to anyone; often his eyes welled with tears at unexpected times. After first hearing the news, Brick had taken Spud for long walks around the ranch, and he had visited the hayloft often. He didn't know how to approach Gerve or how to act. Mike's death was so crushing and so final - what could he possibly say? Brick wanted to confide with Uncle Burnie about the problem, but he refrained, knowing that with Uncle's heart condition, nothing was worth upsetting the man. Besides, he saw the pain clouding their eyes: Burnie's, Sathia's, Darlene's, and Clarence's.

They had no answers, he realized.

A sadness settled over the community. Although people tried to comfort the Hamilton's, tried to assist them with food, calls, and offers of field work, a suffocating heaviness tightened around everyone's heart as the facts spread. Neighbors recalled Mike's handsome features, his dancing brown eyes and the quick smile. And, of course, the unanswerable, gnawing question lingered - why?

The Hamilton's now, were the first local family to have suffered a "war casualty." The reality of it stunned people, made them hurt even more inside. Although Mike had not died on a far away battlefield, he was nevertheless, a hero. American soldiers were being deployed to join the regulars in defense of islands in the Pacific. He had been expendable, one of those fated individuals, caught in some unfortunate mistake or accident. Editorials and city politicians played heavily on the emotions, whipping a wave of patriotism.

Rose returned from the city to be with the Hamilton's. Publicly no one ever saw her cry; yet, her genteel face and rosebud lips looked drained and pale. "She wishes she'd stayed," Toby confided to Brick one day. "She wishes she'd told all the dumb buzzards to go to, and had stayed with Mike - no matter what people thought. She wishes with all her heart she'd married Mike."

Brick just shrugged. "I don't know what to say."

"I think people blame us for what happened," Toby lamented.

"Who?"

"The neighbors. All those in town. Everyone about us. They think we caused Mike's death."

Brick reeled under the thought. "Aaah phooey," he said upset. "Nobody could think that. How could they?"

"But they do. Dad thinks so. He thinks they'll decide we're at fault - maybe not directly; but they blame us, just as if we pulled the pin. Just as if we'd tossed the hand grenade, because we're Japanese."

"Nobody thinks that." Even in his own ears, Brick's words sounded inadequate and unconvincing.

"Dad thinks somebody will try to burn us out, do something to hurt us."

People gathered quietly in the Pioneer Cemetery on a hill where ancestors of the Hamilton's, the Burton's, and the MacQuarrie's, lay interred. Neighbors, relatives, and local officials clumped tightly under a canopy. A soft rain grayed the setting. Military personnel arrived in government cars and Army carriers. From a hearse, six uniformed men carried the casket, draped by the American flag, placing it carefully on a platform above the grave. At command they stepped aside in perfect unison. An impressive crowd gradually gathered; audible sobs drifted above the billows of enclosing umbrellas.

People bowed their heads in silence as a minister rolled out a moving prayer, his words eloquent in the wet breeze, words lost to many. Local, county, state officials, and Mike's commander spoke, nearly all referring to the tragic loss of a young man with so much potential - a potential U.S. officer. All mentioned the great challenges and sacrifices ahead as the so-called axis countries, Germany, and, eventually, Japan, would rise to attempt conquering the free world. Friends and old classmates, then shared happy recollections. A woman, accompanied by a guitarist sang a hymn: "In the Garden."

Soldiers folded the draped flag into a neat triangle; an officer carried the compact structure of red, white, and blue, presenting it to Mrs. Hamilton, as her tearful family closed about her, to steady her, for she seemed to sway as if to collapse. Again, the sisters broke into a bubble of gasps and broken tears. Then, a bugler played "Taps," the sad, tremulous notes floating across the neatly tended vineyards, reaching the surrounding woods. A short column of soldiers with Browning Automatic Rifles moved forward, waited at attention, then came to order at command. At next order, they raised their pointed barrels skyward; then, in unison, they fired a series of shots heavenward. In a field below, a flock of blackbirds burst away in a twist of fright.

For Brick, the ponderous ritual was his first experience with human death. The memory would haunt him, he knew - the images of friends and acquaintances, darkly solemn - and the Hamilton family broken in sorrow, with Mrs. Hamilton under a black veil, and Gerve staring at the ground. Rose with them, strangely standing a few steps to the side, her features empty, uncertain. Toby and Mr. Yamoto holding off a little behind everyone, his arm around his son. Brick would never forget.

12

On Sunday morning, December 7, Brick grumbled into his best outfit, hating the itchy wool, and not liking church because he had to wear a suit and choking tie. Darlene had decided that it would be good if she and her son attended the small country church nearby.

"Hurry up, breakfast's on," Sathia called. Brick, grimacing in exaggerated pain, tiptoed down the stairs, trying hard not to let the trousers rub his legs. "Oh, for heaven's sake," Auntie sputtered, her arms crossed, "quit being an idiot and go see if your parents are ready yet."

"They're still arguing, but, not as loud," said Brick. For nearly a half-hour now, Darlene and Clarence had been talking in her room. The night before he had phoned, missing her, for she had driven to town for groceries. He told Burnie, he was coming early Sunday to talk with her. In the morning Clarence had driven hurriedly into the yard. With an air of intent, he had charged upstairs, earlier than expected, to awaken his wife, igniting her temper, soon calming her with some apparent serious talk.

"Well ask them anyway," Sathia insisted.

Brick bellowed, "You ready, Ma? Dad?"

"For heaven's sake," Auntie sputtered again.

"We're talking," came a tremulous voice.

"They're talking." Brick lunged down the last steps.

"I could hear her. Did you have to yell?"

"Yep." He tugged at his tie. "Aghh, I hate ties."

"Since you are now in high school, you're awfully cocky, big britches."

"Yep." Brick ambled to the kitchen, and stretched his lengthening feet under the table. Businesslike, he flipped a pancake onto his plate.

"You are going to wait, aren't you?" Sathia frowned and looked severe.

"No," Brick said, scooping two eggs onto the pancake. "'Cause I've already started." He placed a second pancake on top, laced that with bacon, drowned it in syrup and squashed it all with his fork.

"Where's your manners, young man? And, best you wait."

"Not if we hungry wolves have anything to say," Burnie said, shuffling in to pour coffee in his initialed mug. Sathia brought him a poached egg on milk toast from a warming unit on the stove. She patted his head and smiled slyly. Uncle looked at the food and curled his nose. "The wages of sin," he moaned.

From upstairs, Darlene asked something emotionally. Clarence replied emotionally.

"Will they ever quit scrapping?" Sathia shook her head and clicked her tongue.

Everyone listened. Brick skidded back his chair and headed toward the living room.

"Where are you going, young man?"

"To hear better."

"Now, is that nice? Is it any of your business?"

"No, but I want to know what's happening."

Sathia pursued him into the living room, where he crept up the stairs, his face a blend of curiosity and mischief. Once more came the raised voices.

Sathia whispered to Brick, "Everything all right up there?"

Darlene huffed, "I'm just now finding myself."

"Mercy, that girl. Young man, let us go back and mind our business," said Auntie, not making a move to leave, her head tilted to hear better.

Brick heard the name, McPeak. Crummy guy, he thought. Then, he heard his dad say bluntly, "You owe it to McPeak as well as to me." Brick was glad, glad they were having it out over the man; crummy guy, he thought, wanting to join them to contribute what he thought of McPeak. "It's unfair to both McPeak and me. You leave us dangling," his father blurted.

"Heavens," exclaimed Sathia.

There was abrupt silence - then sudden convulsive sobbing, followed by soft talk that Brick could barely hear, let alone discern. Thoughtfully, he came downstairs, his fingers trailing the rail. He did not look at Sathia, nor she at him.

"Well, kiddies, happy?" Burnie said devilishly, as they returned. Sathia colored pink around the ears. She took her feather duster, dabbed across the kitchen facilities, swiftly over the potted plants, patted it along the wall into the dining room. "You, Brick, and you, Burnie, eat your breakfast before it's cold."

Darlene's bedroom door closed. Clarence, whistling a jolly tune, jogged heavily down the stairs and into the kitchen. The family watched, their mouths agape. "Won't be joining you folks this morning, thank you," said Clarence, a twinkle in his eyes. "Need to let Darlene think things over - alone." With determined strides, he swept past them. "See you, folks. So long, Lop Ears," he called, closing the porch door gently.

"So long," said Brick faintly, looking with bewilderment at Uncle, who looked even more bewildered at Sathia who had pivoted back to the kitchen.

A few minutes later, Darlene strolled downstairs into the kitchen. Her eyes were red-rimmed, her lips proudly pursed. Without a word, she poured coffee into a flowered breakfast cup. The family waited, but, no explanation came, no comment, no facts. Suddenly, she turned to Brick, and hugged him. "I feel everything's going to be all right, just fine, eventually," she announced, sniffing. Then with stately grace she exited, back to her room.

"What the devil?" said Burnie. "What's that all about?"

"Never mind," said Sathia, following her. "She may need woman talk."

"Don't count on it. She seems to know what she wants."

"You men are so dumb sometimes." Sathia left.

Again, the boy and the man looked at each other baffled. "Well, that takes care of church," Brick bubbled, relieved, tugging his tie loose. A car chugged into the driveway. Uncle stirred. Responding to his duty, Brick said, "I'll get it." From the porch, he watched Mr. Raffetto climb out of the car, faster than normal, his forehead deep-furrowed, the raw, red hands knotting anxiously. "What's the matter?" Brick reacted.

Raffetto said cautiously. "Burnie resting?"

"He's in the kitchen."

"Heard, hasn't he?"

"Heard what?"

"You hain't heard?" Raffetto lumbered closer. Brick stepped outside into the yard.

"No."

Raffetto shook his head. "Figured he knew."

"I don't know what you're talking about," Brick said, sensing something impending.

"Clarence or Sathia here?"

"Auntie is."

"Better get her then," Raffetto suggested. "Don't want to upset Burnie."

"Why?"

"The Japs just bombed Pearl Harbor. They blasted Hawaii!"

In the next 24 hours the world exploded with bombs and hatred. Clarence returned to the Sea Ranch to sit anxiously before the radio. He and Darlene held hands. "I just don't understand," she kept saying. "I just don't understand what's happening." Aunt Sathia mopped the kitchen around the stove, set to roasting two chickens, and baking both an apple and a berry pie. Uncle sat motionless, staring at the floor, and puffing a cigar produced from some hidden cache. Sathia scowled at him, but held her tongue.

Hour after hour the radio news-spotted around the globe; commentators reviewed, predicted, and condemned. Officially, Japan had declared war. With excited voices they described Pearl Harbor, the flames and black smoke, how the devilish planes had roared out of nowhere to scream death bombs onto airfields and into factories. How mysterious two-man subs had torpedoed shipping in the harbors. Appraisals of damage were vague and inconclusive, but conservative reports estimated at least five battleships out of commission, at least one hundred and fifty American planes destroyed on the ground, and thousands of Americans feared dead. The newsmen related tales of valor, of ships turned infernos, of women and children huddling in fear of invasion. They repeated stories about airmen shot down, who swam ashore, patched up a second plane and flew out again.

"Well," Burnie remarked, "if anything will pull our country together, it's this."

Enemy paratroopers, according to Sunday night disclosures, had landed on the hills back of Honolulu. A number of Japanese servants had attacked their white employers; some Japanese sympathizers had launched a guerrilla warfare by setting crucial fires or by raiding important installations, thus creating confusion and terror. Japanese laborers were said to have cut directional arrows in the cane fields. Japanese saboteurs had deliberately blocked the Honolulu-Pearl Harbor Road. The announcers readily admitted that fact and rumors could not be separated, that rumors were wild. But for certain, the situation had grave implications.

Following a desperate phone call from an Army general to the President of the United States, the two leaders along with the Hawaiian governor, agreed that martial law must be enacted immediately.

"I just know Ida will be in the thick of it," Burnie murmured. "She'll be nursing everybody. Poor dear." In those endless hours, Ida's name passed from lip to lip.

The laborious day stretched into evening. Darlene prepared a light supper from Sathia's industrious cooking. Once, she leaned back against the stove and asked, "How did they do it? They must have carriers - big aircraft carriers."

"Bet they're getting help from local Japanese," Clarence spat angrily. "They're probably destroying everything they can."

"Will transport planes come back? You know, to drop troops." Burnie asked more to himself. Two ferocious waves of planes had attacked an hour apart. "Wish I knew about Ida."

From spotty news, they had learned that the Japanese, with dive bombers, had first nosed down, shrieking in to eliminate America's defensive air force on Hickam Field, a bomber base, near Pearl Harbor; striking next, those on Wheeler, a base inland to create havoc, there ripping hangars apart, ruining planes, all lined in tidy rows, readied for action. Then, with precision, they had devastated and destroyed U.S. naval ships in the harbor. The extent was unknown, except that eight battleships, three cruisers, and an unknown number of destroyers and other miscellaneous ships were afire or sunk. The full fury of the attack seemed directed at the battleships, USS Arizona and West Virginia. As the USS Oklahoma capsized, a frightful explosion shook the harbor, the rippling concussions rumbling over the land and up the canyons, striking terror in the countless observers who saw an oil-black inferno of smoke plume skyward, billowing, drifting, to smother the western basin along with orange streamers and a roiling dark of other ships broken, sinking, afire in a pink glow of massive explosions. The reporters and correspondents, enlivened the details with their word pictures, fearing that over a thousand service personnel had been lost on the Arizona alone. Firefighters with congested emotions, told of blood and bullets, of the stench of burning flesh, and the acrid reek of gunpowder.

Frightening speculations chilled the airways that there was a likely invasion of the continental coast, that California, Oregon, Washington, even Canada were targets. While Pearl Harbor was an inferno, rogue planes, low flying, gunned cars on roads, bombed and strafed surrounding suburbs with incendiary bullets, hitting Honolulu businesses to leave gaping holes, while killing residents. Some Japanese planes roved far into outlying districts.

Interviewers told of field workers on the Eva Sugar Plantation above Pearl Harbor, hearing approaching aircraft, and how they looked up to see mustard yellow torpedo planes, with emblems of a red rising sun, coming in so close that pilots were clearly visible in their cockpits. The flyers had apparently used prominent volcanic pinnacles above the sugar rows as a guide in approaching Ford Island, known locally as Battleship Row. The strategic attack had caught America off guard, lasting from 7:55 to 9:15 a.m., with a break between the two waves. The estimated 180 aircraft had been upped to over 350 torpedo planes, dive bombers, and high altitude horizontal bombers. Details continued to be bewildering and ominous.

After sunset in San Francisco, police units received radio calls, "All patrol cars stand by. Enemy planes sighted approaching. Warn the people." Someone ordered lights on the Golden Gate Bridge to be turned off. The family listened in rapt contemplation, struck silent. Sathia and Darlene left the simple meal preparation, to join Brick and the men, to absorb every word. They listened into the night. Later, the Army concluded that the call had been a hoax or the work of an enemy agent.

Next morning, Brick awoke to wheels screeching in the driveway. Groggily he tumbled from bed and peered out. Two helmeted soldiers halted their jeep by the porch, as Spud barked frantically. A sharp-nosed man with shiny insignia climbed out and introduced himself to Clarence, who stood waiting, his arms crossed. He had remained overnight, sleeping on a couch. Darlene, slender in a pink housecoat, met Brick on the stairs. "What could it possibly be?" she said nervously. Together they hurried outside to see the officer point toward the hills back of the farm at the coastal ridge and swales. Next to Clarence, Burnie stood defeated, his chest concave, a twitch moving up his cheek. Sathia, her face composed, but disapproving, glanced at Darlene and shook her head. The officer gave Clarence a polite salute, swung himself into the vehicle and snapped a command. The soldiers roared out of the driveway.

"What is it?" asked Darlene, addressing the two men who returned sluggishly.

Slowly, Burnie chose his words. "We're to prepare for evacuation -- on 24 hour notice, if needed."

His tone odd, Clarence added, "The Army's taking over here. They'll be arriving in another day or so to set up tents on the hills. They'll take over the beach and will dig lookouts."

"Here? Why here?" Darlene gasped.

"Maybe 'fraid of a Jap attack. He didn't say." Clarence's blue eyes were a faded gray. "He said the Army's got to protect the beach. He also said we won't be able to travel in and out of the ranch here -- without permission."

"And just what does that mean?" Darlene challenged.

"That soldiers will check us in and out, that's what. We'll have to have passes."

"For our own place? Will they bring guns?"

"Of course. This is war, honey. They're military."

The family stared dully. Darlene forced a frail laugh. "This must be a dream."

Wearily, Sathia settled into a yard-chair. "I don't know where to begin. There's so much. You mean we actually might have to leave?"

"That's what the officer said. He didn't really know - all depends what happens."

Overwhelmed, Sathia bobbed her head, trying to collect her thoughts. "But where do we begin?"

"We pack only what's necessary," Burnie said simply.

"Pretend you're packing for a weekend," Clarence suggested.

Sathia looked at him. "But, our home here, the ranch. What about it?"

"Can't take it with us. Besides - won't make much difference if the Japs land."

Mesmerized, almost paralyzed, the family enclosed the radio, switching from network to Bay Area news and back again. "Well, life has to go on," Clarence told Burnie. "You stay calm here; pretty soon, I'll take care of the chores - check the feed and water, get the eggs." Burnie nodded in a solemn appreciation.

Following the dramatic day of attacks, in the wake of grim news, growing bleaker, a stoic population waited in a hazy blur of chaos; to assure the citizens, announcements prepared the unsuspecting: the American armed forces were or would be arriving along the Pacific Coast at those places that seemed vulnerable to attack, where an invading force could land with relative ease and gain quick access to the interior valleys. Ground and air defenses were rushed in for day and night readiness around the cities, for the Japanese had torpedoed an American vessel just 700 miles west of San Francisco.

To steady jumpy nerves, the authorities mentioned that large batteries, housing mammoth sixteen inch guns, were being readied. Their casements and firing platforms had been constructed in the 1930's as Japanese military animosity grew. Authorities assured that they had been fired twice in practice. Weighing one million pounds each, and capable of hurling a 2,100 pound shell twenty-seven miles with accuracy, the massive canons were there, waiting. "Good gosh," said Burnie, "Good gosh," a low gurgling in his throat.

Soldiers and sailors were rushing to battle stations, while war vessels patrolled outside the Golden Gate, and Navy planes swept the seas further out. Gas masks, machine guns, rifles, and riot guns were being issued to special police. A few Japanese-Americans had been picked up on the south coast by the FBI, some taken out of stores, or out of fields to be interrogated as possible spies. The concern was not if the Japanese forces were to attack the Pacific Coast, but when. Would local Japanese assist, even join in the invasion? German saboteurs had been landed from submarines on our East Coast. It was not unreasonable that the same could happen on the West Coast.

The Santa Rosa PRESS DEMOCRAT came late. December 8 headlines bombasted the reader from a front-page, filled with a swirling, dizzy display of crushing news: JAPAN WARS ON U.S. - MAKES SUDDEN ATTACKS ON HAWAII - HEAVY FIGHTING AT SEA. Articles elaborated an estimated 2500 people had been killed in the surprise attack, in an effort of the Japanese to control the entire Pacific. U.S. possessions - the Philippines, Guam, and the Marianna Islands had been hit. Japanese forces had landed in Thailand, and the British colonies of Hong Kong, and Malaya. The U.S. was counting the cost of the attack: nineteen warships out of action, including four battleships sunk, 188 aircraft destroyed, and a further 159 damaged. The only positive news: American aircraft carriers had been out to sea or in dry dock and were not vulnerable to the devastating attack. For some reason, the Japanese had not blown up any repair shops, or the vast oil supplies that would be instrumental in reestablishing armed recovery and retaliating in the Pacific.

School was closed, and Brick gladly remained home. After doing chores for Burnie, Clarence drove to work at the apple ranch.   All the fruit had been harvested; the chores, however, never ended - maintenance work, and preparation of winter pruning and spraying lay ahead. The women did their household duties in silence. Brick walked outside, not really seeing anything, wondering what their friends and neighbors were thinking, especially the Yamoto's. Toby had not phoned, understandably. And, Brick hesitated to call him. What could they say?

When Clarence drove home at noon to hear the president speak, the family confronted him before he could step out of the truck. "For heaven's sake," Sathia expelled. "What's happening out there?"

"Not many people on the roads. They must be home, listening to their radios. Saw a caravan of trucks and soldiers, had to pull off the road for them." Everyone trailed him into the kitchen to the sink where he lathered his hands with soap.

"What else? Will they be on our ranch?" Burnie asked.

"I have no idea. Saw them. Never talked to them." Clarence scrubbed, slopped soap from his face and reached blindly for a towel.

Darlene snapped the towel from the hangar and handed it to him. "Then what do we do?"

"Wait."

Sathia set a platter of cold beef and chicken on the kitchen table with bread and all sandwich necessities. "Make your own. We're eating early, ice cream or pie tonight. Eat good now, 'cause after you hear old Roosevelt, you won't feel so good."

Her face creasing with gladness, Darlene added, "Nice you got back soon enough to hear the President."

"Wouldn't miss it. No doubt he'll declare war. Make it official, so we can get started on the Japs and Germans." Clarence wiped his face and arms briskly.

Brick took a piece of bread, smeared it with butter, arranged some Swiss cheese on a slice of beef, coated it with mayonnaise, mustard, and catsup; then structured it with pickles, lettuce, tomatoes, and a second bread slice.

"Look at that guy dig in," said Burnie, with his usual blend of pleasure and amazement.

Almost meekly, Sathia interjected an inquiring, "Burnie?"

"Uh huh."

"Burnie, I think it would be nice to say Grace."

"Huh?"

"Yes, Grace. It's been a long time. And, I can't think of a better time."

"It's a fine idea. But now? On Sundays I'm prepared."

"We'd appreciate it," said Darlene.

"Well...." Burnie pawed his head. Sathia closed her eyes. They waited quietly. "Lord....." Burnie cleared his throat. "Lord, thanks for this food, and for our wonderful women who prepared It. Ame---."

"Burnie! Please?"

"Uuuuuh -- and give us the strength to endure this terrible war that has been coming, and is upon us now. And, give us strength, Oh, Lord, to understand and to fight this enemy. Touch the souls of all those boys dead and dying - boys like Mike. Amen."

There came an audible sigh from everyone. Sathia smiled sweetly, obviously moved. "Very, very nice, Burnie dear."

"That reminds me," Burnie shifted his chair back. "What time is it?"

Darlene glanced at the delicate watch on her wrist. "I think it's that time. I could just make out a man mentioning the speech on the radio." All morning they had kept a radio on, turning the volume up and down to keep informed.

"I'll get it." Clarence turned up the little radio on the shelf above the sink. Following an around-the-world - on the spot report, the program switched to Washington, D.C., and Congress. Solemnly, an announcer described the mood, the setting, the confusion and uncertainty. Then, the Speaker of the House introduced the President of the United States. There was tension - a sense of something momentous and historical.

"Yesterday, December 7, 1941, a date that will live in infamy," the President began, his voice rich and infective, "The United States of America was suddenly and deliberately attacked by naval and air forces of the Empire of Japan." A chill laced Brick's spine. The faces now were somber, reflective. "The attack yesterday on the Hawaiian Islands has caused severe damage to American naval and military forces. Very many Americans have been lost. In addition, American ships have been reported torpedoed on the high seas between San Francisco and Honolulu."

"Wow," said Burnie.

"Yesterday, the Japanese Government also launched an attack against Malaya.

"Last night Japanese forces attacked Hong Kong.

"Last night Japanese forces attacked Guam.

"Last night Japanese forces attacked the Philippine Islands.

"Last night Japanese forces attacked Wake Island.

"This morning the Japanese attacked Midway.

"Japan has therefore undertaken a surprise offensive extending throughout the Pacific area. The facts speak for themselves. The people of the United States have already formed their opinions and will understand the implications to the very life and safety of our Nation."

"We'll stamp their buck teeth in," Clarence hissed. Sadly, Brick wondered if Toby were listening.

"Hostilities exist," said the President. "There is no blinking at the fact that our people, our territory, and our interests are in grave danger."

After the speech, applause, shouting, and some whistling shook the chamber.

A nameless sorrow enclosed Brick. Intuitively he knew. Somehow he was standing on the threshold of something terrible and all engulfing.

13

December 9 dawned cold and dim, after the family's fitful sleep. Two radios on and a percolator with strong coffee opened the day in that order. The family pressed around the radio in the kitchen, leaving the console on in the living room to hear if they roamed about. Programmers warned that happenings were flooding the airways nationally, that it might be difficult to separate fact and fiction. For certain, America had never been so unified suddenly, in a sweep of horror and indignation, backed by an instant desire for justification and revenge. The sense of isolationship that had held the nation back from full intervention in a building war beyond American borders, vanished overnight. Recruiting stations were overwhelmed by floods of patriotic volunteers eager to enlist. More specific details of the Hawaiian destruction were coming in: Eight battleships, three light cruisers, three destroyers and four auxiliary were either sunk or damaged. Ninety Army and seventy-seven naval aircraft had been destroyed, with another 128 damaged. Over 2400 Americans had been killed or missing so far, with nearly 2200 wounded. In comparison, Japan had lost twenty-nine aircraft and five or six midget submarines.

Citizens were reacting with anger and frustration around the nation. The U.S. Attorney General announced that there would be no roundup of Japanese. However, the FBI ordered that air, bus, and rail lines refuse Japanese passengers. In Washington, D.C., 3,000 cherry trees, had been mysteriously cut, gifts from Japan thirty years earlier. The Japanese Embassy had plumed into smoky fire. Lights in the White House had been darkened, with 40 millimeter guns stationed on the roof, and sandbags blocking all entrances. The guards had been doubled and gas masks issued to staff members. Private planes had been grounded nationally, and all ham operators had been silenced. Around the country, master power switches had been pulled to darken cities. Crowds here, there, everywhere roamed, tossing bricks, rocks, and bottles to knock out lights, marquees, store lights, neon signs, traffic lights, as crowds screamed, "Blackout. Blackout."

The West Coast was in hysteria. Authorities announced immediate plans to dismiss Japanese-Americans from civil service jobs, to prohibit them from a further practice of law and medicine, and in some cases, doing business of any sort. In Los Angeles, sirens commenced screaming and antiaircraft guns commenced firing in the middle of the night. There was no enemy, but, someone reported seeing planes. Aviators reported observing thirty-four warships between Los Angeles and San Francisco. Investigation proved that the enemy armada was some fourteen fishing boats. A dozen elegantly dressed Japanese at a wedding reception in Los Angeles were arrested and taken to jail on suspicion that possibly they were high authorities instrumental in the attacks.

When a lookout suddenly spotted 30 unidentified planes off the coast west of South San Francisco in the early hours of December 9, alarms went off all over the Bay Area. Fire alerts wailed and police cars raced through the streets amongst the confusion, warning people to turn off lights. The aircraft proved to be reconnaissance planes, not enemy bombers. But the PRESS DEMOCRAT, in a late edition, headlined in red: "Enemy Here!" Air raid sirens wailed in San Francisco every night. The Army announced that enemy planes from carriers lurking offshore had dropped flares. Los Angeles had an air raid alert and the night was made hideous with the sound of antiaircraft guns spitting at imaginary planes. Several people on city streets were killed while driving without headlights, and, one driver, racing across the Bay Bridge, was shot by a sentry. An hysterical woman fell out of a high rise apartment to her death.

That same day, 1300 men of the 17th Infantry from Fort Ord, part of the Seventh Division, arrived at the fairgrounds in Santa Rosa to convert it into an Army camp. Students at Tamalpais High School to the south, were ordered to wear dark clothing to assist in concealment, as pupils and officials practiced heading for the hills behind, in the event of attack.

Not only had Pearl Harbor been surprised and America's Pacific fleet knocked out of commission, but, the British had lost two of their best battleships off Malaya; with overwhelming forces, the Japanese were invading the Philippines, the East Indies, Wake, and Guam Islands, meeting valiant but outmanned resistance. Japanese had seized Hong Kong on the coast of China, invaded Borneo and the Solomon Islands, to dominate the Southwest Pacific, the Indian Ocean, and Singapore, center of British strength in the Far East. All were left helpless to the sweeping supremacy of the Nippon Empire.

To ease the fears of listening Americans, authorities assured that the Japanese-Americans would be scrutinized. Some had been stopped, searched, many forbidden to go out at night. Unfortunately some were beaten by anxious crowds, and some arrested on the possibility they were spies. In fact, a few had been picked up as early as December 8 by the FBI - some had been taken from stores or out of the fields.

The phone rang: one long, four shorts. Toby, the Army, something about Aunt Ida? Curiously, Brick ventured to the head of the upper stairs. Darlene answered. It was Mr. McPeak; he knew by her soft, "Hi." Yet, oddly, her tone was different, reserved. When Burnie ambled in, she waved to him to hold back, but not Clarence, who joined her to lean against the doorjamb, his arms crossed, waiting.

"You're in San Francisco?" A hand fluttered to her throat. "With the National Guard? They called you?" She listened, then covered the receiver with a hand. "He's on emergency call," she whispered to Clarence. "His unit is being activated."

"Figured they'd get him, sooner or later."

"Oh, isn't it all horrible. Everything's just horrible." She chatted aimlessly about soldiers and guns and possible evacuation orders.

"You're avoiding the real issue - what we're doing. Tell him," Clarence insisted. "Get to the point. And, what does he want?"

Curiously, Brick tiptoed down the stairs, but, Darlene saw him and signaled him to stay, while pressing a vertical forefinger to her lips, motioning him to be quiet. He obeyed, waiting, determined to grasp the situation.

Darlene hesitated. Listened. "It was the hardest letter I've ever written, Ed," she admitted. "We've talked and talked, and I know you understand." Brick could see her bite her lips. "I would never hurt you. Not purposely. You know that. But, the world has changed now, totally."

"Get to the point, Dear," Clarence urged.

"No. It's no use talking it out any longer, Ed. Nothing we can say anymore will change what has to be." She was standing a little taller now. Her voice and face had a gentle decisiveness. Her slender fingers moved to Clarence's arm to stroke it. "Clarence is here with me." She waited, listening, nodding. "Of course, you knew he would be. He and I have discussed everything - thoroughly. And, we agree." Brick strained to catch every word. "I hated to tell you by letter," Darlene continued, choking slightly, "but, it was the only way. It was the only means I could say what needs to be said. I didn't want to argue, or end up crying in front of you. You know what I mean."

Clarence smiled proudly. He winked at her.

"I know now, where I belong. And, I know what's best for my family - especially for Brick in these difficult times, which will get far worse. It's been hard for him; hard for all of us, and especially for Burnie with his heart." She smiled tenderly at Clarence. "I know I was just a foolish little girl, in ways. It was you who was strong and good, when I needed someone strong and good."

Clarence frowned slightly. He watched his wife's face relax some, as she listened patiently. "You're a fine man," she said at last. "Thank you for understanding. We knew it's been coming. We've talked about it, for how long, now?" She listened, absorbing whatever Mr. McPeak said. Her expression registered pain, remembered pleasure, appreciation, relief. At last, she finished firmly, "All my family respects you. You have been and will always be a part of us." Mr. McPeak apparently responded with some positive reaction. Darlene smiled, and continued. "Please keep in contact. Let us know what's happening and where your orders take you."

Brick wondered what exactly was happening, for his dad had a confident look suddenly. After replacing the phone, Darlene stood thoughtfully, until Clarence pulled her to him, to hold her.

Impatiently, Brick clumped down boldly to his mother. She loosened herself from her husband.

"Dad and I need you," she said, hugging him. "We need your help now, because we're going to try and be a fine family again." Wiping her eyes, she took Clarence's hand and they walked out to the front porch. Brick watched, speechless, with mixed joy, yet not knowing what to expect.

While Clarence and Darlene walked around the yard, Burnie sat in his big Morris Chair lost in thought. Sathia puttered in the kitchen, listening always to the radio. Brick stood watching his parents. Burnie suddenly uttered, "I'm happy. So happy about Darlene and Clarence finding themselves, gradually. They have a lot to work out."

"It's a wonderful start," said Sathia.

"There's something more in the air. I can't shake the feeling, that things are going to happen."

"What?" asked Brick disturbed.

"I don't know. I keep expecting that Army officer. But, there's more happening, I sense it in my bones. Part of it's in the paper here." He lifted the PRESS DEMOCRAT, laden with world news. "Big article here, says the Japs are gloating; they think their future is just grand; they claim the U.S. has been reduced to a third class naval power after the attack, that we're trembling in our shoes." Burnie crushed the paper slightly. "They've underestimated us. We Americans have a fighting spirit. We'll kick their butts; wipe them out."

Sathia jolted a little, and continued washing a dish without saying anything.

The news kept growing all dark and despairing. A wave of hostility and revenge was washing across the nation, especially, because of the fact that as the attack came, Japanese envoys were negotiating peace in Washington, D.C. That same day, the Pan American flying boat,

Philippine Clipper, landed at Treasure Island in San Francisco, the plane's fuselage riddled with bullet holes from the raid on Wake Island. Within hours, in the predawn darkness, the popular luxury ship, the Lurline, running without lights, edged under the darkened Golden Gate Bridge, her nervous passengers having worn life jackets night and day.

Lieutenant General John DeWitt, U.S. Army, head of the coastal defense, added to the fear of saboteurs, of a native Japanese insurrection, and of ultimate invasion when he stood before the supervisors' chamber in San Francisco's City Hall and said tersely, "Bombing is bound to come. Don't be jittery. Learn to take it. You've got to take it."

Small boats, manned by Sea Scouts, patrolled the piers of the Bay Bridge, watching for saboteurs. Antiaircraft guns guarded by nervous sentries were put up on hills. Soldiers were posted along the beaches and in caves to watch for invasion. Two American ships - one off Santa Cruz and one off Eureka - California coastal ports - survived attack by an enemy sub. A CHRONICLE headline announced: "THE WAR IS REAL AND THE WAR IS HERE." Several Bay Area papers ran informative articles on how to spot Japanese planes, from the front, side, and bottom of five different bombers. They followed with silhouettes of various kinds of Japanese warships. Instructive articles appeared: "WHAT TO DO IN THE EVENT OF AN AIR RAID WARNING." Panic swept through some households of people who feared a gas attack. Other headlines read: PACIFIC BATTLE WIDENS; ROOSEVELT PREDICTS LONG WORLDWIDE WAR; TOKYO REACHES FOR WORLD CONQUEST. Other countries followed the declaration of war - Britain, New Zealand, Canada, China, France. Quickly, the world began preparing for global conflict. Democrats and Republicans, labor and capital closed ranks, to face the enemy, side by side. Editorials, speeches, radio pleas began, demanding the Japanese-Americans be removed from the west coast as they were considered a security risk.

In the Pacific, Wake Island momentarily repulsed the invaders, afterwards telegraphing the message: "Send us more Japs." Japanese warships and planes were sweeping all shipping from the sea, even sinking liners and fishing vessels. Over and over, newspapers featured the ruins of Pearl Harbor, the twisted steel and crushed ships, horror photos of belching flames and wounded civilians bandaged and homeless.

Brick asked permission to phone Toby. He felt sick-at-heart, as he cranked the numbers. When no one responded, he tried several times again. Rose answered.

"Rose?"

"Yes - hello, Brick."

"What are you doing home?"

"It's a long story."

"Is Toby there? I've been worried."

"All so horrible." Her voice caught and she choked slightly. "Dad's out in the orchard, on the tractor, furrowing. I fear he's losing himself from everything." She paused. "I'll get little brother."

Brick waited impatiently. Then Toby came on. "Hi."

"What's Rose home for? 'Cause of all the troubles?"

"That, and she lost her job." Toby whispered the last words.

"What?"

"Her supervisor said her services were no longer needed."

"Why?"

"The attack, the war, and she's a Jap, I guess."

Brick changed the subject. "Probably won't see each other, except at school."

"Yeah, school could start tomorrow."

"Radio said that it would be announced if any are open. Mom's gonna phone the high school tomorrow."

"Would like to see you," Toby said earnestly. "But, dad won't let us out. He's afraid. We saw lots of military trucks - a convoy or whatever, moving along Highway 1."

"Well, I better let you go, then. See you." Brick stumbled his words, fought with them. "Don't know what to say or even think. You know?"

"I know, and I don't know."

"See you." Brick replaced the phone heavily, as a car turned into the open gate and drove up the lane to the porch. A man in a cap and gray outfit stepped out, holding a brown envelope; he was not in a military uniform. Clarence and Burnie walked out to meet him, Burnie shuffling more than usual.

The man made a practiced smile of greeting. "Mr. Burnie MacQuarrie? Route 1, Box 775?"

"Yes, I am who you are looking for." Uncle took the porch rail for support and headed unsteadily down; he looked pale and shrunken.

"I'm from the telegraph office in Petaluma. It's a wireless from Hawaii. Hard to get through with all the censorship and attacks." The messenger licked his lips. "I was told to prepare you, that it may be worrisome, but nothing tragic or fateful - that's the words my boss used." Sathia and Darlene moved back of the men, with Darlene continuing down beside Burnie. Brick pressed in behind his family. "There's lots of military vehicles on the coast highway. They stopped me, at first, until they understood I had a telegram." The man laid the envelope into Burnie's puffy fingers, stood back and folded his own hands in front of him, waiting. Burnie tore at the flap and removed the message. He scowled and blinked, his glasses seeming to steam, before handing the paper to Darlene, who scanned it; her mouth tightened, her eyes narrowing. She looked at Burnie, up at Clarence, at Sathia, and at Brick. "It's from both a naval officer and the Head Nurse at Kapiolani Hospital in Honolulu."

"Where Ida is working again," Burnie interposed.

Darlene summarized its essence, before passing the telegram around. "Ida MacQuarrie was injured in the attack on Hickham Field. Apparently a bus carrying nurses had turned on its side. Ida has a broken arm and a mild concussion. Because of her age, she will be confined for a time. Details will follow."

Burnie sucked in air.

"Are you all right?" Sathia twisted her apron that she was clutching.

Burnie trembled. "Yes. I want to send a return telegram." His request was gentle, but urgent.

"Certainly." The messenger took a pad and pencil from his inside coat pocket.

"You do it in telegram words?"

"We always do."

"Thank the naval man and the nurse. And tell my sister we love her, that she's in our prayers. That we want to know more about her condition." Burnie ftumbled for his wallet. "How much we owe you?"

"We'll bill you. Depending on the number of words and such." He leaned around, hearing, his legs bracing wide. All the family looked to the inland hill. "You got visitors. Time I get back."

Burnie's uneasiness was further justified. The Army arrived. A motorized caravan wound noisily down the country road, led by the colonel in the jeep, driven by his orderly. He lifted an arm, signaling a halt. The trucks filled with armed soldiers, some carrying machine guns and antiaircraft barrels, each wrapped in canvas, but not so completely as to hide what they were. A few vehicles hauled caissons on big wheels. All rumbled and squeaked to a halt, stretching from the front gate through the tree-lined drive. The colonel's jeep bounced up to the side porch. Clarence walked out to meet him. "Just wait, Burnie. Don't get yourself upset any more than you have to," Sathia warned. Burnie did hold back, deciding to let Clarence learn details. Everything was getting to Uncle, Brick decided: the war, the soldiers, now, especially, Ida.

Clarence conversed with the colonel, his pointed nose twitching over a fine mustache. At last, the orderly started up, as the colonel waved to several more jeeps that followed, holding both sergeants and officers, the gold or silver bars gleaming in the sunlight. The jeeps continued up the ridge and side hill. The caravan remained, the soldiers relaxing, smoking and chatting. Clarence returned. Before he spoke, he walked into the kitchen with the family trailing. "Talk," Burnie ordered.

"For now, until they unload, they will be in the yard and around the buildings; eventually, they will set up tents and latrines, kitchens, away from us. Colonel Mathias said they will have guards, emplacement guns and lookout posts, gradually. Like he told us before, we will need passes to come and go to town. There's going to be a guard station up the hill near Highway 1, where the road turns toward our place. Remember, they told us that. The colonel said it probably won't happen, but, should we have to leave, we should have emergency clothing and toiletries packed. He's assigning a corporal Harry to assist us."

"Jumpin' Freckles. The animals, the poultry, will be scared to death," Burnie mumbled, a little befuddled.

"Burnie," Sathia pleaded. "Don't worry now."

Clarence braced himself, waiting. "Auntie's right, Burnie. The colonel claims we can go about our business as much as possible - take care of the chores and such."

Spud was beside himself, yapping, and racing about. "We've been invaded," said Burnie bitterly. "The colonel said we could be invaded. He sure meant it."

The colonel and his officers and sergeants returned. "Those are the new Willy-Overland Jeeps," Clarence said, impressed. "Heard about them, seen pictures, but this is the first time I've seen one. They can go anywhere."

"Glad you found something nice," Darlene said, sarcastically. Clarence ignored her.

Immediately, the men encircled the colonel, listened to him as he studied a clipboard of papers; then barked orders, his pointed nose twitching again. Frequently he would gesture toward the hills and the Stemple River. Another caravan of trucks, large and small, rumbled through the yard, their heavy motors grinding. Mud spattered up to whack against the windows of Clarence's and Darlene's parked machines. "For heaven's sake," Sathia choked, and looked at the splotched windows.

Another caravan brought tractors, bulldozers, and more high-pointing 40 mm guns. Numerous vehicles trailed more caissons that creaked on their big, many-spoked wheels. They, too, pulled into an upper pasture and swung into a circle. "Gracious, did you see those ugly cannon?" Sathia shuddered. Brick felt an instant rage mixed with dread. He kept pressing against the window to stare at the big guns, so formidable - so shockingly out of place in the beloved setting.

Darlene asked softly, "But, why the Sea Ranch? Why us, here?"

"I don't know, exactly," Clarence said seriously. "If the Japs take over Hawaii, California will be next, you know."

"But, that still doesn't explain all the military here," Burnie remarked. "More than most other places on the coast, I imagine."

Clarence nodded. "Yes, something strange is going on here."

"I feel so sorry for Rose," said Darlene, gloomily.

"Well, don't feel so sorry yet," Clarence countered, "we don't know what the local Orientals will do yet."

Quickly, men poured from the military machines, gear and duffle bags slung over their shoulders. A few wandered into the corrals and poked into the sheds to startle cattle and scatter chickens. The hens cackled uproariously. Haphazardly, the soldiers dumped some of their equipment in the yard and along the fences. Most they carried to the first pasture above the barn where they began spreading small tents. Several trucks continued past the chicken houses to the back hills and the terrain above the sea. There men dispersed, some exploring the ridges and checking the shallow gulches, others vanishing over the cliffs, doubtless descending to the beach below.

In the next hours, trucks moved back and forth bringing poles and lumber, boxes of food, and mysterious gear covered with canvas. Burnie stood hollow-eyed with disbelief, his face growing longer and sadder. To the upstairs, he, Brick, and Clarence had ventured together. "I worry about you climbing those stairs so much," Sathia scolded.

"Doggone it, Woman. I'm interested, and a man's gotta do what he's gotta do," Burnie voiced. From Brick's upstairs window, the three could see bulldozers pushing dirt into mounds near the river. On the beach, beyond the mouth, a couple of tractors scraped out shallow pits. The blunt-nosed machine guns and the antiaircraft guns, still pointed upward having been lifted from the carriers, doubtless to be strategically placed later. The caissons had been lined up in a pasture. "And we can see only part of what they're doing," said Burnie, distraught. He had been looking through his binoculars, except observing made him too nervous, so he handed the glasses to Clarence and returned to the kitchen.

"I'll make you some more tea, if you don't pace," Sathia called.

Brick wished to burst from the house and pick his way across a yard scarred and mushed from heavy traffic. There in the barn, he would crawl into the hayloft to try counting the hornet nests and suck on some straws, which would probably taste like mildew. His sanctuary, he knew, would not close out the shouts and the clatter of working men.

The knock at the front door sounded firm, in authority. Not knowing what to expect, family members followed Clarence to the door, with Darlene taking his arm. Burnie attempted to join them, but, was unsteady. The door opened to two soldiers, a corporal, tall, handsome in face, with blond sideburns. Beside him was a private, shorter, darker, with an apologetic smile. They wore flat helmets, puffed trousers, and knee-high boots. Brick had seen some soldiers in leg wrappings; why the difference, he didn't understand. "I'm Corporal Harry Sanders. This is Private Joe Golden." The latter saluted, smartly. "Colonel Mathias has assigned us to you personally, for any of your needs, concerns, questions. You name it, we are here at your call anytime. We will be passing your front door many times. If you wish our attention, please hang this on your porch." He handed Clarence a bright red star. "Here, too, are some passes, please print your names and sign. The boy does not need one, as yet. You, of course, can carry on your work and shopping, inland and on the ranch. We hope you have extra cloth or sheets, that you can put up temporarily, to darken your front windows. Private Golden will bring some black crepe paper, but you will need to purchase more."

"Why so many guns and shooting irons?" Burnie called.

"There's around 400 men - seems like more, I know. This is war and we just don't know what to expect. Your long beach here, is a natural landing site that could lead enemy forces inland, right into central California."

"God," Darlene uttered.

"I don't mean to frighten you half to death, but, that is why you have been asked to pack. I doubt very much if you will have to leave ever. If necessary, however, pack enough for a few nights, as needed. Any questions?"

Each of the family looked at one another. "We just don't know what to ask," Clarence shrugged, his face pale.

"I totally understand. We don't know what to ask or say either. We'll be in touch." He smiled and the two soldiers slipped away.

Reluctantly, the family began packing clothes and personal belongings in suitcases dusted off from years of storage, should orders necessitate an evacuation. In his room, Brick folded his gray sweater and tucked his bird guide in the luggage bag. Sadly, he turned away, drawn to the light of his window. The sea looked the same, deep and blue, restless as always. A creeping mist was washing the shadowed cliffs. Spumes of foam drifted with the wind, where the waves met jagged shore. The old familiar scene, Brick's world, its cozy comfort shattered, wisped away like the foamy spray. Brick slid onto his bed and crushed a pillow to him. For many minutes he stared vacantly at the wallpaper design that had amused him during many days of sickness. There were varied prints: redcoated men, who sat streamlined horses, sailing them over a fence. Before them raced a pack of loose-tongued hounds. In another scene, two red foxes hid behind a stump. In yet another, an elegant hunter held aloft a battered little fox. Brick saw the sketches differently, somehow, in a new way he did not comprehend. A burning filled him, deep inside from the silent place where fears crouch. Does Toby feel this way, he thought.

14

That evening of December 10, ironically the same day that the Army arrived, Brick experienced a terrifying, surreal night that would possess him, live within him indelibly. Following a boxing exercise, with Clarence supervising, he trotted upstairs, feeling growing strength in his body. He washed, changed his shirt for supper and awaited the dinner call. Combing his hair, and pressing a few waves into place, he heard shouts and rumbling noises, with the multiple roar of truck ignitions firing up. Darlene and Clarence had assisted a fussy Sathia in darkening the front window with closed curtains, lined with rags and old towels. Brick parted the curtains as carefully as possible, held them aside to see soldiers running about, some swinging a cannon on wheels around - the figures jerky like a film reel gone out of control. A faulty searchlight came on, its beam thrusting into the night to splash over the water, only to go out and come on again, and out for good.

Brick lifted the windows to the cold night to see and hear better. The cursing of men in the yard punctuated the action. He caught what he later learned was the throb of a diesel engine. From below, his father cried out, "What the hell? Get the flashlights and turn off all the lights." There came orders and counter orders, and a dizzy movement of vehicles without headlights. From near Sathia's garden, he heard a man bellow, "Enemy ship." Brick grabbed his flashlight from the bed stand and turned off his lamp; then, rushed back to the window; the breathless babble of men echoed here, there, afar. Beyond Tomales Point, a narrow peninsula that arrowed toward Bodega Head, six miles distant, a big form had emerged in the purple dusk, low, lengthy, vaguely visible against a shimmer of sea, its engines throbbing steadily, clearly visible through the dip of bluffs.

"Dad, come here, quick, look," Brick called. He heard Clarence clamoring up the stairs.

"Don't you run up there, Burnie. Don't," Sathia warbled in an anguished way. "You peek out the window on the front porch."

As Clarence reached Brick's side, with binoculars, Darlene not far behind, the world erupted in explosive light and gunfire - the howitzers from wherever, the antiaircraft from truck beds and spots on the back hill and ridges where they had been temporarily placed. The soldiers attempted to point the barrels seaward, their struggling actions indistinct in the pinnacles of flash. The pump and rumble of artillery and the crackle of small firearms deafening. The ground trembled, shaking the house and rattling the windows, until one feared they would collapse. Brick recoiled with a frightened cry and pulled back. Spud disappeared under the bed.

Spitting white flashes punctuated the coastline with ear-splitting fury. Most terrifying, were the tracers, hundreds, white, interspersed with red, that arched into the ocean, like shooting stars gone wild, some crisscrossing, most centering off the point, exploding into watery plumes that reflected the flaring gun blasts. In the flickering intensity, all Brick could think was - the invasion has started. "It's a sub, a sub," Clarence hollered.

Darlene screamed hoarsely, her voice gagging in a throaty way, as she dropped to the floor, crouching. "Oh, God, help us." Her words had an empty, forlorn sound, a part of her reaching, straining. Clarence stood watching, but, not before pushing Brick down. He had come back on his knees to peer over the sill.

"Best you keep back from the window, son." For fifteen to twenty minutes the shelling continued. And then, the rapid bombardment ceased as abruptly as it had begun. The cannonading had seemed like an eternity. Stooping over, running awkwardly in the dark, Brick moved to the stair edge, anxious, fearful about what it all meant and fearful of what the shock would do to his uncle. He saw Sathia standing with an arm around Burnie; they, too, were peering through parted curtains. Their side features drawn with terror in the glow of a low-turned flashlight. "Clarence, just what do you see?" Burnie managed.

An eerie silence fell, while eardrums still rang. "The sub is still there." Clarence paused. "Just a minute, I'm adjusting the binoculars. Wait a minute now. It's just sitting out there. The sub is just sitting there rocking kind of. Apparently, our guns - what the military just brought in, nothing we got can reach it. It must be out of range of all that fancy stuff they've tossed at it."

Apparently, with an arrogant confidence that they could not be harmed by ineffective coastal batteries, the Japanese officers held their ship steady, bobbing slightly. "They're lowering a light - a light over the side." Brick saw his father readjust the glasses, as Spud emerged from under the bed.

"What's happening?" Burnie rolled his words more in an alarmed acceptance, than a question. "What are they doing - anybody doing? Us guys - the Japs?"

"Dang it, Burnie. I'm trying to see. I'm trying to see." A painful silence followed for all. Clarence then said, slowly, "They're some rafts, or boats, spreading out from the sub. I can see what may be flashlights - big flashlights with long beams. They seem to be looking around."

"Is it the invasion?" Darlene inquired, her voice soft, uneasy, almost resigned.

His voice tight, Clarence said, with a registered anger, "I don't know. I don't know."

Shortly, those upstairs retreated to the first floor, grouping to support one another, hopefully to rally their spirits. A knock resounded at the front door. Expecting the worst, the family crowded back of Clarence as he slid the latch. Corporal Harry Sanders silhouetted the doorway, his face tight with concern. "Are you all right?" he asked, somberly. "Is Mr. MacQuarrie okay?"

"Yes, we're surviving, I guess," Sathia said.

"What the hell happened?" Burnie asked from the dark.

"A sub - an enemy sub - the spotters sighted a big one a couple of miles offshore. We've learned that they're prowling our coast - 350 feet long with over 100 men, we've been told. We sent over 1700 rounds of sizeable ammunition at 'em - all we have, but couldn't reach 'em. What we brought in doesn't have the range we need. Got to bring heavier stuff in. The colonel radioed headquarters for planes to strafe, but, so little available - few and far between right now. We'll just have to see." The corporal was excited, adventuring in his first combat duty, and probably talking more than necessary.

"Are they going to shell us then?" Clarence had a direct, sober question, adding, "We can't stop them, apparently."

The family could not see the corporal's face clearly, but, his voice was assuring. "No. If they had intended to harm us - to shell us - they would have by now."

"I saw little boats leaving the ship, men holding flashlights. What's that all about?" Clarence pursued.

"We don't know. Could be the Japs are trying to intimidate us; or study our shore batteries - or look over the area as a landing site. I don't rub shoulders with the big wheels, so, can't say. I tell you all this, 'cause this is your place, and you folks are in the midst. I feel I owe you that much."

"What do we do?" Burnie asked.

"Just keep your curtains drawn and all lights off until morning. Get some rest and if you have to move about, keep the flashlight beams pointed at the floor or where you're going. There will be a sentry passing regularly. If you need attention, put the red star we gave you on your porch. We will be in touch." The corporal left. For nearly an hour the family sat in the dark, listening, wrapped in blankets, waiting, fearing the worst, their imaginations running rampant.

Finally, Clarence said. "I'm going upstairs. I've got to see what's happening. Best you all get some rest - you especially, Burnie."

"Who can sleep at a time like this?"

Brick laid on the couch, but could not sleep either, until he dozed off in early morning. The sub waited out the night as the crew accomplished whatever purpose they had, and disappeared before the first glow of dawn. When the threat had eased and the military personnel ceased their frenetic activity, the family members opened the curtains and sat, sipping coffee and chocolate.

A persistent knock pounded, startling the family, causing Sathia to choke on a sip. Clarence opened to the Corporal Sanders and an officer with a gold bar on each shoulder. He introduced the man as a Lieutenant Burkhart. The officer apologized and asked how everyone was holding up. "I'm sorry for the chaos and the horror; all this is beyond us. We are at war with a diabolical enemy at our doorstep."

"We understand. It's beyond us. However, feel assured we will support whatever you do - but, we must keep running our ranches," Burnie said. "You know that."

"That's one of the main reasons I've come here. Despite all the confusion, we want you all to carry on as best you can - travel wherever you need around the ranch or out for groceries and such. You might be stopped or detoured - you know - for heavy equipment, guns, troop movement." The Lieutenant's face softened.

"My chickens probably won't lay for a week. Guess that is not very significant in light of things. We'll do what we can," Burnie said, with appreciation.

"Also, there will be a lot of rumors circulating, a lot of people that are aware of the shelling, but, don't know exactly what happened. You saw things. It would be wise if you and the boy, when he returns to school, not give details of what you witnessed. There is much fear out there. We don't want a panic." The officer paused, then said directly, "We'd appreciate your cooperation on this."

Speaking out, calm now, Darlene said, "We will cooperate in any way we can, officer. Yet, I know there will be a lot of calls inquiring as to what we know or saw. How do we handle that?"

"Easier said then done, certainly. It's best to say that it was scary, that you don't know what happened, except that something triggered an alarm. It happens all the time. Everyone's spooked. After all, no one was killed or injured - a few sprains and bruises - that happens daily in the service. The fact there was a sub out there will only terrorize people - make our problems more difficult. Believe me." The Lieutenant stepped back, and saluted. "We will be in touch."

Local schools remained closed for a few more days with all the confusion and disorder. After the shelling, hearsay ran wild. Telephone calls came from the Rafetto's, from the Hamilton's, from others, all questioning, wondering, all sharing concern from anxious neighbors. Even Gerve called Brick - but not the Yamoto's - too embarrassed, the family figured. None of the callers had seen the sub - their only awareness had been the frightening bombardment.

So, Brick phoned Toby, and Rose answered. They shared a polite greeting, and Brick learned that Toby and his father were working in the orchard. Suddenly Rose asked, "Did you see anything? One of our friends thinks there may have been an enemy ship out there." She avoided the word Japanese. "Did you or your family see anything?"

Remembering the officer's warning, Brick answered, "Guess something out there spooked the soldiers." He wanted to share the horror, tell about the terror, and about the big sub - but, he didn't, proud afterwards that he had remained professional.

"Isn't it terrible - all so sad. Dad has just withdrawn into himself. He's really just closed himself off from everyone. I doubt if he ever takes another picture near the coast. His hobby is over." An awkward pause followed, as she struggled for words. "I will tell Toby you called. He'll appreciate it." Another pause followed. "We don't want him to disturb your family - not just now - so. understand, it's probably best he doesn't call you right away. Considering all that's happening right now with your uncle's health, if you know what I mean."

"Yeah, I guess I understand," Brick said flatly, hanging up slowly.

Air raid sirens continued howling off and on in San Francisco and Los Angeles every night as reports of enemy planes shook the airwaves and antiaircraft guns dotted the night with bursting shells. Sea scouts continued searching the wharves and piers for saboteurs. Soldiers clambered over coastal shores watching for an invasion. German and Italian citizens were picked up on suspicion as enemies that would collaborate. To avoid being mistaken for Japanese, Chinese wore big buttons: "I am a Chinese American." On December 11, Germany declared war on the United States.

Mr. McPeak phoned Darlene, having heard from cohorts about shelling - that something - a sub possibly had been sighted near the ranch. He wanted to know - would explore further the facts, for he had the authority. Darlene assured him that something happened to set off all the new gun emplacements, terrifying the family; soldiers afterwards had assured them, that it was all a mistake - jumpy nerves in a time of chaos. Someone had seen something on the sea that wasn't really there. Darlene assured Mr. McPeak that they were fine, not to be worried, that she appreciated his concern. After she hung up, Clarence commended her for handling the issue to perfection. Burnie agreed. "He seemed skeptical, not sure if I were leveling with him," Darlene confessed. "He said the West Coast was virtually without defenses."

The good news in a depressing day, came as a telegram over the phone. The reader stated that no one wanted to deliver the message personally. Nobody wanted to encounter the confusions and the difficulties in working their way through military interrogations. The words from his sister's supervisor delighted Burnie, brought tears to his eyes. Ida was improving and would remain in convalescence. "Lord, oh Lord," Burnie raised his eyes heavenwards. His face enclosed the family, as he returned the phone gently. "I'm so grateful she is alive - alive." He shouted the word. "She is such an active woman." He directed his emotions, taking control. "For a time, it will be a living death for her." He then hugged and kissed each of those before him.

School was in a turmoil with swirling rumors about the shelling, which had been heard far inland; and, for a time, Brick became a kind of celebrity, for he had been an eye witness. Mary Ann embraced him, kissing him on the cheek, after hearing about his Aunt Ida - plus she figured him a kind of hero. Brick was floating afterwards. He wanted to tell her the excitement, share with her what had really happened. As yet, however - apparently for security reasons - the authorities would not admit that a sub had surfaced; they would concede only that, "There was cause for military response." Like his mother with Mr. McPeak, Brick hadn't suggested that anything happened other than confusion and momentary excitement, although he anguished to tell - to be someone in the know.

Nobody could concentrate on school that day, with kids skipping class, not studying, and with everyone excited. Disinterest in school was an ongoing problem. Brick's algebra and Spanish grades had been slipping even before Pearl Harbor. His subjects seemed pointless and remote. Even escape-reading, which had always been his favorite hobby, proved dull with little pertinence. No pirate yarn, no cowboy and Indian tale, no outer space, was half as exciting as the activities around him and in the news. Most of the men teachers were too old for active duty, except Mr. Conan, the natural science teacher, the one all the girls had a crush on. He was leaving to take officer training in the Air Force. The majority of senior boys were considering quitting school, the oldest to join the Marines or the Air Force, those seventeen, volunteering for the Navy.

One morning, Principal Huff called a special meeting to plead that the boys hold out until June graduation. On the way to the auditorium, Gerve confronted Brick. "The Dallases said they're gonna punch you out after school - beat you up good." He chawed into a jam sandwich, then licked some peach drip from his wrist. "Watch it. But don't let them know I told you."

"But why now? With the war and all?"

"Don't know, except you and Toby are friends." Brick gulped as Gerve melted into a blur of students.

Principal Huff was barely into his plea, when Joe Kelly, star quarterback for their beloved football team, stood up in the audience and said he was an American, and Americans didn't take this stuff lying down; that he wanted to fight Germans and Japs. Over six hundred students cheered him and cheered again. Somebody started the school fight song. In open rebellion the entire student body rose as one, clapping, and singing full-voiced. Mr. Huff looked dumbfounded. He raised his hands, trying to silence them, but to no avail. The Vice Principal leaped up, ran to the back of the stage and rang the dismissal bell. The students sang on. Angrily, he waved his arms and shouted orders to go back to class. Students took their time, however, singing and whistling as they left. A few sophomores jumped up and down on the seats. Others chanted, "Beat the Japs! Beat the Japs! Beat the Japs!" until it pulsed from nearly every lung. Seventy some students burst through the front doors and scattered into the street. A few thrashed a nearby restroom and carved up a wall with, "Kill a Krout, Kill a Jap."

Firming his shoulders, Brick headed back to English. Well, was this the inevitable, he thought, a sickness creeping through him. Bunched outside the room, at the edge of a flowing crowd, they waited: Ray, Jay, and a couple of cronies, were visibly agitated by the excitement of the assembly. Ray wolf whistled, as Jay announced loudly, "Isn't he pretty?"

Brick started past, but Ray intervened. "What's the matter, Curly? Put your hair up in curlers last night? Got 'em too tight?" He spat his words. Anxiously, he looked around for support; a kid laughed. But, the tension from the assembly remained so high and talk so sustained that most students gabbled incessantly. Frustrated, Ray repeated himself. "How many hours you curl your hair, Burton? Burton? You hear me, Burton?"

"Better than having pig bristles like you!" Brick hissed. A few students were watching and heard.

Ray went blank. He tried to retort, but couldn't think. Aimlessly, he drummed his fingers up and down his Levi's.

Satisfied, Brick entered class. He heard some kids laughing - laughing at the Dallases! The twins swaggered in, flushed with anger. For the next twenty minutes class dragged unbearably: lousy grammar and lousier Dallases, Brick thought. Twice from behind, spit wads stung his neck. Unaware, Mrs. Hoyle chattered aimlessly about verbs and nouns, whitening interminable sentences on the blackboard.

Outside, somewhere on the grounds, male shouts and female shrieks penetrated the sanctity of closed windows. Heads lifted, rotated, cocked here and there curiously while Mrs. Hoyle elevated her voice. In the halls the sounds of doors opening and students exiting began shaking the walls. Mrs. Hoyle darted her severest look in the direction of chaotic sounds: slamming lockers, thundering feet, and shrilling voices. In defiance, she peppered and streaked the blackboard with sentence diagrams, the chalk tattooing the dark space.

Suddenly a willowy girl with big glasses walked into the room and timidly handed Mrs. Hoyle a message. She read it carefully and frowned while the class sat hushed, frozen in expectation. At last she said, "School is cancelled." The roar of joy drowned her next words. Reacting, she held up her hands, tempering the near mutinous group. "But the Principal states - very emphatically, that we must all proceed as a class downstairs and out the nearest exit. Now understand, we are not to leave here as is normal. But we are all to proceed in an orderly fashion downstairs. Hear me. Hear me." She broke her composure. "You hear me - you animals?"

Brick felt some relief as Mrs. Hoyle slammed her hand on the desk in dismissal. But his heart caught as the grinning Dallases rushed ahead, their faces bloated and menacing. "Don't you boys push." Mrs. Hoyle slapped her desktop with a book. Ignoring her, kids giggled and elbowed out into the hall where many lined the corridor to watch Brick emerge.

Fortunately, Mr. Condon, herding his own class, prompted them to move on. "No loitering here. Get moving. Clear the halls," he ordered. Reluctantly, the Dallases and a couple of buddies sluffed along, mumbling remarks that Brick could not hear.

Outside, the growing crowd broke ranks and surged toward the shops where apparently a dozen juniors had challenged some Japanese kids. Dazed, Brick followed an ugly, thirsting crowd. In the street, a Japanese who had been a star halfback, stood with doubled fists, his nose oozing blood - a wetness glittering his eyes. Huddled behind him, frightened, humiliated, hunkered a half-dozen more Japanese. One had his face smeared with dirt, another his shirt ripped. Those responsible were taunting them. Brick could not see them all, for the crowd tightened about them like a hangman's noose. Some white kids yelled, "What's the matter, Japs? Hey, sneaks! Going to fight, monkey faces?" The white boys were livid; a few laughed hysterically. One youth squatted to flop his arms and hop loosely. He squealed, crossed his eyes, and bloated his cheeks. The crowd roared. "Go on, Charlie, make like a monkey." Charlie went through it again. The crowd clapped and cat-called.

"Like that, Japs? Look good at that, Japs," screamed a tiny, freakish boy, his throat cording with fury. He looked over the crowd - waited. Finding them with him, he continued, encouraged, suddenly ignited with a fire of belonging. "Because we're going to beat the hell out of you - yellow bellies." He shook his shrunken fist.

Repulsion shuddered through Brick. He looked at the Japanese, defiant but cowering, still holding together - their features tight with fear. Toby was there. The fact startled Brick. Their eyes met suddenly as if drawn magnetically. Toby shook his head in disgust and hurt. He looked away. In a distorted flash, Brick recalled the Brown boys, battered by the Dallases, after the baseball celebration - the memory disorienting him momentarily.

The Dallases appeared beside Brick, their faces furious, for the hostilities were contagious. "Hey, kissy, why don't you join your Jap friend over there," Ray snarled, knocking the English book from Brick's hand. Brick stooped over to retrieve it, and swung a right fist from the ground up. The blow thudded into Ray's cheek, staggering him. A wild left hook knocked him against some outside lockers with a resounding smash. Students turned around. "Another fight," someone shouted.

Stunned, Ray pushed himself from the lockers, and Brick clobbered him again, catching him on the nose in a sickening, crunching sound. Blood gushed from both nostrils, then streamed over his mouth and chin. Ray's eyes rolled up, and he sagged, teetering for a moment as if he might go down. From behind, Jay hit Brick on the head with a fist. Swinging blindly, Brick swarmed over Jay, forcing him into some bushes, punching him again and again, until the brother threw his arms over his face and slumped low for protection. All the buried hurt and rage erupted from Brick.

"Stop it," Mrs. Hoyle commanded. She had been faithfully accompanying her class to the busses. Furiously, Brick hit Jay again, slicing open an eyebrow. "I said stop it this instant." But, the words were lost. Jay swung viciously, missing.

"You dirty bum, I'll kill you," Ray screamed, hurling himself on Brick, hauling him down. They rolled on the cement in a flailing of arms and legs.

"Oh, somebody stop them, please." Mrs. Hoyle wrung her hands.

Ray twisted astride Brick, pinning him, then pummeled him to split a lip. A tousled Jay, rocky on his feet, kicked at Brick's ribs, grazing him - frustrated - angling again with his pointed sneakers, his mouth grimacing, determined. Brick gasped a silent scream, blood oozing from a corner of his mouth, around his teeth, where the lip had parted.

"Cowards," Toby shouted, appearing out of a gathering crowd. "Two against one, you gutless cowards." The little Japanese, compact and muscled, jerked Ray off of Brick and flung him away to dance loosely, almost toppling.

"Yeah, cowards," a football guard shouted. "You two are gutless cowards - should never have been on the team." The crowd enclosed them. "Yeah, cowards," the kids chorused.

Toby was in the midst now, swinging, landing squarely in Jay's battered face. Brick struggled to his feet and went for Ray. Both clutched each other, gasping in exhaustion. Indifferent to his own pain, Brick pushed Ray backward. Clumsily, almost desperately, Ray came back and swung. Brick ducked. The missed blow nearly lurched Ray off his feet. Consumed by the interminable days of indignation, of embarrassment, and of frustration, Brick retaliated with everything he had, landing a solid fist in the stomach. The bigger of the twins belched out air as he doubled over. Brick caught him with a left on the head. Ray staggered brokenly to the side and tried to shuffle away, his face white in surprise and confusion.

Toby turned around and stood back to back with his friend. As he did, he landed a resounding blow to Jay's head. The latter howled and plunged away, again, taking refuge in some low shrubbery, hunkering there, his fists thrusting outward, defensively, his eyes bugging. Suddenly, he clutched his head in quaking hands. As Toby headed after him, Mr. Conan appeared from nowhere to halt him. Then Conan grasped Brick and Ray by their shoulders as the two again grappled - and jerked them apart. "What's the matter with you two?" He looked around at Jay who was emerging from the bushes. "With all of you. What's the matter?"

"Boooo, boooo," the students hooted, sorry a good fight was over.

"Who started this?" Conan exacted, his fingers pressing the boys in his hold, his back to the hisses and catcalls.

"He did," Ray shouted, his face gummy-red. He pointed at Brick. "He's a mama's boy - a scaredy cat - a teacher's brownie." Mr. Conan smiled slightly; then tightened his grip on the twin, making him wince. The heat of a fight abruptly ignited one portion of the crowd into a spontaneous explosion. "The Japs, get them, good this time," someone screamed. Flushed, twisting faces looked toward the knot of Japanese-Americans that waited, frozen with fear. A clump of bodies surged forward, past the young fighters, seemingly unaware of Toby who had shown his mettle.

A loop of white boys entangled themselves in the Japanese. The sharp voices of panicked girls pierced the air. "God, we've got to do something," Mr. Conan uttered, as he left the four combatants to themselves and was carried along with everyone else. Without a word, the Dallases vanished. And a shaken Brick and Toby edged up behind clustering students.

A police car wheeled through the crowd, splitting it, so that people hissed and booed even more; several slapped the rear fenders. The car slammed to a stop, and three tough-faced cops emerged to bulge their shoulders. More boos and jeers greeted them as the students fell back. Another black and white car came up. Principal Huff crawled stiffly out. The police had managed to pick him up and were delivering him to confront the crowd. He looked nervously over the youths, his thin face white, behind spectacles. "Go home, you kids," he announced indistinctly. Clearing his throat, he tried again. "Go home, get on your busses, or in your cars, or start walking, whatever - before the police chief here starts arresting." His slender hands jerked.

"Get old fuzzy-top, too," somebody yelled. An electric silence gripped the crowd suddenly.

Huff looked hawk-eyed over them, but could not locate the caller. "Go home. Get out before you're sorry." He was having trouble controlling his voice. No one budged - all faces remained a sullen wall. "For the last time, go on, get, go," he ordered. A few snickered, defiant at the commands. The students bunched tighter, charged with combustive power that seemed to sizzle in the air. Huff's mouth trembled; sweat pimpled his forehead.

"You heard him. Go - get," a husky cop barked, and walked into a parting crowd. Wearing the badge of an officer, he looked about like some meat-eating animal searching for prey and whopped a nightstick against his muscled palm. The two other cops joined him, including the three that had accompanied Huff. In the background, a few more officers arrived, their motorcycles rumbling behind the mass. The students retreated, confused, milling, and breaking reluctantly.

"Jap lovers!" someone spat.

The big cop swung his stick. Kids scattered; a student yelped. Another cop grabbed a fist-swinging boy and spun him against a line of taunters. They flushed like startled quail.

From the first police car came a loud puff, followed by a decreasing sound, like escaping air. "The cop's tire," a voice croaked. Kids rushed past Brick, away from it all, bug-eyed, pushing, some laughing savagely; one student tripped and two others sprawled over him. Someone yelled, "Let's get out of here." Everyone ran - Brick and Toby with them.

15

Authorities suspended Brick and the Dallas twins for five days. The Vice Principal visited the family at the Sea Ranch. Brick sat glumly in the living room on a couch, his hands folded, waiting. "Ordinarily, for fighting, we would have suspended those involved for at least ten days," the V.P. explained, his eyes magnified and intent through thick glasses, his bald head reflecting Burnie's floor light. "Face it, times are terrible - just terrible - so many pressures - so many families strained - nothing is normal. The Principal and I decided, under circumstances, five days were enough." He sank some. "We might make it a day or so less. We will arrange with his teachers for assignments. Our decision remains a warning to future rabble-rousers that we won't tolerate troublemakers and riots."

"It was coming," said Clarence. "Those twins and their buddies have been picking on Brick for a long time."

"I know, Mr. Burton. We had heard about it. Before we could do anything, the world went insane." The Vice Principal spoke slowly choosing his words with care.

"I'll take a lot of the responsibility," said Burnie, firmly. "I told the kid he had to stand up. He had to fight back."

"I, too, was with Burnie on that," Clarence added, immediately.

"I'm proud of our boy," Darlene added. "As a woman, I can't abide violence. I've known for sometime what's been happening."

The Vice Principal nodded, receptively. "We're transferring the Dallas boys out of Mrs. Hoyle's college prep class. They need a more basic English - that's in confidence, of course, but the fact will alleviate any future tension."

"The little Yamoto boy, I understand he joined in on Brick's behalf," Sathia questioned, standing primly in the kitchen doorway. "Is he suspended too?"

The Vice Principal rubbed his chin, trying to balance decisions. "No, he was one of the minorities being put upon - defending himself we figure."

"And Brick," Burnie's words snapped like a hand clap, "he is white - not a minority."

Although only five days, the time would seem interminable for Brick.

The Vice Principal left, after first shaking all of the family members' hands, including Brick's. Sathia, Burnie, Darlene, and Clarence then enclosed the young man's shoulders in a squeeze, without a word, only an understanding acknowledgement that Brick felt deep inside.

Darlene and Clarence took Brick to their dentist to check his teeth and then to their doctor who probed his nostrils and placed salve on his swollen lips. Dr. Thurlong avoided any questions, but wryly commented, "Had a difference of opinion with someone?"

"Yes, sir," Brick felt a strange mix of embarrassment and of satisfaction.

"He came out okay," said Clarence, boldly. "You should see the other guys."

"Would hate to see the other guys." The doctor chuckled and grinned broadly.

Afterwards, home at the Sea Ranch, Rose phoned Darlene. Brick sat near her, in a comfy lounge chair, nursing his swollen features. He perked up, listening intently, momentarily forgetting his battle wounds. "Don't apologize, I'm so glad you called. I've been thinking about you." Darlene listened. "Yes, it is a horrible time. Yes, Ida is surviving, improving, doing well; apparently; at her age, it will take time." Darlene winked at Brick. She listened intently, nodding. "You say Toby wants to phone Brick - maybe even be with him for a time?" She listened again. "I see no problem." Darlene stiffened and wiped her cheeks with a hanky. "Yes, he was suspended, and we know Toby came to his defense." Brick sat up, bigeyed. "No, his call or a visit won't upset anyone here. Burnie's worried about the war and Ida, but, he's not intolerant. I'll take care of it." She listened further, seriously. "Yes, for Clarence and me, things seem to be working out. We're trying - hard. The world is going crazy except for Clarence and me right now. I'm living at the Sea Ranch close to work and to help Sathia and Burnie. But, I have been going to our fruit ranch to help, to cook and clean for Clarence - to keep things in order. You know bills and such."

His mother absorbed whatever Rose was conveying. Brick leaned forward, his face squinched, trying to hear, wanting to know what they were sharing. At last she said softly, "I feel awkward - not knowing what to say, except I'm always here for you, if you need. You've been through so much - you know, with Mike." For an eternity it seemed to Brick, Darlene remained on the phone in mixed silence, her face registering pain, pleasure, concern, sympathy.

"Wow," Brick thought.

"You are a beautiful person, Rose." Darlene set the phone in place, sat down, and held her face in her hands, looking up in contemplative thought.

"What's going on?"

"She regrets that she didn't marry Mike - that she was afraid of public opinion. She claims it all made her much stronger, however." Darlene fluffed with appreciation. "I know and understand what she's saying."

"What's all that mean?"

"That she must live to help her people, her friends, this country. She said she and Mike loved each other. That the least she can do is support his memory and his family, for what he believed in, all that he committed himself to. He joined the Army for purposes beyond himself. How can we ask more of anyone?" Darlene patted some eye tears. "Toby will be in contact."

During the miserable days that followed for reinstatement in school, the world and news darkened. In ways the war was exciting; in ways it was terrifying. Washington, D.C., buzzed with emergency meetings. Around the nation, businesses were booming suddenly with the promise of unlimited production; factories were revolutionizing; car manufacturers were planning for tanks and armored vehicles. Shipyards were turning from launching luxury liners to battleships. Millions of people were on the move, to new jobs, to new assignments. They crammed bus and train depots, overwhelmed recruiting stations. Newspapers printed full page advertisements: JOIN THE SERVICE OF YOUR CHOICE, NOW. Between programs, the radio filled the airwaves with "The Star Spangled Banner," and "My Country Tis of Thee." Authorities predicted: rationing - a term for limiting gasoline, rubber, and such foods as sugar, coffee, and meat. Even dresses and children's clothes and shoes would be rare. Predicted: massive farm and ranch produce needed to supply the military, as well as destitute people on every continent. Predicted: heavier taxes, families split, women assuming home jobs left by men. Predicted: heavy construction, a great need for minerals, water power, and timber. Predicted: A massive population shift to the West Coast. Change here and now. War, once the rumble of distant thunder, poured over them, unleashing its dark storm.

Up in Joy Woods, near the picnic grounds, ripsaws wailed through the hours, tearing life from the giant trees. Tractors and huge logging trucks hauled the great timbers away to a nearby mill, for later marketing and war. Each day, Brick listened to the sickening whine of blade against living wood; the ripping crash of the thousand-year-old monarchs echoed daily in the canyons. "Some of those trees were enjoying the sunlight before Christ was born," Burnie stated one day. Sathia fretted, fearing it would upset him, might overstimulate his heart, but he ignored it, losing himself in his hobby, as he traced on maps the advance and retreat of armies. Uncle accepted the change and the chaos philosophically; where once, the cutting of great redwoods would have aroused him to write Congress, he now viewed the action as an inevitable tragedy of war.

One evening, despite female protest, Burnie joined Clarence and Brick as they drove to the various chicken houses. "I got to get out - feel trapped," he said, slipping his binoculars into the truck. "Besides, I want to see what's going on around here." While Brick and Clarence checked the food and water in each yard, Uncle remained obediently in the cab. "Hi, friend chickens," he greeted at each stop, to flocks of white leghorns that pressed against the wire. They clucked and cocked their heads curiously. "Think they remember me?" Burnie asked.

Upon reaching the last chicken house on the hill, Burnie handed Clarence the binoculars. "Here," he urged, "you got better eyes. Take a close look."

"I want to look, too," Brick said, excited. Clarence braced his elbows on the truck door and steadied the binoculars. Slowly he surveyed the miles of structured defense. "I feel like a spy," he laughed self-consciously. Below them stretched an array of trenches and machine gun pits, enclosed by sacks of sand, built into bastions toward the ocean. Behind, in the large dunes, rose emplacements of heavy artillery, the wide muzzles pointing seaward. All the guns lay cloaked in green netting, sprinkled with grass, blending them with the mauve terrain. Miles of barbed wire paralleled the shore in haphazard coils.

In the cliffs to the north, soldiers had dug lookouts, little dirt rooms with observation slits, the excavations braced with timber, then buried under layers of earth, so concealed that a casual visitor would never know. Brick and Gerve had watched the military build them, had watched the soldiers enter and exit through tiny trapdoors.

"What all d' you see?" asked Burnie.

"Nothing that we haven't already," said Clarence. "Can see those big guns a little better. They got some fifty caliber machine guns down there. And I can see some soldiers now. They're just sitting back of the guns,"

"We probably could get in trouble sneaking on 'em like this," Burnie remarked, "except it's our land, and they're allowing us to work it."

"Seeing it close up -- gives a kind of wallop," said Clarence, still viewing intently. "I can't explain it exactly, but it makes this war business hit home. If you know what I mean."

"I know," said Burnie, despondently.

"You want to look?" Clarence offered the glasses.

"No," said Burnie. "I've seen enough."

"I do," Brick piped. His heart began pounding as he swept over the machine gun nests, many more than his naked eye had discerned. Olive-green artillery filled his view, the big mounts bulky in the dunes.

"Why us?" Burnie questioned. "It doesn't make sense. The Rafetto's got ocean frontage. And so do the dairies south of us. But they don't have all these guns and stuff. The Army hasn't taken over their ranches."

"Maybe it's because we got so much more beach," Clarence suggested.

Brick adjusted the glasses on a nearby lookout. "I can see a soldier in there," he said. "He's got a pair of binoculars, too."

"Then, let's get out of here," said Clarence. "It's our land, we have permission to be here, but, I feel someone is going to report us as spies."

Depressed, the three returned to the ranch house. "I don't know what the world's coming to," Burnie lamented.

"Well, we told you not to go." Sathia refused any sympathy. "Now you'll probably have a setback and be sick."

"I'm fine. It's just what I see outside there. All this change. Here at the Sea Ranch. It's just hard to believe." Burnie sat heavily in his chair.

"Well, forget it," said Sathia. "Nothing you can do. Nothing any of us can do. Right now I got some hot chocolate for everybody."

"None for me," said Brick, excusing himself.

Sathia gazed at him. "You not drinking chocolate? You sick?"

"No, ma'am." Dejectedly, Brick began strolling upstairs to his room. He wished he were far away. Someplace where there were no restrictions, where guns and soldiers and barbed wire no longer enclosed one.

"Incidentally," Darlene shouted from the living room, "while you guys were gone, Toby called - remember, Rose said he's been wanting to phone you."

"He called?" The fact lifted Brick's spirits. "Okaaay!"

"I told him you'd get back to him. He's waiting."

Quickly, Brick cranked the handle, measuring the necessary counts, long and short. Toby lifted the receiver immediately. "Brick?"

"Yeah, me - so glad to hear you."

"Feel bad you got kicked out."

"Was worth it. Family has been behind me, and our old Vice Principal said he saw it coming."

"I should have been expelled with you."

"No, it was my problem; but, thanks for sticking up for me, for coming to my aid."

"What else could I do? Lots of kids at school are talking about it. Surprising how many think the Dallases are bullies - that they got what they deserved."

"You heard that?"

"Got it by the grapevine."

"Well, like me, they're out for a few days."

"Look forward to you comin' back."

"I do, too, should be better now."

"Well, for you, pal. For some of us, maybe not."

Brick was bored with war depression, catching like a contagious disease. His eyes strayed around the room for something to occupy him. Something to lose himself in. His old junk drawer opened sluggishly from disuse. He pawed through the entanglement of broken toys and miscellaneous gadgets. He examined his old slingshot. Kid's stuff, he thought, tossing it back. The same with a tiddlywinks set, and a Tom Mix holster. Then his eyes settled joyously on a forgotten duck call, the one he had spent three hard-earned dollars for, the one he had never learned to use, although the manufacturers had supplied directions and a musical arrangement. The process looked easy enough. One simply played the basic calls -- the greeting, the feed, and the comeback on a piano, then accompanied the notes with the duck quacker. Brick examined the call, turned it over and over to admire the bulbous shape, hand carved and varnished to a gloss. "No time like the present to learn," he decided.

"You help me?" he asked Sathia, after charging downstairs.

Gamely, she sat before the piano. "You mean I play these notes?"

"Yes."

"And it's supposed to sound like a duck?"

"I have to follow you, with my call."

"I see," she replied, skeptically. But, she obliged, picking with one finger. Plunk, plink, plunk.

Brick paused, adjusted the call to his lips, cupped it professionally in the palms of his hands, like the drawings showed, and blew. Sqwack, quack, sqweek, squack.

"Good heavens!" said Sathia.

Brick blushed. They tried again. Plunk, plink, plunk.

"Does this call ducks or pigs?"

Brick glared at his aunt.

"Sorry," she said. "How about trying the feed call. I'm sure we scared them away with the greeting."

Brick waited, refusing to dignify her comments with an acknowledgment. Plunk, plink, plunk, tinkle, tinkle, tinkle.

Brick set his mouth in determination. Squack, squeek, sqwack, tucka, tucka, tucka, tucka, tuck, tuck, tuck, quack, quack, queeee.

"Step on it before it multiplies," Clarence warned, poking his head in the living room door. Darlene was beside him, covering her mouth, giggling.

Uncle Burnie came in from his bedroom. "The Japs have landed!"

Brick took down his call and flushed angrily.

Clarence chided, "Eureka! The secret weapon! Pass 'em out to the Army, and the Japs will never land."

Brick wanted to throw the call at them. Who -- just who were they to insult his duck quacking?

Sathia chuckled. Darlene laughed heartily. Burnie guffawed. Suddenly they burst into a release of mirth. Affronted, Brick watched them, until finally yielding with a grin.

For all the dark of war and the unknown, Brick felt one light of hope. Darlene and Clarence were back together, despite the world's turmoil, joining each other on the fruit ranch some nights. Darlene, however, remained mostly at the Sea Ranch - for proximity to work and to assist Sathia and an unsteady Burnie. Brick continued his residence at the ocean to help with chores; and, of course, he had better access to the school bus, and a constant need to remain in clean breezes to ease the bronchial problems.

To his surprise, Brick found himself somewhat of a hero amongst the guys upon his return to high school. He remained in English with Mrs. Hoyle, while the Dallases were removed to a less accelerated class. To his relief, at least temporarily, he seldom saw the twins. He continued to share with Toby on the phone; at school, they nodded at each other, shared notes sometimes in the corridors, without really conversing. The

Japanese boys and girls had isolated themselves in tight groups. Even their parents were having difficulties hiring itinerant workers to prune and spray their orchards, the latter choosing not to indulge the "enemy," forcing the Japanese to help each other.

In English one morning, Mrs. Hoyle read aloud a dramatic essay written by Brick - the assignment: bring alive some scene or action you have observed. Brick had attempted to recreate the setting of the Sea Ranch with the battle practices - the artillery; the roaring planes; the big trucks and even tanks; the soldiers behind machine guns. He had attempted to impart the presence of a military force. He had tried to paint with imagery - apparently successfully, for the teacher read with emotion, obviously relishing his words. In honesty, he had written it from the heart trying to capture every impression. This time, without the Dallas twins and buddies to heckle, his classmates listened closely, smiling, even oohing once, and a number clapping when Mrs. Hoyle finished and looked up.

16

In the hectic weeks that followed, the military abandoned the tents to build temporary barracks in the upper pasture. The Sea Ranch became a busy city with soldiers lounging against fences, digging "foxholes," or spreading telephone lines over the hills. Along the beaches, back of the tidewater, they stretched more coils of barbed wire; they began preparing bunkers with sacks of sand where bulldozers pushed the earth about, disrupting the rhythm of wind and surf, while tearing and rupturing the gentle sand dunes. Trucks and trailers lined the entrance way. Equipment and stacks of boxes and gear littered the yard and the grazing field beyond the barn. Trampling feet and grinding wheels marred the slopes and mushed the wet earth.

The family watched sadly, wondering if the world would ever return to normal. "I'll be so happy when those soldier boys go," Sathia remarked. Brick agreed. The newness was over, the initial excitement gone. But, with the Japanese advances in the Pacific, their presence might remain for some time. The war had settled into a tedious period of waiting, the future unpredictable. In exotic -sounding places: Hong Kong, Malaya, the Philippine Islands, U.S. and British forces were reeling under Japanese assaults. President Roosevelt confessed, that the news in the Pacific was, "all bad."

"No doubt about it," Burnie lamented, "they're licking us. At least for the time being." With the somber presence of the military, and the depressing news that filled the airwaves daily, a heaviness settled over the family. Early one evening, a dignified officer with a gray mustache arrived to meet with the family after making rather formal arrangements over the phone. Graciously, he took a place at the dining room table with Sathia, Burnie, and Darlene to discuss what was happening on the ranch. He handed Burnie a complex list of what the family could do, could not do, and what they had to do. "Why? What is happening?" Burnie demanded. Brick stayed back in the kitchen listening.

"All I can tell you," said the officer, "is that we are at war. And all that is being done here is for national security. I'm sorry that we must dictate limits on your own property, but we must have your cooperation."

Meanwhile, in response to the list, Sathia and Darlene sewed heavier black coverings for each of the windows. At night, all the homes along the coast were ordered into secure blackout. Should a thread of glow escape, soldiers would knock at the front door and politely suggest that the problem be corrected, immediately. What troubled Brick most, he could no longer walk down the beaches, or fish the Stemple, or hike the far hills. His precious play land, except for the upper chicken houses and the routes to them was off-limits to all civilians. "But it's our ranch," Brick complained to Burnie. "Why can't we go where we want?"

Burnie listened and tried to cover his own bewilderment, his own indignation. "It's wartime, Boy," he explained, sympathetically. "It's a time when man goes a little insane. Happens ever so often."

Continuously, small boats, yachts, fishing trollers put out to sea, with Navy radio men aboard; any make of plane, military or private, that could fly was launched. Observation planes, Coast Guard ships and dog patrols scoured the shores day and night, while pursuit aircraft, even medium bombers joined the growing forces.

The Coast Guard, which had begun preparing before the war, now coupled with civilian volunteers, began establishing lookout posts, especially in all lighthouse stations. The four crew signalmen, equipped with twelve inch lights, operated on a twenty-four hour basis. Their purpose was to prevent the landing of enemy agents, to sight and report submarines, unidentified ships and aircraft, and to observe and report attacks on coastal shipping.

All along the west coast, other means of providing warning and protecting against enemy attack went into effect. Radar stations were to be installed soon in limited numbers; from atop buildings: school belfries, church steeples, and forest lookouts, civilian volunteers watched and called in what they saw to filtering centers.

In the towns and cities, block wardens were instructed on how to fight fires caused by incendiaries and how to help people successfully blackout their homes.

With time, the military activities and use of equipment became more sophisticated and structured. After the first battle practice, Brick wondered if the world really had gone insane. His family and neighbors watched with disbelief, as if everything were a bad dream from which they would soon awake. Each morning, dark planes circled beyond Bodega Head, then zoomed in over the beaches in mock attack as if strafing the shoreline. Sometimes they roared in so low one could see the pilots silhouetted in the cockpits. The soldiers in the sand dunes, and on the bluffs where they had installed lookouts, would take positions. Some would dive into newly dug pits, as the planes banked high and wailed down in angry dives. Along one curving headland, the caterpillar tractors had gouged the earth, spacing and blocking between rocky outcrops. There the men had installed a number of five inch guns pointed seaward, all draped with green netting covered with dune grass. In the various pits, and on the hill above the buildings, they had placed smaller, long-barreled armor, four to a mount, that Burnie learned were 30 and 40 millimeter antiaircraft guns. In addition, Burnie recognized a howitzer, numerous twelve inch mortars, and 75 millimeter field pieces - all of World War I vintage. When the planes hurtled in, the soldiers followed their flight through big rounded sights. Since the military hustle and bustle was taking place on the family's property, the Army officers made little effort to conceal their maneuvers.

The unusual activity was having its negative effect, however. Cattle bawled and raced about the fields, their tails high and crooked. The chickens ceased laying and fluttered about the yards or huddled under their long houses, whenever the planes racketed overhead. Wildlife disturbed by the influx of military reacted in terror - deer and rabbits were seen bounding and skittering frequently over the hillsides. Shorebirds bunched and twisted in flight, flashing black and white, back and forth along the beaches. Enormous flocks of Black Brant, a delicate sea goose, swarmed in dark masses out to sea and back seeking refuge. Burnie telephoned the authorities and complained. County and state officials simply shrugged it off - admitting that it was beyond their control. One military office apologized, but warned that worse was to come.

It did - with artillery fire and practice bombing. The soldiers pulled back the netting and began pumping salvos out to sea at rafts anchored in a zigzag pattern. Then planes buzzed in over the isolated sand dunes near the mouth of the bay, zooming low, the explosives hitting dully, spraying sand and sometimes water in graceful plumes. They and the salvos rattled windows, jarred doors, and even crumbled some dishes once. Aunt Sathia became peevish when the plaster cracked in an upper bedroom one morning after an intensive shelling.

"What are they expecting, an invasion?" Burnie would ask, punching a fist against his rocker. Auntie would click her tongue and wag her head and condemn the Army, the President, and the whole Japanese Empire. Darlene, when she was present, would flatten a hand to her throat and check and recheck her business records.

After school, whenever the trucks and planes and guns rumbled the earth, Gerve came over to help Brick feed the nervous heifers or gather what eggs had been laid. But his interest wasn't really in helping. Each time, after a few minutes of work, he would say, "Let's cut out and watch the planes and stuff." Brick understood, for sometimes, late in the afternoon when the sun pressed low, the armed forces simulated an invasion. The action was unreal, like some sweeping movie that had come alive - action that they not only could see and hear, but could feel and smell and experience. With barges and makeshift rafts anchored offshore, the Navy planes dropped low, their torpedoes slicing the water - igniting the floats into orange flames, often blowing them from the water, the splintered debris littering the area. Fighter planes followed in single file, splattering the remains with machine gunfire, the furious spurts flashing from their wings. Afterwards, the compact little planes dogfought, swept high overhead, to peel and plunge, their motors screaming as they chased and eluded and rechased. On some days, a plane would trail a long white canvas target shaped like a huge cigar. The squadron would attack, shredding it with bullets; the rat-a-tat-

tatting, the smoke, the shrilling roar, the planes gleaming in a sunset glow - all a fantastic spectacle.

As the boys watched, Gerve loved it, hidden in the thick grass near the far chicken house on the bluff. And Brick was glad. He wanted to reach out and help his old friend, although they were not as close as they had once been. So seldom anymore was there a trace of joy in Gerve's face. Since his brother's death, and because he had remained so small, almost runtish, he had withdrawn into himself, more and more, and away from friends and school, leaving him seedy and morose. For some reason, unlike all the other kids, he had not developed. And in contrast to the handsome Mike and his two attractive sisters, he was somewhat apart and a little ostracized by his family. His face had narrowed; his nose had lengthened; and his neck had thinned, giving him a cartoon look with his prongs of black hair. Some of the kids at school had cruelly nicknamed him, "Pinocchio." He was still skipping school much, so that his grades had dropped. And he continued hanging around with some younger kids in the neighborhood, some surly seventh and eighth graders.

But the change was not just in Gerve. The whole country was entangled in a wild fervor of patriotism, confusion, and change. In the towns about, bands gathered on the streets to squawk and blare dozens of John Philip Sousa favorites. In all the village squares, every police chief, every fire deputy, every mayor, gave rousing speeches lauding America, and assuring quick victories. Citizens clogged the streets, applauding with vigor, experiencing a oneness that gave them supreme confidence for a time.

Emotional words entered the everyday vocabulary: rationing, blackout, war effort, shortages, mobilization, and slogans such as "Remember Pearl Harbor." Across the Atlantic, the Germans, led by a madman named Hitler, had conquered Western Europe and North Africa; troops were now pushing rapidly toward the rich oil fields of the Middle East. In Southeast Asia and in the Pacific, the Japanese were advancing, overrunning anything or anyone that stood in their way. Before the end of December, Guam, Wake Island, the Gilbert Islands, and Hong Kong fell.

Often the nights were a mysterious time of droning planes and muffled explosions far out at sea. Ship to shore lights were reported.

Wild rumors continued circulating that, under a Japanese owned chicken house, the foundation for some large artillery had been found, all in range of San Francisco. Oil and debris had apparently polluted a beach south of the Sea Ranch, sure signs that an enemy sub had been sunk. Five submarines had been sighted surfacing, ready to shell the towns and cities. Sections of the beach were now placed off-limits with the free talk of invasion. Fliers had been circulated, posted, many distributed to all the coastal schools, warning people, and, especially children, not to pick up any strange objects. The Japanese subs were sending in balloons and floater bombs that could detonate, that could injure or kill. Authorities claimed that not only could they drift onto shore, but, they could work into the inlets or up rivers at high tide.

Neighbors babbled about the Japanese endlessly. Shiro Yamoto continued as a prime topic. An ironic fact revealed that Admiral Yamamoto, who masterminded the attack on Pearl Harbor and was directing the assaults in the Pacific, had a last name spelled almost like that of the Yamoto family. A coincidence, of course, but something thoughtfully disturbing. The fact that Shiro Yamoto had won awards for his photography of the coastline, continued to seethe in people's suspicions, flagging the embers of accusation, as serious talk of incarcerating all Japanese began to rumble more seriously. Just maybe Shiro Yamoto was working secretly for the enemy as could many others.

Clouds of dark days ahead loomed ominously.

At high school, a number of kids eloped, driving to Reno, Nevada, arriving home after a few days so that the boys could make it to boot camp. Early joiners returned in uniform to parade the halls like knights-in-armor, most in Army or Navy dress, but, a few sporting Air Force wings, and a couple in the snappy outfit of the Marines. Brick and his classmates watched with pride and with much envy: most girls sighed and regarded them, dreamily, as heroes.

To Brick's consternation, Mary Ann, the first love of his life, the first beautiful girl that had ever noticed him, ever flirted, hugged, kissed him, although not on the lips, which he fantasized about a lot - was betraying him. She was enamored with a senior - an old man to Brick. The old man was considering joining the service upon graduation. Brick had seen them all cozy, holding hands in the halls - worse, the old man had driven her to a dance - driven her! Something he couldn't do yet. Driving a car - a world that separated a man from a boy. Yes, Brick had been betrayed. First by his mother with Mr. McPeak, and, now, with Mary Ann and her senior service boy.

Often, Brick wished he were old enough for the armed services. Not the Army or the Coast Guard - he had already seen too much of that. Possibly he'd join the Air Force so he could buzz the Germans, fanning them dead under machine guns from the wings of his P-40. But he didn't like the Air Force song as much as the Marine hymn. Trouble with the Marines, they fought hand-to-hand combat with bayonets which looked mighty mean. He guessed the Navy was the best for him with its big ships and the vastness of oceans. Brick lost himself in dreams. He longed to be in the action. And he knew how it would be. He'd march to war with all the other local fellows, each in uniform, the bands playing, the girls crying, waving hankies and throwing kisses. He'd march in his spiffy Navy uniform, his white sailor cap tilted cockily to one side, his bladed gun polished, uniting him as one with steel. Then, after a few battles, probably somewhere in the Pacific, but most likely in the North Atlantic against the Nazis, he'd become a commander, with his own destroyer to prowl the seas looking for subs.

The war soon touched the young people in a personal, more sobering manner. School officials drew up plans to evacuate. Students were ordered to wear dark clothes to conceal them in the nearby orchards during attacks; students not properly dressed were forbidden to board school buses or to enter classrooms. Plans called for heading into the hills and beyond in case paratroopers landed. Practice evacuations were held twice a week with the help and suggestions from a Lizzy Wong, who told reporters that, "In China, evacuations aren't practice."

On a positive note, the war meant extra business for local merchants with a land-office trade: candles, kerosene, blackout materials, medicinal equipment, and canned goods. One newspaper ran an ad, under the headline, "First Fashion for Air Raids," showing a picture of a woman getting out of bed. The caption said: "When and if Japanese bombers do stage a midnight raid on San Jose, pretty Mary Helzer will be ready to leap from bed with bonnet and booties, and dash for the basement."

On a meaner side, the Buddhist Temple in town burst into flame one night, and a sluggish response from the fire department resulted in the building nearly burning to the ground. West Coast senators asked that the federal government consider restricting civil liberties for all Japanese natives. Newspaper editorials supporting the action appeared immediately.

A wave of destruction occurred - young hoodlums, thrill-seeking punks, and angry citizens shattered windows in Japanese Town. On another night, some beer drinking patriots decided to run the - - - out of the country and returned to their homes for hunting rifles and shotguns. Meeting later that night, the patriots marched down a street and shot into some shacks. The unarmed Japanese responded by firing off firecrackers. The "return gunfire" so stunned the tipsy beer-bellies that they fell over each other in a panic of retreat - one toppling over a sprawled buddy to break a leg. Two days later, a three year-old girl suffered severe burns from exploding gasoline.

When the high school administration cancelled the basketball schedule, because four first-string team members had just announced their joining the services, Principal Huff submitted and called a special assembly on the last period of the day. On the way to the auditorium, Brick felt a tug at his sleeve; Toby gestured him out of the flow of pushing, giggling, chattering teenagers. The little Japanese, his face strained, slipped into a side alcove that opened onto a second-story balcony.

"Aren't you going to the assembly?" Brick inquired.

Toby shook his head ponderously. "I got an inkling what it will be."

"What?"

"You'll see. Walk a ways. Talk to me."

"What if you get caught, cutting?"

"It doesn't matter much at this point. You want a ride home afterwards?"

"Anything's better than riding the bus. Somebody picking you up?"

"Rose."

"Rose? With all the problems? With all the, you know."

"With all the hatred."

"Guess that's what I'm tryin' to say."

"She wants to be near the Hamilton family, to help them. But, she's more concerned about dad."

"What do you know?"

"I overheard her talking to dad last night, after she came home. Dad was awful mad."

"About what?"

"It's all part of this war thing. Nobody will work for us - not even the Oakies - the fruit workers. Nobody. Only our Japanese friends are helping each other - pruning, spraying - you know. And buyers are pressuring dad - offering to pay a lot less than our ranch is worth. And you've heard all the talk about moving us to camps somewhere - with barracks and wire fences, we hear."

The last of the students had meandered down the staircase. A teacher looking for the tardy, rounded a corner and glanced suspiciously at the boys. Toby speeded up and stepped into a darkened stairwell. "We're worried about my dad. Rose and me, we want to see your uncle. We got to talk to him. It's real important."

"Why?"

"About what's happening - like what's happening to dad. Your uncle's been good to dad. They like each other. Maybe your uncle can help get dad's head together, if you know what I mean."

"I see what you mean. Okay, when?"

"Soon as possible. Maybe after school today. Is he well enough to have us?"

"Sure. He's doing good. He's been upset about our Aunt Ida, but, he doesn't blame your dad, no way."

"Then, we'll be waiting for you over by the ice cream store."

"Okay," said Brick. Toby exited a side door and was gone.

This time, from a podium on stage, Principal Huff said, "I'm proud of these boys." He referred to the four basketball players seated in a row behind him. They sat tall, proudly, smiling widely. Huff added in a booming voice, "They have fought for our dear old High, now they're going to fight for a bigger team." Huff, a good guy now, got a standing ovation, while the band played a jazzy version of "God Bless America." Cheerleaders skipped about waving blue and white pompoms in a well-rehearsed routine. Everyone sang. A lump filled Brick's throat. All over the auditorium, girls were crying, some streaming big, free tears. The boys were frowning and gulping, trying hard not to cry, too.

After the assembly, Brick saw Rose sitting behind the wheel of Mike's Chevy coupe, Toby beside her. She had pulled off the street and had backed into a dirt side road, doubtless to be less conspicuous. Seeing the students streaming noisily away, many gathering in shifting clusters at the bus-wait, Brick thought of the recent fight with the Dallases and of the nasty scene with the Japanese. Never again, he realized, could he cross this end of the school without recalling all the sights and sounds - frightening, indelible impressions of fear and raging hatred - a world insane, as Uncle Burnie had described it.

As he approached the Yamoto's, a heavy sense of doubt engulfed him suddenly; the fact surprised him, made him feel guilty, clutched at him. He walked along, almost as if he were outside himself, looking at himself. Surely people would see him get into the car, a white boy, with two Japanese - cause and source of so much suspicion and fear now, with the talk of invasion and uprisings, especially with sighting of enemy submarines and the sinking of ships off the coast. He had already been called a Jap lover. Was this continued befriending going to heap further abuse upon him? The thought jolted through him, stung inside him, and went all whirly. Brick tried vainly to dismiss the idea. He felt ashamed of himself, ashamed that he should wish to shun what had always been a solid friendship. But the provoking thoughts lingered as he approached, lingered gnawingly.

Brick crawled inside the car beside Toby. He tried not to look at Rose. But her pretty face was as open and as sweetly receptive as ever. If indeed, she feared, she gave not a hint.

"Well, how was the assembly?" Toby opened. "Huff give a big, rousing speech?"

"Yeah, you were right, it wasn't worth the time," Brick flipped a hand in dismissal, not wanting to admit that he had been moved by the patriotic scene.

"I don't know if I'll ever go back to school," Toby said, his voice desolate and distant.

"You wouldn't quit school? You're not talking about quitting are you?"

His eyes strange, staring beyond, Toby watched the carnival of students in the front parking lot. Some mouthed loudly, others stood sullenly, their hands sunken into the front pockets of their Levi's, so low that their shorts made a ridge of white. All watched the cars grinding out of the lot, screeching, spraying gravel. Most cars were overly packed with waving, laughing, occupants who shouted catcalls at those staring. "What's left here?" he said forlornly. "They hate us."

Brick searched Rose's face. "He's not serious is he?"

She looked protectively at her little brother. "He's terribly upset right now. We're both terribly upset."

"Rose is talking about dad," said Toby, his eyes riveted on the parking lot.

"As Toby told you, we were hoping that maybe we could talk with your uncle," Rose added. "I know he's not well, and we don't want to upset him, but I need to ask him a favor. He's the only person now - the only being that can help us." Her voice quivered with emotion suddenly. "And I want to do it in person, not by phone." She licked her painted lips. "It's so important now."

Brick felt uneasy, an unexplainable heaviness weighting him, for fear of what she was leading up to. However, he said, "I'm sure he'd talk with you; it's getting past Aunt Sathia, you know that. She guards him like a bulldog."

Rose smiled. "I think they'll both understand. You see, we need a place to rent; we've got to get our dad away for a time, someplace where he can think and talk, and hopefully see things clearer - like in that cabin of your Uncle's, you know, the one in the redwoods." She added quickly, "For just a few days - to save his sanity."

"What's happened?"

"He's not like dad anymore, that's what," Toby interposed.

"He's not the steady, easy going father we've all grown to love," Rose explained gently. "It's true, he's not dad any longer."

With an edge of bitterness, Toby said, "It's all getting to him."

Brick nodded. "I'll call my aunt, tell her you're taking me home." With apprehension, Brick walked to the phone booth next to the store and plunged a coin in.

Sathia's "hello" seemed a little abrupt, even harsh, Brick thought. When he informed her that Rose and Toby wished to confer with

Burnie, she hesitated. "I don't know if he wants to see their kind at this time," she said coolly, "not with Ida in the condition she's in. You should certainly understand that." A silence followed. "Don't you realize that?" Her tone had a cutting harshness to it.

Brick felt a sinking sensation, but he persisted. "They still want to ask him something."

"He's resting. I don't want to disturb him."

"Well, they're going to bring me home, anyway, which is nice of 'em, considering they're going out of their way and all. Maybe when we get there, he'll be willing to talk to them."

"Don't be surprised if he won't."

"But that's not like Uncle Burnie," Brick said huffily.

Once again, a long silence ensued. Then Aunt Sathia replied, "Your Uncle Burnie isn't the same man he used to be." Her words had the thrust of a sabre.

17

At the top of the hill, above the Sea Ranch, two soldiers from the guardhouse sided against the driver and passenger windows, one signaling roll down the windows, which Rose had commenced. "You're Japanese," he barked - "pretty, but, Japanese. This area, you know, is off-limits to foreigners and strangers." His jaw squared. "Sorry, lady. It's off-limits."

Rose handled herself with dignity. Blinking with understanding and straightening with pride. "I am Japanese-American - born and raised not far from here. My father owns a big fruit ranch, just over the hill - Shiro Yamoto? My brother's in the backseat, and we are taking the MacQuarrie's nephew home, Brickford Burton. She nodded toward the boys behind. May I reach in my purse - I have passes?"

"I do, too," Brick joined immediately. "I now have a pass with my name on it, and my parents' and my Uncle's and Aunt's names, too." He offered them a ticket-like form from his left pocket.

The young soldier wilted around the shoulders. "You're Burnie's and Clarence's relative?"

"Yes, and these are my good friends."

The soldier removed his cap, stroked his hair, and gestured toward his associate whose rifle remained slung over his shoulder. "They're okay. We've watched the two kids coming and going over the hill and down the draws."

Sathia, somewhat aloof, admitted the three. Rose held out her hand. Sathia hesitated, then took it. "Burnie's tired."

"We know that, but, Toby and I need your husband's advice. He's really all we have. He and our father have always been good friends. And they respect each other."

"It's okay, Sathia. What can I do for you, Rose?" Burnie appeared from the kitchen, holding a mug of tea.

"We're embarrassed to come in on you," said Rose, carefully, "with everything the way it is."

"The world's in trouble," Burnie agreed. Brick shuffled his feet, and waited, as his uncle observed, and smiled slightly. "I'm up to whatever."

Rose tightened her lips, considered her words, and said directly, "Dad is hurt and depressed by all the hatred. He detests the Japanese government that did this - that attacks us. Dad's worked so hard here, proud to be an American citizen, gratefully paying taxes, supporting organizations, and causes. All that you know, of course."

"I know," Burnie said, waiting. Darlene appeared from the kitchen, baking powder dusting her cheeks. She leaned against the doorjamb, her eyes touching Rose, encouraging her.

"Dad fears our lovely ranch will be taken - with no compensation for us. All kinds of sales people - some not so nice - keep phoning him, even knocking on our door, wanting to buy before everything is taken. But, worse, there is serious talk of shipping us out to camps. Horrible stories of possible barracks and wired fences, with guard towers - a prison really."

"I've heard all that. I fear, too." There was comfort in his tone. "Problem is, I don't, I don't know what I can do except lend a sympathetic ear."

Sathia cocked her head, listening, her features shifting with conflicting emotions. Toby clasped his hands in anticipation, as Rose paused, her eyes rolled up, as if seeking help from above. "We would like to rent your cabin in the redwoods, Ned's old residence - just for a few days. Toby and I will clean it up. If, we can convince dad. We feel he could be alone, in an area he loves - a chance to think things out. You know, get a perspective without all the pressures. That's all we ask."

"Sounds reasonable. The place is just sitting there. Ned took all his personal belongings. I doubt if he'll ever return. He's doing real great - making good money in Mare Island - working on warships." Burnie winced, seeing Rose jerk at the word, warship. "Shiro is welcome to use the place, whenever. It's a great place to just get away. I'll phone him for you. And, I don't expect him to rent it."

"Oh, thank you." Rose stepped forward and took Burnie's right hand, pressing it to her cheek. Darlene advanced to embrace Rose. "After Burnie calls, I will help you and Toby clean the place."

"I will, too," Brick popped.

Rose stood taller, queenly, her graceful fingers caressing Darlene's face. "Thank you, sweet friend." Darlene seemed to melt inside, to address Rose in some feminine understanding that Brick could not fathom, but, that he realized was above and beyond himself.

Darlene released the tension with a giggle. "That old cabin is dusty and in need of mopping. You know how men are? I'm sure it has all the whiffs and smells of an outdoorsman there."

"Oh, yes, I know." Rose giggled, too, as tears emerged. The women laughed and embraced.

Toby rolled his eyes at Brick, who stood back, sluggishly, feeling a satisfaction for the moment. "I'm ready - I'm ready, let's get started." Toby clapped his hands. "Let's find dad."

"Let me know how things go," Brick whispered.

"I sure will."

Burnie waved to them.

"Thank you, Uncle." Brick bubbled. "We have to help them now."

"In many ways, the problem is beyond family concerns." Burnie sounded forlorn, his voice trailing. "People get hurt, and die in war."

"But, Toby and Rose, and Mr. Yamoto have their rights," Brick countered. "I've heard Mr. Yamoto say that."

"Did the Japanese think of Ida's rights when they bombed Pearl Harbor?" Burnie's retort had a slam to it. He softened after a moment. "I will call Shiro for you, after awhile. Storm's coming in. See it on the horizon." He disappeared toward his bedroom.

"Get under the covers. Get warm," Sathia ordered, charging with purpose into the kitchen. "I'll get you some hot chocolate."

Abandoned, Brick watched his friends drive away. As Toby signaled a farewell, Brick experienced a twinge of despair. Suddenly, he found himself shivering. Outside the sky darkened. He turned on all the lights and built the fire to blaze gloriously. Black clouds, sagging with rain, twisted into the Stemple to unleash. Gust after gust tattered the hills and muddied the streams. Gulls buoyed up on the wind, to slide back, forced by the driving wet to hunch patiently on the shores. Brick watched, absorbed in the moodiness, as the rain made silver sparkles in the black puddles.

Spud trotted in circles, his throat rumbling, until the first crash of lightning. Down he sat to howl. "You nutty hound." With a palm, Brick shielded his eyes in loving disgust.

With the second sound-shatter, Spud raced to the wood box in the kitchen and hid. "Bad storm," Sathia called. "It's scaring me and the pooch."

Brick coughed then, a redness congesting his face. The familiar chest tightness was beginning. Brick shuddered, breathed deeply, and felt a rattle in his lungs. It would not overwhelm him this time, he decided.

"Come with me," Burnie said to Brick next morning before school. "Let's call Shiro - probably can catch him, or certainly interrupt him at breakfast." He grinned with a slight devilment.

"Wow," Brick gloated, following him.

Burnie rolled the necessary numbers on the crank phone. Rose answered. "Your old man there?" he asked lightly. A simple conversation followed, with Uncle offering the cabin at no expense. "No, I won't accept any rent, but, yes." He looked around, his eyes darting naughtily, as Brick remembered back, which gave him a dizzy feeling of joy - of his uncle in better times. "Yes, I would like to share a little glass of you know." Again, his eyes darted for someone overhearing, like Sathia. "Best payment I can think of. Good reason to visit the cabin, after you've settled," Burnie chortled. "Won't bring Sathia though. And, you're right, it's best I don't."

Brick kept leaning forward to listen, almost falling. "Saki?"

"Shssssh, Kid." He turned back to the phone. "Kid almost foiled me. True, best I don't bring her." On a serious note, he said, "Darlene and Rose will clean the place up. They'll probably bring some stews and casseroles. They're planning that you know." He winked at Brick. "The boys want to visit and help, too." He listened intently. "I know how much you appreciate this, Shiro." Suddenly, his face clouded. "I don't know what you mean exactly, that things are going worse than what I know. To be honest, I suspect that. Promise me, think things out. Don't hurry. Stay as long as you need." He looked affectionately at Brick, and turned back to the phone. "We'll keep in contact."

The days progressed brokenly. It was an exhausting, mysterious time. Some nights echoed with the dull muffle of explosions far out at sea; low planes droned offshore, sinking depth charges that rumbled like distant thunder. In addition to medium bombers, PBYs, a hefty pontoon plane, searched consistently along the coast and could be seen daily - a comforting sight for uneasy civilians. The sinking of oil tankers out of San Francisco made headlines. And always, rumors persisted, especially of night activity, of ship-to-shore signal lights, of Coast Guard cutters investigating reports of mysterious detonations and concussions from the ocean depths that were never explained. Many citizens recounted seeing ships burning on the horizon - a chilling sight. Someone from "good authority," told someone that Japanese bodies had washed ashore on the Great Beach at Point Reyes. A persistent story circulated, claiming a life raft and a shortwave radio had been found in a cave on the outer side of Tomales Point, across from the Sea Ranch.

Hourly, men with police dogs patrolled the shores. Kennels were soon built to house the animals, their barking echoed disturbingly at night, sending Spud into a "fit," to sometimes hide under Brick's bed. The Coast Guard, nicknamed, "Coasties," were assigned to handle the dogs, in what they considered a cold and boring duty of walking the beach from sunset to sunrise.

The Army ran telephone lines to the mouth of the Stemple, where more big guns had been established, with additional mounts on the hills overlooking the sea. In the flat little canyons, that flanked the river, soldiers banged away daily with their rifles at targets set against the embankments.

Late one day neighbor Raffetto drove into the Sea Ranch. With greater haste than normal, he approached Burnie and Brick on the front porch.

"You know what?" he opened.

"What?" Burnie sat alert, bundled in a quilted blanket.

"They seen a couple of Jap submarines off the coast here last night."

"How you know?"

"Ezra Hamilton heard it from some soldiers." He hesitated. "'Course I shouldn't be talking like this with your pumper like it is."

"Keep talking and lay off the malarky."

Raffetto leaned close, his manner confidential. "Well, he heard it said that before the War the Japs planned to hit that long beach just south of the Sea Ranch. I've said it before. Pretty soon them Japs will be in Australia, Alaska, Hawaii again, and then on the coast of California, and then right here."

"What do you mean?"

"An invasion of California, that's what I'm saying."

Burnie shook his head. "Now, just a minute. You say somebody saw submarines off the coast last night, and then you talk about invasion. What gives?"

Raffetto sat down on the porch. "Hamilton heard that the Japs made plans to hit a beach north of San Francisco and one at Half Moon Bay."

"That's south of San Francisco."

"That's right."

"A kind of pincer movement?"

"That's right."

"Surround San Francisco, then split the state in half," Burnie said, half to himself.

"But hang on, Burnie. Again, as I told you, them plans I hear was made back in the thirties. That's right, according to the story the Japs plan to hit your beach."

"The Sea Ranch? You kidding?"

"That's what Ezra heard. All them rolling dunes supposed to be easy to land tanks an stuff on. Easy to get inland fast."

Brick sat quietly, the talk unbelievable.

186

"Impossible," said Burnie. "However, it figures - maybe that's why all the guns and soldiers are here."

"I think so."

"And Ezra Hamilton heard all this?"

"Yes."

"Who from? And how come he's so special?"

"I told you. From some soldiers - some guys that are supposed to know."

"He could be wrong. Or those soldiers could. Could all be rumor."

"Don't think so. Not after last night."

"You say the Army saw a couple submarines?"

"That's what Ezra heard. A couple. Well, one soldier said two or three. They surfaced a mile or so offshore."

"That many? You really believe it?"

"These guys are servicemen; they should know."

"Scary," Burnie sighed, with an uncomfortable tightness of mouth. He wanted to say, "It's true, we did have that one sub come up out here. For what reason, nobody knows." He didn't, respecting orders.

In addition to dogs along the beaches, there was a noticeable intensification of military routine. Guards stood watch at the ranch entrance twenty-four hours a day. At night, total blackouts remained a must. Now most of the shoreline remained off-limits, except on specified hours, if the weather was clear. Officers again warned Brick not to pick up any shiny article, as enemy submarines were setting adrift booby trapped objects -- pens and bright little trinkets. One had killed a sixteen year old boy in Oregon.

Then after a night of sporadic bombing at sea, in which planes hummed constantly, Clarence asked a young guard on the road, "What were they after out there?"

Said the soldier innocently, "There was lots of oil and junk washed in on the shore south of here, I understand."

"By junk, you mean litter?" Clarence inquired.

"I'm not talking about seaweed," the soldier bantered. "They sank something out there."

Soon after, the military issued orders forbidding all unauthorized personnel from trespassing within one hundred yards of the shore.

In the first month of the war, makeshift arrangements (small boats, local yachts with Navy radio men aboard, observation planes, patrols, medium bombers, and such) were proving an effective deterrent. Although rumors persisted that nine Japanese submarines had been ordered to bombard the Pacific Coast cities on Christmas Eve, which unsteadied nerves. The season had become a bittersweet time of goodbyes as thousands of young men poured into military training camps. Special services and elite personnel began building bases, roads, airstrips, and pipelines throughout the world.

Just before Christmas, Brick hurried toward the house with a letter postmarked, Honolulu. For Uncle Burnie from Aunt Ida, Brick knew, elated, for they had not learned details from her, and then only a few scrawled notes after the Pearl Harbor tragedy. Christmas would be meaningless, the dinner dull without her. Brick understood that she could not visit because of the war; and, he hadn't really cared that her always memorable presents would not arrive, because she was incapable of shopping. What counted - she had survived the terrible bombing attack.

"I sure miss her," said Brick, handing Burnie the letter.

"We all miss her," said Darlene.

"Maybe she'll tell us what really happened," Burnie retreated into himself. He began reading slowly, his eyes serious.

"What is it?" asked Sathia. "Something wrong?"

"She's a little under the weather, that's all," he replied vaguely.

Brick sensed a reluctance to talk. "Well, what's she sick from?" Sathia demanded.

"Pains and maybe a little Island flu. She sends her love and will be thinking about us and keeping us in her prayers." He faltered, his words stifling concerns. "Keep thinking she's holding something back." Burnie folded the letter and left the room.

"We will pray for her," Sathia called, darning worn socks with an intensity that was not her usual controlled reserve.

18

On a January afternoon, the two friends trudged up the old wagon road, scuffing rocks and mud until their shoes were caked blobs. Rose and Darlene had cleaned up the redwood cabin, with their help now and then. They had settled Shiro Yamoto in for a time. Uncle Burnie had driven the short winding road, upsetting Sathia, as she felt he was not up to the effort. Burnie, in his boyish way, had ignored her, delighting in the chance to be engulfed in cathedrals of big redwoods, and to be helpful. Several times the boys visited, finding Yamoto in better spirits, fixing them one day, a rich dinner of vegetables and lamb stew over rice. He had baked chocolate chip cookies all fixed on and in the ancient wood stove. The crackling wood, chopped originally by Ned Benucci, filled the kitchen with a cozy warmth, that had eased the winter cold. The boys and Shiro had played Chinese checkers, the father proving he was a formidable competitor. Toby had mentioned his friend sharing the story about a big rainbow trout in the Tannery.

"Yeah," Brick had gloated, "it's the Wallopoloozer."

"The what?"

"You know, the biggest trout you've ever seen," Brick had reminded, explaining with authority.

"Probably too smart to catch on a fly or bait," Toby had saddened.

"No doubt." Shiro had smiled, entertained.

"Yeah, he's an old one - learned to survive long ago."

"Maybe we could jig him." Toby was referring to a method used in the ocean, with a heavy metal cylinder lowered into the depths, bristling with big hooks; the object was to tease fish - cod and snapper. Then jerk the weight up suddenly, or let it swirl in the shifting currents. Those bottom fish, attracted to the movement and brightness could be jigged or caught by hooks, even if they didn't bite, and thus dragged to the surface.

"No, that's illegal in our creeks and streams - only out in the ocean," Brick had corrected.

"That's true," Shiro Yamoto had smiled at the boys in paternal warmth. "Burnie, Ned - I think your father, too, mentioned the big fellow. I say, leave him be. He's earned his place here in the Tannery. He deserves to survive."

Now the boys saw smoke from the cabin far up at the end of the road; Burnie would be there with his truck parked in front. They could hear the Tannery swelling with rainwater, making a symphony of music through the twisting plunges. Ahead, a pair of Douglas Squirrels tumbled from their perch and scampered away. Small, reddish, they chirped in play, scooting up a small maple to flatten on a limb, protesting the boys. "Let's scold them back," Brick charged ahead.

"Wahoo," Toby howled, joining.

Brick cut through the brush and stopped, his whole being, cramping. The man was standing at the creek edge, where it glinted in the ashen light. The stranger regarded him with a superior overbearance. "Hi, kid."

Recovering, Brick managed a weak, "Hi," instinctively disliking him. The man held an expensive fly rod, darkly glossed and finely bound with green and white threads. His buff coat and dusky waders radiated newness.

"You must be a city slicker," said Toby, jogging happily out of the brush. The man ignored him. Like Toby, Brick figured he was out of the San Francisco area. Each spring and fall the city people came to hunt or fish. Seldom did they take home game; usually they just managed to scare the cattle and break the fences. This trespasser was out of season.

"Good trout stream, huh, kids, even in the winter?"

"Nope," Brick said with devilish satisfaction.

"Just big pollywogs," said Toby. "Any fish are tiny."

The man arched a brow. "Don't give me that, kids. I got a sure tip on this place. Besides, it looks good. More water running than I prefer, though."

"Not many over this big." Toby measured his forefingers apart three to four inches, as the man cast and worked a spinner from the riffles. He withdrew a cigarette from his breast pocket, tapped it against his wrist, lit it, and tossed the match into the water. With indignation, Brick watched it curl about the eddies.

"How's it look further up? Faster water?"

"About the same," said Brick.

"Deeper holes?"

"Smaller," said Toby.

"Well, I must admit, I've thrown 'em everything - Royal Coachmen, Black Gnats. Even tried a McGinty." The man's bloated face looked sour. "What do they use around here? Huh?"

"Worms," Brick said, honestly annoyed, when the man belched a laugh. Brick wanted to shout viciously, then wanted to cry, "Get out, get out." Instead he turned away, sulking, back toward the narrow road, but deciding to follow the trail skirting the creek.

"Don't get discouraged," Toby said to the man, "nobody's caught a fish here for three years. Too many cows splashing around."

When they were beyond hearing, Brick said, "Who's that guy think he is? Who's he to fish our place?"

Toby shrugged. "I don't know, but, face it, he's bigger than we are."

Brick stalked up the trail toward the cabin. "This is our place. Uncle Burnie's, anyway," he consoled. "No guy like that could ever catch the Wallopoloozer."

"The Wallapo, what again? Oh, yeah. That big rainbow. Nutty name." Toby was grinning, enjoying it all.

"Well, I've seen him - lots of times - well, a few times. Well, maybe once. He's a giant. Uncle and I know where he hangs out. It's not far from here." Brick grew remorseful again. "Wish I'd brought Spud. I'd sic him on that guy."

"You kidding?" said Toby. "Yell sic 'em to that dog, and he'd roll over for a scratch."

"Yeah, Spud isn't much of a fighter, I guess. Dumb hound."

They moved through an aisle of lacey ferns. The Tannery gurgled. Brick could see it through the brush, swift, glittering across white gravel. "I'll show you the pool again," Brick cried exuberantly, dismissing all problems; for the Tannery was like that, a happy fantasy world where one could lose himself. They slipped along the bank, plucking strips of pepperwood leaves as they went, crushing them, rolling them in their fists, until the pungency tickled their noses. Brick signaled. They dropped to their knees, and crawled to a loop in the brook, where the water piled behind a trapped log. The resultant pool was deep, sun-dappled, inviting one to swim in the summer and fish in the spring, now building in runoff.

"He's still in here, huh?" Toby whispered.

"Right here."

"I'd sure like to see him; then I'd believe you."

"Think that guy will fish here?"

"Naaah," assured Toby, "that guy couldn't catch anything if he did."

Brick wondered if the man would follow, if he'd find the spot -- lonely still, but, not so much anymore as more people came, people and more people. That bothered Brick. Uncle wouldn't post the Sea Ranch like other ranchers did. "If God gave us a beautiful place, let us share it," he had said. During summers and holidays, families traveled miles for picnics; lovers strolled the banks; kids splashed joyfully in the pools. At first that had pleased Uncle; he wanted people to love the Tannery, to know its charm, to hear its laugh. But now Uncle was growing disillusioned because kids chased the cows; people knocked over fences or left gates open; everybody dropped papers, and garbage, and cans.

Brick's heart pounded to his throat. It was happening - right before them like he remembered. A blunt form nosed powerfully into the light, against the water rush, its back darkly speckled, the ventral fins undulating. His breath catching in little pains, Brick tried to speak.

"Holy cow!" Toby dropped his jaw. "It must be three feet long!" The trout drifted gently back into the shadows, lolling there.

"You see him? You see him?"

"Yeah. Yeah," Toby uttered. They watched for a time, speechless, until Toby said, "Let's get him."

"Now? Want to?" Brick's voice went high with excitement.

"Yeah, right now. I want the Wallapo---" Toby hesitated. "Gooper?"

"Wallopoloozer," Brick corrected with disgust. "You think we can catch him?"

"Sure we can. I know we can."

Quivering in anticipation, they crawled back from the bank, onto a moist carpet of moss. "I'll go home - get my old pole and stuff," Brick said giddily, "while you dig the worms."

"Gee, thanks."

"I'll show you where, screwball." In a moist glade, Brick scraped handfuls of dark humus from the stream-edge. Carefully he picked out a half dozen stringy, yellow worms and a wriggly pink one which he dumped into Toby's shirt pocket. Toby giggled, his nose wrinkling, pulled his shirt front out, and peered into the squirming pocket. The boys laughed in a relieving moment of total companionship.

Brick started to rise. "I don't know; it's a long ways back. And with that fisherman here."

Toby grew morose, his eyes concentrating on the open earth, with the little creatures writhing to escape. His warm, brown, eyes intensified as he addressed Brick. "You know, my dad didn't want that big fish taken. Not that we can. And your uncle, he likes that fish."

Brick felt an inward tightness, as he sank to his knees. After a painful moment, he admitted, "I know you're right." He bellied next to the bank top, beside his buddy to gaze down. A skeeter drifted lazily over the cool greenness of a protected eddy, free from the stream flow. A few gnats plinked the moving surface. Brick imagined readying his pole, a weatherworn rig used years back by Burnie. He imagined impaling the pink worm, while Toby puckered his face. He imagined plopping it, sinking it enticingly. He imagined jerking and dangling the bait, sometimes deep, sometimes near the surface, circling it, rolling it under the logs, or tossing it into a scrambling falls to let it drift over the riffles.

"That guy, here he comes," Toby warned. "He's movin' this way." The city man wandered up to a bend below them to cast evenly. "He'll be here soon," Brick said, a flush of anger creeping over his face. He glared at the stranger.

"Look," exclaimed Toby. The great fish pushed from where the water was swelling against the logs; they watched him at the bottom, big, holding himself where the sun lighted the spot. His back was mottled, his side flashing, the fins fluttering. "We've got to save him, scare him off," Toby warned, his voice urgent. The fisherman was looking at them now, curiously. He took a flask from his vest and swigged something. "I'm going to slide off the bank, to the sandbar down there. Pretend I fell."

"I'll be right behind," Brick assured, his eyes dilated, looking at the fisherman, who seemed to be listening, despite the noisy water. "Just be careful."

"Grab one of those long poles down there. You may need to pull me out." The twisting water had packed broken sticks and limbs against the shore to pile haphazardly. The two could see the great trout settle protectively in a slow pool of water beneath a temporary dam of debris.

Toby looked back in preparation, his eyes a mixture of glee and concern. "Hope I know what I'm doin' - your mom and aunt will kill you if you get soaked." Toby pushed off. "Whooo," he howled, dropping swiftly, but landing upright, some twelve feet below.

"Wow. Wow." Brick gasped. Toby looked down creek, but apparently could not see the fisherman. He looked back up at Brick and signaled toward the enclosure, where the trout rested, undulating, still holding in place. Toby plunged recklessly, determinedly into the pool. Instinctively, in a flurry of fright, the Wallopoloozer shattered the surface, rising in a sliding roll, twisting savagely - trying to escape the human form threatening him. Down again and up the trout arched, roiling the water, sending concentric waves to wash the bank.

"Chase him out," Brick throated, his eye rotating toward the fisherman, who continued working his lure in the rumpled flow, while curious about the strange activity of the boys. He started slowly reeling in his line.

As Toby floundered deeper into the pool, Brick shouted, "I'm coming down now." He plunged off the bank, to splash in the graveling rifts. "Wheee," he exclaimed, surprised at the exhilaration of a sailing drop.

"You okay?"

"Yeah. I'm with you - I'll help."

"Gotta chase him upstream." Toby threw rights and lefts like a boxer, slapping the water.

"Get him over the dam. Get him out."

"He's trapped by the logs, I think."

Brick lurched after the great fish, his pants, mud splotched, his hair matting over his eyes. The trout rose in a shaking jump that sprayed the pool in glinting droplets. His sides flashed iridescent pink and green as he cleared the barrier and burst up the Tannery to freedom. The boys buckled in relief, then whooped deliriously, at last collapsing on the bank, gasping and soaked.

The stranger secured his line on the reel and stepped onshore, where the bend rose a couple of feet above the creek. He disappeared along the trail. Toby and Brick looked at each other. "He suspects something. He couldn't see me and the fish, I know," Toby grumbled.

"Yeah, he was looking our way." Brick's face darkened. "I don't want him here," he added hoarsely. Toby reached for a loose alder sapling that had lodged in the dam, one of which he had asked Brick to secure.

"What are you doing?"

"Just a chance. Here take this." He handed the sapling to his perplexed friend.

Shortly, the stranger appeared, casually slapping the low brush with his rubber boots. "What were you doing, boys, diving after a fish?" His eyes devoured them.

"No, sir, I fell off the bank; my friend here, he jumped down and pulled me out."

The stranger looked down his nose, and studied them. "Come on, kids, I heard you yelling. I saw something breaking away, up above you. Could have been a big trout that was spooked."

"There was no trout," Brick joined. "No, sir, no trout."

"Give you a buck - a whole big dollar - to tell me about that trout. Bet you know all about him."

"No trout up there," Brick pursued. "This is my uncle's property. There are sometimes little trout found, six or seven inches at the most, but, nothing like you think."

"A dollar and a half."

Toby entered the fray. "Well, to tell the truth - it was a river otter we saw. I went down to chase him and fell in. My partner came to help."

"Two bucks."

"That's the truth. That otter's probably up there someplace grinning at us."

The fisherman looked skeptical, disdainful at the couple. "Guess I'll have to check it out myself."

"My uncle doesn't like people prowling around, sir."

"Don't see a 'No trespassing sign.'"

The boys looked at each other and remained silent.

"You know, kid; yes, you, kid," the man pointed a finger at Brick. "That little partner of yours - he emphasized the word partner - he's slick." His eyes narrowed. "Take it from me, you got to watch these Japs. He'll sell the shirt off your back someday."

"Not my friend."

"Well, this place looks promising. I'll be back, when the water settles out."

"What happened to you guys?" Burnie looked aghast, when the wet boys reached the cabin. He and Shiro were sitting on the rickety porch, with small glasses, partially filled.

"There was a trespasser after the Wallopoloozer," Brick explained, hurriedly.

"We chased the big fish away," Toby blurted quickly. "Got him out of a pool, before the guy found him. The rainbow - think he came up this way, so he's safe."

"Proud of you boys protecting the land, and the fish." Burnie looked warm, and fuzzy, and comfortable.

"It's not easy nowadays. Somebody's always out to take what belongs to somebody else." Mr. Yamoto's voice slurred with bitterness.

"Problem now is, the women in our families are going to clobber you, when they see you soaked, and gooey with mud," Burnie snickered. Both adults looked at each other and chuckled, their voices somewhat slurred.

Toby muttered to Brick from the side, "Saki."

Darkness was closing in scented purple as the boys finished their baths and commenced batting caked mud from their trousers and socks that had been drying before the big woodstove. "Shoes will take a little longer," Burnie mentioned.

The sound of a truck chugged up the road and slammed to a halt before the porch. Clarence rolled from the cab, hurried up the steps, knocked and entered, before anyone could admit him. His eyes had a fixed expression - deadly serious. His face had yellowed, with a hollow gaunt look. He scanned all before him, settling on Shiro Yamoto, apologetically. "Your apple drier was set afire. I'm sorry to tell you."

Mr. Yamoto rose, his mouth open. "Set afire?"

"Your neighbors rallied with spray outfits, put it out, before it got out of control."

"Lots of damage?"

"No, nothing that can't be rebuilt - gutted here and there."

"Got some good neighbors," Yamoto sighed, sinking back in his chair.

"Best we get back with you, Clarence. Help Shiro here," Burnie advised.

"Where's Rose?" Yamoto asked anxiously.

"She and Darlene are with the Hamilton's right now. Someone threw a big rock into your living room, knocking out the front window."

That night, at the Sea Ranch, Burnie received an anonymous phone call cursing him for collaborating with the enemy.

19

In mid-January, presidential dictate ordered that all aliens register with the government. This included not only Japanese, but, German and Italians; the majority of U.S. citizens agreed, that this was the beginning to move Japanese-Americans to internment camps.

The days seemed to bunch in misery. February of 1942 went badly for the free world. Singapore, Java, the Dutch East Indies, Malaya, and Rangoon in South East Asia crumbled. In the Philippines, the Americans, outnumbered and outgunned, held on suffering from malnutrition, tropical diseases, and decreased medical supplies as casualties increased. The newest premier, General Tojo, announced that Asia and the Pacific would soon be under Japanese control.

In Europe, Hitler's western and eastern fronts continued smashing every allied defense. The massive air attacks and blitzkreig of spreading armor and trucks were thrusting toward precious oil fields in the Middle East, as British and German armies continued sparring in North Africa, with a Field Marshal Erwin Rommel landing the more effective punches.

In the U.S., as President Roosevelt spoke to the nation in a fireside chat - his subject: America's coastal defenses in event of a Japanese invasion, a huge submarine emerged west of Santa Barbara, California, and commenced a leisurely shelling, the concussions more alarming than destructive. A full blackout followed, as all traffic was halted and planes dropped flares. Too late, the sub had vanished. Authorities concluded that the ironic incident did not happen by chance, that Japanese intelligence had learned about the President's subject and their Navy responded accordingly.

Sentiment soared against all Japanese, with growing fear of invasion and uprisings. There was a sharp upswing in gun purchases. A Japanese section of one town in Oregon was shot up. Congressmen, editors, business leaders, and citizens joined, their voices united: protect us; remove the Japs; isolate them; clear the coast of them; intern them for the duration of the war. No evidence surfaced that Japanese-Americans were anything but overwhelmingly loyal to the United States. Yet, two thirds of them, native born, were suspected as lying low, waiting for a coming invasion. Also lobbying for evacuation were white businessmen and farmers, who resented economic competition. A congressman from Mississippi, made a speech in the U.S. House of Representatives, saying, "Once a Jap, always a Jap. You can't anymore regenerate a Jap than you can reverse the laws of nature. I'm for taking every Japanese and putting them in concentration camps." He got his wish.

On February 19, President Roosevelt authorized military officials to declare security and exclude anyone they believed a threat. Citizens with at least one-sixth Japanese blood were barred from living, working, or traveling the West Coast.

"A Jap's a Jap," declared Lieutenant General John L. DeWitt, new commander of the internment operation. "It makes no difference whether he is an American citizen; theoretically, he is still a Japanese, and you can't change him."

Espionage and sabotage were becoming more feared, white citizenry convinced itself, believing still, that the large Japanese population had aided the Pearl Harbor attack. On the Pacific mainland, ignited grass fires; guns stolen from homes; and, shadowy people sneaking about, to many, revealed a pattern of insidious sabotage.

One afternoon, Toby appeared at the Sea Ranch. "How did you get through all those soldiers?" Sathia asked, somewhat abruptly.

"Oh, I just walked from our orchard down over the hill."

"Nobody stopped you? You might have been shot."

Toby smiled. "They're used to me and Brick," who he glanced at.

"Yeah," Brick piped. "They know us, and wave at us."

Sathia frowned. "Well, I don't know. I'd sure be careful."

Toby appealed to Brick. "You and me. We got to talk." He had a heavy, dark look.

"Sure." The boys stepped outside, off the porch, in a pale sunlight out of hearing.

"My dad's bought some handguns - or at least got some from a few friends. He doesn't know, I know."

"Handguns?"

"Yes, handguns. He has a shotgun and a twenty-two rifle, which I've never seen him use - but, no handguns."

"Why handguns?"

"I don't know just yet. I do know he doesn't want to be forced to leave, to lose our ranch and all he's ever worked for." Toby looked away at the sheds and at the braided folds of broken hills, radiant green.

"How do you know he's got handguns?"

"I just got suspicious, when I saw him take a sack from one of our neighbors; another time he brought a small box home. He kept looking around, as if to see if anyone was watching. Rose was gone, but I was up in the drier."

"So, what does that mean?"

Toby held his words, shifted his feet, and rolled his eyes up in a twisting anguish. "When dad was gone one day, I sneaked into his bedroom. In his closet, he has a trunk with a lock. He hangs the key on a rack in the kitchen."

"You took his key?" Brick's mouth rounded in disbelief. "Your dad's stuff? You could get into real trouble."

"I took it," Toby said solemnly. "Dad would have been hurt, so disappointed in me. But, I had to. I opened it. Yes, there were a couple of pistols and bullets. I just slammed it closed."

"Collecting handguns. Wow. You better stay with me. My room's big enough, or maybe at Ned's old cabin." Brick spoke with sincerity, knowing that the problems were too immense to allow such.

"No. You - you're a great friend, but, no. Dad needs me now. I just don't know what's going to happen," Toby looked shrunken, his body curled in a despairing way. "If it comes to an evacuation and looks like it is, I don't know if dad's going. I think he would die first. He and Rose now, are at odds over it all. Dad claims it's like being shipped to a concentration camp. Already, some of our Japanese friends were arrested. They were officers in some ranch organizations, especially for Japanese. I'm glad dad's just a rancher."

"All getting to Rose pretty bad, huh?"

"She's been going through all old letters and pictures. Anything written or sent from Japan. Even stuff real personal."

"What did she do with them?"

"She just sat in front of the fireplace, crying. She burned anything that she thought might make us look - as she said, disloyal."

"Gosh."

"She made me keep guard at the windows for any strange cars that might turn into our driveway. She was scared that there might be FBI agents coming to take dad away."

"I don't know what to say."

"Nothing you can." Toby brought up something buried deep inside. "I haven't told you, but our family was just given numbers - five of them - to identify us when we arrive at wherever we're going."

That night, Brick dreamed that he and Toby lay on the otter point at dark. Both watched the figure of Mr. Yamoto crouched along the shore - or it seemed like Mr. Yamoto. "Don't go," Brick implored.

"It's too late. Too late. Too late. Too late." The words echoed and faded in the murky air; then clearly, Toby said, "Everybody hurts everybody," his voice cold and desolate.

"We - you and me - we don't."

"We're the only ones in the world, then."

Brick tried again - the setting unreal before him. "You've got to come with me. It's your dad they want."

"I'm an enemy, too, now."

"We don't owe anybody, anything," Brick begged desperately. "This war isn't ours - we didn't start it."

"I've got to go with my dad."

"Why?"

"Because he's my father. I don't understand what's happening, but still, he's my father."

Brick sat up, confused, the room whirling in a wild way. He ran fingers through his hair and waited - the alarm clicked steadily - the hands lit up at 2:21 a.m. He lay for a time, dully, unable to think; an uneasy tiredness weighted him - a sinking, dusky enclosure.

Then in his dream again there came a dull sloshing sound of displaced water, suddenly tumbling into foamy waves that slapped against the shore, then returning, to curl white and turbid around an emerging tower. Brick and Toby sat erect in stunned silence. Within the curve of the point, where the water lay deep and mysterious, the ocean erupted and parted; a dark outline took form, looming larger and larger, until filling the entire inlet. "Oh, Lord," Toby uttered. Brick could not move, could hardly breathe -- before him, a submarine, long and black, rose gracelessly like some prehistoric monster. The strange ship settled to ride gently in the rhythmic swells. Hypnotized, Brick watched, watched, watched - the scene dotting and streaking like a film gone bad. Brick twisted, writhed amongst his blankets, fighting them.

Now, the images became confused, blinking on and off. He thought he saw Mr. Yamoto. Then, he did: Immediately, Mr. Yamoto sent a light beam flickering over the water. A cold light-wink returned from the sub. In the faint glow, Brick saw two men launch a raft from the deck. They floundered into the puffy, oblong contraption and began paddling rapidly toward shore. "They're coming for us," Toby said, woefully.

Again, Yamoto flashed his light. He turned, came back near the caves and pulled two suitcases from the rocks. "Toby," he called softly. "Come now. Hurry."

"Don't go," Brick said with agony.

"It's no use. There's no place for us here. Not anymore." Toby started away. In the contorted dream, Brick saw and didn't see. Then, a sizzling ignited the air overhead, swept past and sank into the headland beyond. Toby gave a cry and threw himself flat against the embankment. White flashes lit the sky as the shore batteries opened, punctuating the coastline with ear-splitting ferocity. Water plumed about the sub, then hit, renting it, buckling it, as the middle exploded in a geyser of orange flame and smoke. Brick burrowed into the brush, buried his head, but looked down, determined. "Run," Brick shouted, unable to move; in the jumbled, fractured chaos, fading, clearing, appearing and passing, he saw Toby's small form, pelted with shrapnel and broken steel. He wiped his eyes, tried to see, and then saw - his friend tattered, cradled as if asleep, in his father's arms.

Jerking into a sitting position, with a rueful cry, Brick felt his body shudder all over, a cold wetness of perspiration soaking him. He fumbled on the bedside light and looked about, half expecting shells to explode on top of him. The clock ticked monotonously and the ocean wind rattled the windows with a steady throb. And, then, he knew for certain he had been dreaming - a nightmare so remarkably vivid that he could not shake its numbing effect for the next hour. And, he knew for certain, that it would return again in some form to horrify him.

The days tumbled past. Spring, usually a joyous time of renewal, of cherry and apple blossoms, had become a world full of threatening doom. In the Bay Area, an oil refinery erupted, shelled by a Japanese submarine. Days later, a Japanese fleet nearly destroyed the American and British fleet in the Java Sea. School work seemed less important. People in the stores, on the streets, even in the quiet countryside, showed the strain and worried concern that grew rampant. The Philippine Islands were being overrun by the Imperial forces. Names like Bataan and Corregidor dominated the news as last bastions for beleaguered American soldiers.

On the Russian front, the Nazi Army, which had been pushed back, began a counter offensive. In North Africa, Field Marshal Rommel continued to seize Africa and beyond, into Palestine and Arabia. Hitler seemed unstoppable. Would the Germans join Japan, now sweeping through India and Southeast Asia?

Toby shared his fears and confusions even more with Brick. "You're the only one I can tell anything," he confided. His father and close friends were upset, feeling that the Japanese had been singled out. No action had been taken against people of German or Italian ancestry, even though they outnumbered the Japanese-Americans, and the United States was also at war with Germany and Italy.

The Japanese-American Citizens League sent a letter to the President, reaffirming their loyalty, pledging fullest cooperation in repelling any invasion along with their fellow Americans. "We're Americans," Toby swallowed his words in pain. "Dad said, if he was young enough, he would join the service and fight against Tojo and his bullies."

Again, General John DeWitt, head of the Western Defense Command, defended all removals. "A Jap is a Jap - it makes no difference whether he is an American civilian or not. I don't want any of them." He offered an insight: "The very fact that no sabotage has taken place to date confirms that such action will be taken."

High officials supported such a contention. Relentlessly, the white farmers along the Pacific joined the condemnation. Some skeptics said that many were envious of the high success with their Oriental competitors. Austin Anson, head of The California Vegetable Growers' Association, told the Saturday Evening Post, a popular national magazine: "If all the Japs were removed tomorrow, we'd never miss them, because the white farmers can take over and produce anything the Japs grow. And, we don't want them back when the war ends, either."

A columnist, Henry McLemore, in the San Francisco Examiner, urged the military, "To herd 'em up, pack 'em off, let 'em be hurt and hungry." The nation's most respected columnist, Walter Lippman, warned that, "The Pacific Coast was a potential battlefield."

"We've got to do our part to support the war effort, and help all those boys losing their lives out there in the Pacific," Burnie announced one morning. "There's been wide talk of sabotage." Uncle was basing his concern on rumors and vague facts. Here and there, along the coast, trees had dramatically burst into flames. Electrical poles were mysteriously cut, severing power for miles. In the Bay Area, at the huge Mare Island Naval Yard, where Ned Benucci worked, the FBI swooped down, arresting some Japanese-Americans, claiming that signal flags, radios, guns, and cameras had been found. Nine cooks, waiters, and laundry workers were booked, but, were never charged for lack of proof. Concerned officials noted that Japanese lived near roads, airports, railroads, defense plants, ports - all over California - proof that many were planning something. A curfew was imposed on Japanese, on both "Aliens" and "Citizens."

The rising sun, the Japanese flag, rose over more and more of Southeast Asia. In the steaming heat of jungle, British, Chinese, and American soldiers suffered from malaria and painful wounds as food and medical supplies further dwindled. Four million men joined the services in what was now a global war. Americans bought war bonds; collected cooking fats that could be used in making explosives; rationing became an anticipated sacrifice. Citizens commenced using any available ground to plant Victory Gardens, even in towns and cities, to produce vegetables for families, leaving the commercial produce to feed the armed forces. Many inexperienced town people phoned Burnie asking for his expertise on planting and tending. The fact pleased Burnie and made Brick proud.

20

In the early spring, March 2, before the April 7 deadline, the first Japanese came to assembly points, quietly, without resistance - houseboys, doctors, fishermen, gardeners, lawyers, businessmen, women, and children, all in respect of authority.

Letters began to arrive from the first internees, the facts circulating rapidly throughout the Japanese communities and spilling over into the surrounding ranches and towns. Orders listed simply: they were to take only what they could carry in two hands, no pets, and nothing could be shipped ahead. They sold their holdings, their businesses at whatever minimum was offered, for they had no choice. Some just left properties behind for others to claim, having less than 24 hours to sell or store possessions. The families were given numbers. The early evacuees were taken to holding facilities, the Rose Bowl and the Santa Anita Race Track, in the south state. Those on the North Coast, were bused to the Central Valley, to a holding center, with muddy grounds, mosquitoes, and cockroaches. They soon would be loaded onto trains (the shades pulled down), and shipped to open desert country in Northern California, under the watch of soldiers with guns; then later to Amache, Colorado, near the Kansas border, one of ten bleak camps in six western states: California, Arizona, Idaho, Wyoming, Colorado, Arizona, and

Arkansas in the South, which had been established by a new agency, The War Relocation Authority. President Roosevelt referred to them as concentration camps. The term disturbed many. In the dictionary, concentration camp is defined as, "a camp where persons (as prisoners of war, political prisoners, or refugees) are detained or confined."

Some Japanese were given a few days to a few weeks to turn themselves in. One hundred and twenty thousand would eventually be incarcerated. Two thirds were American citizens, their civil rights denied or ignored. Tar-papered barracks had been partially erected. Letters told of workmen still hammering on rooftops. They were placed in block sections and given two rooms, if the family was large; Army cots and a potbellied stove were the only furniture on plank floors, with bare light bulbs hanging from the ceiling, but no cooking stoves or running water. Eating was in a "mess hall," with hundreds of others. The restrooms and shower facilities were centered in a common area in each block. Privacy became impossible. Japanese women sometimes had to bathe in front of sentries.

The entire camps were surrounded by barbed wire fencing with watchtowers and armed guards on duty. At night, searchlights explored the setting. The prisoners often hung blankets to add privacy in their crowded quarters. All the selected camps had been located in barren deserts that historically were subject to freezing blizzards of snow in the winter, and sweltering blasts of pummeling dust in the long summers.

Some evacuees fled eastward to the Rocky Mountain states, only to be met by prejudice and hatred. Fearful for their lives, they had no place to hide. In a common sentiment, the Governor of Idaho said, "The Japs live like rats, breed like rats, and act like rats. We don't want them." The War Department submitted and supported the only practical solution: Internment.

These facts and incidents were being filtered through special reports and informative articles, some called undercover, others called sensational. The most solid facts for the family, came from the Yamoto's. Rose confided in Darlene, seeking assurance and advice. Darlene passed on to the family, only those confidences that she assessed were not too personal or private. Of course, she elaborated on what information other Japanese had revealed; about assembly centers; the transportation;

the impressions and first experiences in the camps. Under pressing questions, she admitted that Rose was living between her home and with the Hamilton's.

"Toby told me that," Brick inserted, feeling important.

Darlene's lips spread, framing an appreciation. "There is strain between Rose and her dad. She claims she will be obedient, will go quietly on the assigned date, probably before. She believes her Christian faith will sustain her."

Unexpectedly, a few hours later, Mr. Yamoto phoned Burnie to thank him for graciously allowing a temporary sanctuary for thought in the redwoods. Burnie assured him that he had good friends around who had saved his drier. "Just sorry that somebody torched it. The sheriff will find out who."

"I don't expect so, not with all the feelings running wild."

"I feel bad all this is happening to you. It's the tragedy of war that affects everything." Burnie listened for a time, his face pained.

Afterwards he had paced the living room floor in front of the family. "He told me much of what Rose told Darlene." Burnie showed spiraling emotions in his stumbling narrative. "I hate the sneak attack, what the Japanese are doing to the country and our boys, and what happened to Ida. But, it is sad what's happening to Shiro. He said, 'We will be prisoners in our own land.'"

"Maybe it's for their own protection," Clarence defended.

"Yeah, but he's frightened. Local realtors, officials, speculators are trying to wheel a deal to buy his ranch for practically nothing. He fears everything he has built and lived for and for his kids - all his hard work and dreams of a better life are gone - the same for his friends." Burnie stopped his pacing and turned to his rapt audience. "I asked what he planned to do. He said he would not be herded off like cattle to slaughter, whatever that means."

"Heaven help him," Sathia blurted.

Burnie rubbed his arms as if cold, or to relax himself. "He did tell me one nice thing." The family leaned forward, waiting. "He said he would send Toby with his prize fishing rod, the ocean pole, for me to keep, depending on what happens." Burnie made a muffled, unconvincing laugh.

Several days later, Brick entered the house with a letter for Uncle Burnie, postmarked Honolulu, with a Kapiolani Hospital return. Brick felt good, for they had not heard from Aunt Ida as much as hoped, her well-being still unsettled.

"Maybe she'll tell us what really happened," said Burnie. He began reading slowly, his eyes serious.

"Well?" asked Sathia.

"She's still a little under the weather."

Brick sensed a reluctance to talk. "Well, what's she sick from?" Sathia demanded.

"We'll talk about it later. Right now I need to telegraph Ida."

"What is it? What did Ida say?"

Suddenly Darlene hinted to Brick, "Can't you clean up your room or something?"

"Why?" Brick challenged, determined not to be dismissed.

"Because I said so."

Brick flopped on the couch and draped himself over it, in defiance. "Well, I have a right to know what's going on."

"Apparently this is adult business, nosy britches," Darlene huffed.

"Let me talk to the ladies, Boy," Burnie ordered. "You and I can talk later."

Brick slammed out of the front door; stopped and slammed it again, the way he did as a kid, the way they hated.

At lunch, the family ate in silence. Brick devoured both Auntie's and his mother's pie and no one even noticed. Auntie was more attentive than ever to Uncle. She set a pillow in his rocker, and even got his slippers and a magazine for him. Clucks over him like an old mother hen, Brick thought disgustedly. Yet he understood that it all had something to do with the mysterious letter.

After the women had cleared the dishes, Brick again confronted Burnie. To his surprise the words that emerged were not about Aunt Ida, but about that which troubled him so deeply. "It's terrible what's happening to Mr. Yamoto and Toby."

"I suppose it is," Burnie replied.

"We gotta help them, someway. I been real worried."

"It's beyond us now, Boy." Burnie set his lips and looked down at his magazine.

"Why?"

"We'd only be interfering. The government knows best."

"But they're having a terrible time. With fires, and threats."

"I know. I know."

"Well?"

"I don't want to talk about it. I don't want to hear about it anymore." said Burnie sharply.

"But they need us, Uncle Burnie," Brick pleaded.

"That's war, Boy. People get hurt." Burnie looked at Brick through moist eyes.

"But Toby and Mr. Yamoto got rights, too," Brick argued, "and Toby's my best friend."

Deliberately Uncle attempted to absorb himself in the magazine.

"And what happened to Aunt Ida? Why was I kicked out?"

Burnie turned to Brick, seriously. "She's just a little sicker than we thought."

"What happened? Will she be okay?"

"She'll be fine. Nothing to worry you about."

The days flowed torturously, as the grim news of war threatened. General Douglas MacArthur left the Philippines for Australia, vowing, "I shall return." Mr. McPeak phoned off and on, to see how the family was holding up. (Brick had dark suspicions that McPeak's real concern was to keep in contact with his mother.) He was stationed in Washington, D.C., on some diplomatic undertaking.

For the majority of Japanese left, the apprehensive date, noon, April 7, approached rapidly, as thousands of evacuees reported. There was no rioting, no armed resistance, no impulsive guerrilla warfare as expected. Adding to the daunting removal, was the inevitable collapse of the Philippine Islands, and the surrender of seventy-five thousand American/Philippine troops, which cast a gloomy pall over the populace.

"But why take them away? It's like going to a prison," Brick said.

"Because they're Japs. And we're at war."

Brick remained untouched. "But most of them are friends. We're not at war with our friends."

"Well, people are scared of them now," Burnie said abruptly. "And maybe some of them are dangerous. Look what happened in Hawaii. Some servants turning on their masters. Who knows?"

"Is Toby dangerous?"

Burnie rubbed his eyes. "I don't know, Boy. I just don't know."

A worried Brick had not heard from his friend, who seemed to be avoiding him at school, until one bleak afternoon, when Toby appeared at the Sea Ranch to tap at the door, lugging his dad's ocean pole. Burnie looked up from the fire, where his thoughts had strayed. A usually aloof Sathia had softened some at sight of Burnie's face suddenly alive with pleasure. He took the pole, pressed it to his chest. "Your dad shouldn't have."

"He wanted to."

"Of all his collection, this is his pride and joy." Burnie rotated the 7 foot piece of art; once again, Brick and Toby admired the split bamboo, brightly glossed and finely bound with a roller tip, the 30-inch butt, hand carved, with intricate patterns: curling waves, elongated fish; a sea hawk with spread wings; the black and silver drag reel, still oiled and polished to a shine. "Beautiful. Beautiful. Don't know how to thank your dad. I'll hold on to it. He may come back and get it some day."

"Oh, he'll come back. Right now, Rose has packed and left. She and dad tear me up," Toby said solemnly.

"You and your father packing, too?" Sathia asked almost urgently. Burnie frowned at her.

"Dad's trying to find somebody to leave our property - but, it doesn't look good. Everybody just wants everything for nothing."

"That's too bad," Burnie said weakly, still admiring the pole.

Brick rescued his friend. "You want to go upstairs?"

"I'd rather go for a walk, like down to the Stemple, and just talk." A fidgety Toby rocked nervously.

Sathia looked skeptical. "Didn't the soldier boys try to stop you, carrying that pole? You can't go down to the beach, you know, if they thought that's where you were going."

"I know. They just waved at me. Like I keep telling you, Brick and me, we're pretty well-known around here."

"Put on a warm coat, young man. You know how you catch colds."

"Don't worry, I'll put a big coat on." said Brick flushing in disgust. Burnie prodded the fire, for he could not combat both boys - their uncomfortable uneasiness.

The two walked beyond the barn and along the road in silence, toward the Stemple under a gloomy overcast of filtered sunlight, with the trees dripping and the fog low and slate-colored, the sun poking through here and there. They slipped down to a river cove hidden from view, rimmed with white beaches and gold-lit water, shallow where smelt darted through the quivering eel grass. The enclosing ridges were laced with azaleas and laurel, their leaves shiny. Here Tannery Creek tumbled from the back hills, through a canyon of ferns to purl musically, blending at last with the salty tides of the Stemple. In the quiet of inlet where the trees were mirrored, the boys often hid, replenishing themselves with the beauty, fishing for bullheads, and snagging crabs to later boil over a driftwood fire. They had watched deer browse daintily and coons explore the lapping shore for clams. There had been days of storm-pushing winds, and biting fogs. But the spot remained a haven, worlds away. And the boys had shared. It had been a time of foxes on the sand, of herons wading languidly. Days of grebes streaming dark wakes over the glassy inlet, of ruddy ducks drifting like toy boats. It remained always a time of oneness. Brick was glad, yet saddened for his friend, sensing that those simple pleasures had come to pass.

"I don't know what to say," Toby choked,

Brick stared at his friend, waiting.

"We're supposed to leave tomorrow by noon."

"Supposed to?"

"It's my dad."

"What about him?" Brick's voice caught the tension.

"A couple of days ago, I found him - just staring off at nothing. Just sitting and staring. It was the way he looked. I just knew something had happened. He turned around and said to me, 'I'm through crawling'. That's what he said." Toby wiped his mouth; a twitch traveled one cheek. "When I asked what he meant, he got mad, said he was going to fight fire with fire."

"What'd he mean?"

"He says he's not going."

"Not going."

"He says he refuses to lose everything. He's not going to be a prisoner out in the desert - some place called Colorado."

"What's he going to do?"

Toby licked his lips and scrunched his face. "I don't know. He pulled most of the window shades down, and barricaded the doors with chairs, except a back one he left for me."

"Wow, he has the guns?"

Toby contorted his face again. "I don't know how to say this."

Brick waited, letting Toby explain in his own way and time.

"At one point, dad just went crazy - never saw him like that."

"What did he do?"

"He threw stuff - lamps and vases; said he wouldn't be herded like a dumb sheep; said, he'd kill 'em before they took our place."

Brick saw rare tears in his friend's eyes. "What about the guns?"

"He's laid 'em out, around the house - set 'em out all loaded - with more ammunition by 'em."

Brick shook his head with disbelief, a shudder racking him. Such things happened only in the movies or on radio dramas. "What will you do?"

"I don't know exactly. Dad will be furious if he learns I told you all this."

"Didn't he expect you would?"

"Can't say. Maybe he doesn't care. He wanted to get the pole to your uncle, and for things to look normal, I figure."

"You can't go back."

"Have to."

"Maybe you could come back with me." Brick knew much of his family was caught in crossing emotions, and realized that he didn't sound convincing.

"Wouldn't be fair to your family."

Brick struggled for ideas. "You could come back to the house, phone the sheriff."

"Couldn't do that to my dad."

"You could find out where Rose is, maybe, and join her."

"Don't know how."

"You could try. My mother would help you." Brick pleaded, almost desperately.

Toby wagged his head. "I've got to go back, old pal. He's my dad. I can't desert him. Not now - nor ever." He punched Brick's right shoulder, and, Brick punched him back in a shoulder, lightly. "You'll always be my best friend," Toby grinned sickly. "So, long." He saluted and spun about.

Brick stood shivering in the encroaching cold, watching Toby move ponderously away up the shadowy hill.

21

Noon, April 7, came and passed.

Toby was nowhere at school, nor were any other Japanese. From a phone booth, Brick attempted to call Toby - no one answered.

An overwhelming fright exploded inside Brick as he reached the Sea Ranch. Uncle engrossed in the fire, as usual, looked up, his eyes penetrating. "You okay?"

"Yes," Brick lied.

"Come in. Sit down, Boy. Relax, you'll live longer."

"I want to talk," Brick said, torn inside.

"Sure, Boy, it's been a long time."

Brick wanted to tell, wanted to beg help, but he faltered. No longer was Uncle as receptive. No longer did he really seem to care about the Yamoto's. Instead, Brick burst out, "The point down at the end, where all the water comes in …."

"Yeah, Boy. The old Schooner Cove."

"Toby and Gerve and me, we discovered some sea otters there. They sure looked like sea otters."

"Sea otters?"

"Real honest to goodness otters. It's been our secret for a long time now."

Uncle listened skeptically, his hands folded.

Tears oozing, Brick said, "Something awful is going to happen to them, with all the soldiers and shooting. I know it."

Burnie said carefully, "Those ones with round faces? The speckled ones?"

"We saw some swimming around, when Toby went fishing with us - you, me, and Toby."

"Before my attack?"

"You saw them then?"

"Partially, yes. It's just that I don't want to disappoint you, but, I'm sure those weren't sea otters." Burnie tongued his words. "Although, I admit they kinda looked like 'em; however, I just saw the heads stickin' up, out of the water. But, they couldn't be. Otters are so rare - nearly extinct possibly. So don't keep your hopes up. You'll just get hurt."

"I was certain." For an instant, Brick forgot about Toby. "They had light faces and long whiskers, like in the pictures I've seen."

"If you don't believe me, look 'em up in your nature book. Sea otters are found way south of here, Boy. Down around Monterey County." Burnie reflected on his words. "Although Ned Benucci said once, that he thought he saw some near here, up in Sonoma County."

Brick shook his head. "We were so sure."

"We all make mistakes," said Burnie, sympathetically. "Now just don't worry about those old harbor seals. They're the toughest creatures in seven seas."

As Brick reached his room, he heard Darlene and Clarence drive up, then hurry into the kitchen to talk rapidly, both at the same time. From his bureau, he took his <u>Mammals of North America</u>, thumbed to the pages on otters and seals, and studied the pen-lined sketches. The rare sea otter, slight and dusky with droopy whiskers shielding a white or yellowish face. The common harbor seal, chunkier, gray speckled with shorter whiskers. Funny he hadn't seen the difference; maybe hadn't wanted to, he concluded. He wished Toby were beside him to assure him, that what they had seen those times, looked like the pictured sea otter. He slammed the thick book.

"Come downstairs, we got to talk," Clarence called, the voice demanding. Brick responded slowly, his mind clawing at a hundred tangled thoughts. "Important conference," Clarence spat, his eyes blazing queerly, as Brick reached the stair top.

Someone had turned on the radio; the only available news concerned fighting a continent away. "Nothing local," said Sathia, turning it off. Clarence took a gulp of fresh poured coffee and mugged his lips, waiting. Brick sat down in the cowhide couch, his sides shriveling.

Darlene commenced chattering in her nervous way. "We are just worried about you, darling, with Toby such a good friend." Darlene started toward him, but, Clarence checked her.

Brick stiffened. "What's Toby got to do with anything?"

"Makes no difference now," said Burnie, who had been watching glumly, "long as this family sticks together, nothing else makes much difference."

"You and Toby, that's what we want to talk about," Clarence approached cautiously, his expression regretful. "You know, I expect, Mr. Yamoto didn't meet the deadline. He didn't move out, as ordered. Rumor in the neighborhood - he's holed up - armed."

"Better tell the boy what you heard," Sathia advised, "because, I think he can tell us something. Toby was here yesterday afternoon, and seemed awful upset."

"We know," Clarence assured, as Darlene sought her husband's hand. "You realize, Son, Mr. Yamoto has to accept government decree."

Brick listened, expecting the worst.

"I talked to Ezra Hamilton; he, too, had heard that Yamoto remained - he saw some sheriff's cars patrolling around - unusual for this neck of the woods."

"Tell them about the government men today," Darlene urged.

Clarence paled with strain. His eyes floated over the family. "Today, some government men came to the apple ranch. They asked all kinds of questions. They showed me their credentials: FBI."

"No, kidding?" Burnie sat erect, "FBI?"

"Yes," Clarence paused and caught his breath. "They asked what I knew about Shiro Yamoto. Rumors are wild about his picture taking."

Brick glowered at his father. "Toby said over and over that his father knows he's suspected. But, he does it, takes pictures cause he's an artist. It's his hobby. Pictures are his hobby and he's famous for it. You know that, Dad." Brick's hands clutched convulsively.

"Son, those men said they'd been suspicious of Yamoto for months."

"What did Toby tell you, honey?" Darlene said anxiously.

Burnie interrupted, "Toby did seem mighty upset - secretive, too."

Clarence shook a finger, "Son, you got a responsibility - this is bigger than you know, than any of us know. Bigger than a boyish friendship, that's for sure."

Brick couldn't hold back any longer. The nausea of fear, the jumbled thoughts spewed forth. With tears welling, he cried, "Toby and Mr. Yamoto - they're going to hold onto their ranch." In despair he looked at the taut, resistant faces. "They don't mean to hurt anybody," he reacted. "That's all Toby said, and he's scared."

"What else?" Clarence's eyes had a frustrated shine.

"He must have told something more," Auntie offered, "they share everything."

"Honey." Darlene slipped next to Brick and embraced him. "You're a fine, brave boy, but you must tell us."

Brick pushed her arms away with such determination that she blinked and stepped back.

"Now look, young man." Clarence was flushing. "He's not a friend to you or anybody else. He's dangerous. Get that through your thick skull. And get it fast."

"They've always been friends," said Sathia, acidly, "the child is blind to what's happening."

"This is war, Brickford," Clarence voiced. "Grow up. The Japs hate us, and apparently Yamoto has chosen to resist."

"The Yamoto's - they don't hate us."

"They're Japs."

Darlene tried again. "Toby is a nice boy - but he isn't really like you, honey." She groped for a word. "He's - he's just different."

"Look at it this way," said Burnie. "Yamoto has separated himself from America and his own people, who are doing right by giving up. The best way to protect him and us, is to stop him. So he's got to surrender. If he's really barricading himself, that's insane. He's gone crazy." Provoked, Burnie continued, "You know what that last letter from Ida was about?"

"No, nobody would tell me."

"She didn't let us know until that last letter, because she didn't want to worry us, as we didn't want to worry you," Burnie said heatedly. "She got crippled - wounded in the attack on Pearl Harbor - worse than we knew."

Brick's heart sank. His features whitened. "What happened?"

"A window blew out in the bus when they were hit and crashed - cut her all up. She's still in the hospital. Hopefully, soon, she'll be able to go to a convalescent home."

Brick's voice went scratchy. "I'm sorry, Uncle," he tried, knowing his consolation, empty and lost. "Wish you'd told me."

"She's confined to a wheelchair. As I said, she didn't tell us everything, until that letter."

"A wheelchair? Will she be all right?"

"Who knows?" Burnie turned his head aside. "That's what the Japanese have done."

Brick's words were throaty, heavy. "All I know is that Rose left, and, Toby is going back to his dad."

"Who is staying against orders," said Clarence, his voice like a finalized clap.

Brick nodded in submission. "Who is staying, yes."

Clarence leaned back. "I hope you're telling the truth. If you're not - someday you'll regret it."

"Tut, tut," Sathia admonished. "The boy's had enough."

"I have no sympathy. None whatsoever," said Clarence, striding about. "War is no game."

Burnie looked earnestly at Brick. "Remember, Boy - unless Yamoto is stopped now, others like Aunt Ida could get hurt. Thousands of innocent people could die, especially if Yamoto has turned against us. We don't know what he's done. I, too, don't think he's a spy, but let's not take that chance."

"Will they shoot Mr. Yamoto?" Brick questioned, his mouth open and set.

"That's not our concern," said Clarence, warming his hands before the fire. "He'll get what he deserves. He could be shooting Americans right now."

"I doubt they'll try to shoot him," Burnie interjected, as if convincing himself. "They'll just arrest him. I'm sure that's all. Just arrest him."

"But what about Toby? Will they hurt Toby?"

Clarence scoffed. "He's a kid. Nobody hurts a kid."

"Look at it this way," Burnie explained. "By resisting our government and our orders, Mr. Yamoto has turned enemy. Let the authorities take care of him. The Good Book says it best, 'An eye for an eye, and a tooth for a tooth.'"

In disbelief, Brick looked at his family, and lastly at his uncle. "Why, you?" he asked plaintively. "Why you, Uncle Burnie? You always understood."

Burnie retorted, the harshest he had ever been to his nephew. "You're blinded by friendship. You are a naïve young man. How can you protect those people after what they did to our country and to Ida?"

Brick dashed upstairs and sprawled on his bed. Through clouded eyes, he stared at the wallpaper, at the bright coated horsemen, and the loose-tongued hounds, at the little fox huddling. The family was right; he knew, that if Mr. Yamoto had chosen to resolve his conflicts by force, he had to be stopped. Brick wondered, was he wrong in defending his best friend? Had he betrayed his relatives and neighbors, and classmates?

No matter how he approached the dispute, it was an adults war, caused by adults, and fought by adults. And, now, he and Toby were involved, forced to take sides in a war they had not made.

Somewhere in the darkness, Toby would lie frightened, his life endangered.

No doubt the patrols, usually guardsmen, the FBI, and the sheriff's men, all with guns would focus quickly. There would be no mercy, only efficient annihilation, if Mr. Yamoto refused to surrender. Hadn't he, and Toby, for months, watched the accurate harmony of men and weapons? Despite his family, despite the whole world, Toby was his responsibility. After sunset, he would slip out his window, down the escape ladder.

"Hold fire," the man on the bullhorn ordered. "Let the boy come out. The Jap's going to let the kid out."

Mr. Yamoto called, "I beg you, let my boy go. Don't hurt him." His voice went high with emotion. "Don't harm my son. This is not his cause. You understand?" Brick heard the pleas distinctly this time.

"It's okay," said the lawman on the horn. "It's okay. We want your boy. We won't harm him. Now you be smart. You come, too, Yamoto. You come with him."

"No!" Yamoto's voice seemed to rip through his throat. "No, just my son."

Brick saw the officer with the horn look around at the armed force, and survey it. He took a deep breath and said firmly, "Come on out, son. Come out into the yard; we won't shoot. Come on out into the light. Don't rush. Just come out slowly." The guardsmen and a few regular soldiers pointed their rifles. The lawmen leaned over their cars and pointed sidearms, steady in both hands.

A long pause ensued. Nothing moved except for the writhing shadows that the trees made under a steady sea wind. Then the front door opened and a small, chunky figure appeared. Toby Yamoto raised his arms to shield his eyes from the glare. He stood for a time, blinking, looking about as if trying to orient himself. Hesitantly, he moved down the steps and into the yard with short, uneven steps like some robot. He stopped and squinted into the light. "Please don't kill my daddy," he called. Suddenly the boy turned around with his back to all the firepower. "Dad - I'm coming back for you," he cried, his arms outstretched, reaching toward the house.

"For God's sake, no, Toby. Please don't," came an anguished, frightened, voice from within.

"Halt," shouted the man on the bullhorn.

"I'm going back," Toby screamed.

Brick had fought his way from the Sea Ranch, through the tangled brush, the beam of his flashlight splashing, penetrating the dark. He knew the family had found his bed empty, for his father was among the force of men and guns before him, no doubt, seeking him. He envisioned his mother, near hysteria, blaming herself. His father, angry, first phoning authorities. Brick tried to ignore the images; tried to make his mind a comfortable fuzzy blank. Toby, now, was all that mattered. Brick lay, body stretched, belly down, reaching, clutching the soft earth, kneeding the rich furrows.

The man on the bullhorn, threatened, "Come back, boy. Come back."

"Not without my dad."

An unexpected silence, strange, unnerving, struck the men, immobilizing the clustering intensity of might.

The man on the bullhorn mumbled something, found himself and shouted. "Now, go for it, now, Boy." The loud words, a gritty order. The officer raised a hand, palm back toward the force with guns, controlling, cautioning them. A heaviness engulfed the setting, seemingly for an eternity. The intimidating lights pierced grotesquely in the eerie night, distorting hostile features.

Then a small form emerged again, followed by a second, larger form - hesitantly, guarded. Pointed rays found them, blinded them. Toby led his father into the yard. The man holding his hands shoulder high. "I don't want anyone hurt," he called simply, "especially my son." He waited, to push his hands higher and wider apart, his wrists out, wavering, white in the shocking rays.

Suddenly his voice rolled high, rippling, "God forgive me. God forgive us all."

Brick stayed home with a cold.

Several days crawled by, spring greenness touched the coast. Meadowlarks flew joyfully over the slopes in swift, long glides, their voices sweet and clear. Back of the sea cliffs, marsh hawks dipped curiously among the netted pockets where black-eyed guns stared ominously. Flowers now splotched the fields, spreading more each day, blending reds and yellows, sometimes streaking or dotting with blues and oranges. Flowers bloomed gaily between the jeep tracks that crisscrossed hills; they bloomed next to the gun mounts; on the beaches, sand verbenas sent flowered strands around the trenches and into the machine gun pits.

In Santa Rosa, in Sebastopol, in Bodega, in all the villages and on all the ranches the rumors spread. Was Yamoto a spy? Could he really have been? If not, then why did he resist? Whispers spread among the surrounding neighbors, even those who had known him, experienced clashing views. Did such resistance now justify the removal of all native Japanese? Or was he a mere mortal passionately devoted to saving his land? He should go to prison some asserted. I'd fight to keep my ranch, too, others confided. But the facts remained perplexing. The dark, the flashing lights, the sirens, the dogs barking, the men shouting. We thought it was a night practice again, a few explained, still befuddled. The Bay Area newspapers gave no notice - a local weekly, on the third page, mentioned briefly, that a deranged Japanese, possibly drunk, had been arrested.

"Figure the Jap just flipped out - went berserk," an investigator told the family. Flanked by two formal-looking Army officers, he had talked briefly, his words firm with a taint of bitterness. Brick would never forget him, standing inside the living room door, a sag to his shoulders and his face sallow and lined with fatigue. "War is hell," he said evenly. "The Japanese everywhere pose a threat. And you people here - you especially have learned how really close war is. We must all remain alert." The family members nodded dully in compliance, their faces registering dismay and anguish. "Loose talk about what happened here might hurt American morale. Do you understand?"

"We understand," said Clarence.

"Continue then, as if under normal conditions," the inspector ordered. He snapped his head in a dismissing salute, and turned back into the yard with the officers following.

How, Brick wondered, how could he ever play, or hike, or fish, or view the ocean again, as if the incident had never happened?

A detention officer phoned, surprising Sathia and Brick. He wished to find if it was convenient to bring Toby to the Sea Ranch, to say goodbye - he was being temporarily housed at a juvenile facility. "Of course," said Sathia, her voice more cordial and sympathetic than Brick had heard from her in months. Upon replacing the receiver, she fingered it absently; then, addressed Brick with an embracing comfort. "Your mom and dad won't be back until after work. If I could drive, I'd take you two up the hill to find Burnie."

"It's okay, Auntie, we'll walk." Brick was ecstatic that Toby was safe and would be visiting; of late, Burnie was climbing up the hill - pausing often for breath and for a needed rest - his eventual goal, to reach the last chicken house overlooking the cliff. He was determined to strengthen his heart and body. But, Sathia worried, fretted constantly.

Brick was waiting at the gate to the front yard, when a car carrying Toby arrived. Toby climbed out and the two boys punched each other's shoulders, joyously. "Uncle will want to see you - he's up on the hill and doesn't know you're here."

"Good, he's getting out and walking."

"Yeah, it's good."

Toby leaned toward his escort, a serious looking man, with a pencil mustache, in a gray suit. He wore a tilted Stetson. "It might take a little longer than you expect. Gotta walk up the hill to see Uncle Burnie."

The man nodded. "Just don't take too long - we have that bus to meet. If I think you're forgetting me, I'll blow the horn."

Brick saw a small suitcase. "Where you goin'?"

"To a bus in Santa Rosa - and then on - a government man is taking me and a couple others to Colorado - to be with Rose."

"That's great - doesn't seem you're takin' very much."

"Oh, a toothbrush, some pj's, and a few clothes, tossed in a Field & Stream, a Popular Mechanics, and some Bugs Bunny and Donald Duck comic books."

"I was there at your ranch - saw it all - sneaked there."

"You did?" Toby looked astounded, yet embarrassed and apologetic. He sought his words. "You must have got into big trouble."

"Yeah, well, it's a long story. My dad was there, too, but, we didn't go together, that's for sure."

"You sneaked off because of me?" The two strolled toward the house.

"Yeah, I wanted to help you somehow. Dad came looking for me. Found out I'd got out the window, down the fire ladder."

Toby hung his head. "You shouldn't have."

"Glad I did. You're a hero, you know."

"Only did what I had to do. Is your family real mad?"

"Thought they would be. But, dad, being there. Seeing. He really never said much, except that he was proud of you."

"He did?" Toby puckered, as if holding tears.

Sathia was standing on the porch with a pan of fresh cookies. "Thanks, that's nice of you," said Toby, "but I don't feel very hungry." Brick started to reach; then decided not to.

"How are you doing?"

Toby explained that he was being shipped off to be with Rose.

"How is your dad?"

"He's in jail. I guess there's going to be something like a hearing. The judge said that dad would be sent to one of the camps - hopefully to where we will be holed up."

"He won't have to go to prison?" Sathia pursued.

"I guess not. The judge told me not to say anything to anybody. I'm telling you, because you're my only friends now. The judge said people would be upset and could riot or get awful scared if dad didn't go to jail. About bein' sent to a camp, shortly, he said, 'what they don't know won't hurt them or anybody,' whatever that means."

Silently, Brick, Toby, and Spud walked side by side up the slope toward the cliffs near the far chicken house still empty and ghostly. Almost daily, Brick had strolled to the site. Above the spreading water, he could seek the clouds that bordered the horizon, watch them pile higher and higher to hump magnificently. He sat there often, quietly lost in his own world, trying to escape the chaos around him.

Daily, Brick had observed Burnie shuffling toward the bluffs. He watched him as Auntie had requested. The man would pause to rest, and then move on with effort, determined to work his way up. If Sathia or Darlene knew how difficult his endeavor, they would be disheartened with concern. Probably by now they suspected, Brick figured, but knew Burnie had to get out and prove himself. As the boys reached the rise, they saw him sitting, contemplating the sea's movement. A rush of engulfing warmth filled Brick, soared through him, "Uncle Burnie - you rascal," he uttered. Self-consciously he glanced at Toby who kept looking ahead, smiling with satisfaction. Startled by their feet slapping the grass, Burnie turned and rolled slightly on his amble belly. Spud bounced ahead to lick at his face and to avoid playful swats.

"You made it! But maybe you shouldn't be up here," Brick said, having sudden doubts.

"I want to," Burnie answered with finality, grunting back to a sitting position. He looked at the boys intensely, appreciatively. "It's been a long time since I walked up here. Now that I came, I'm glad you joined me. Happy to see you, Toby. How did you get here? And how's Shiro holding up?"

Brick's face softened with gratitude and relief. Burnie still looked disturbingly tired and dark around the eyes. Toby explained that he had been brought by an official. Before leaving to be with Rose, the judge had allowed a visit to whomever he wished. He had chosen Brick and his family. Painfully, briefly, he mentioned that his dad would face a hearing, and, hopefully, he would eventually join him and his sister.

The boys dropped to the grass beside Burnie. Brick stretched his lengthening legs and watched the gray clouds race overhead. He waited absently through an awkward lull, then suddenly blurted, "Toby's come to say goodbye. This is his last day. He's being shipped by bus to Colorado, to an encampment there - I guess until the war's over."

"We heard." Burnie looked down and pulled aimlessly at some grass. He tried to form words. "It's been rough for all of you - for everybody. And you, Toby, I really respect you." He touched the boy's forearm. "You saved your dad and others. You used judgment and common sense that none of the others did."

"It's going to be a long war, isn't it?" Toby said.

"I'm afraid so," Burnie sighed. "With a lot more hate and a lot of hurt."

"Why must people hurt and kill each other?" Toby asked, with difficulty, his voice catching.

Burnie sat thoughtfully. At last he said, "I'm sure there is a purpose in all things, even if we don't understand. Maybe after all the fighting and shooting are done, a few people become more human. You watch the tide. Regular-like, the sea comes up and sweeps things clean." Burnie's eyes had an inward look. "Maybe that's what hurt and pain are all about - forces a person to start anew with hope."

"Then why don't people know that?" Brick asked.

Burnie smiled at the boys with an amused tenderness. "Because there's an awful lot we adults don't understand."

"Well, after the war, I'm coming back," Toby announced, rising. "We may lose the ranch, but it doesn't mean I can't start again, like dad did."

"Hopefully, some day, you can stay with us for a time," said Burnie, holding out his hand and enclosing the small fingers. "And, good luck, young man." Suddenly, Burnie raised a finger, halting them. "Incidentally, I been aching to tell you two. After we talked about the otters - you and me. Remember?" He glanced at his great nephew.

"Yes, sir," Brick alerted, curious.

"Afterwards, I phoned Ned Benucci where he works at Mare Island; left a message with some secretary. I made a couple of follow-ups. For a time, I didn't hear from him; then he did call." Burnie swiveled his body in discomfort, until beaming pleasure, as if offering a gift. "I asked about the sea otters. Now hear this. He feels certain he did see a pair out in that deep cove. He didn't want to tell anyone, although he did admit it to me. You know Ned, he wouldn't do anything that might harm wildlife, like rare sea otters."

"That's great," said Brick.

"Yes, that sure is," Toby joined. Their excitement was tempered. Obviously pleased, the boys were not exhilarated; the proof, the vindication was not that satisfying now, as they once would have been - not that significant in the scheme of things.

"Better go. Time's runnin' out," Toby said, resigned. "The guy down there in the car will start tooting his horn if I don't show soon. Thanks for telling us about our otters."

"My pleasure, looked forward to it."

"You take it easy," Brick said to his uncle. "I'm going to see him off. He's always been my best friend you know."

"And forgive us for not understanding that," Burnie replied softly. He watched the two boys and the dog until they vanished over the knoll; a knowing smile played across his lips.

CPSIA information can be obtained
at www.ICGtesting.com
Printed in the USA
FFOW03n0417250716
26180FF